POWER

FOUR CLASSIC BOOKS ON HEALING, COMPLETE IN ONE VOLUME

by

Lilian B. Yeomans, M.D.

Harrison House
Tulsa, Oklahoma

Unless otherwise indicated, all Scripture quotations are taken from the *King James Version* of the Bible.

Scripture quotations marked (WEYMOUTH) are taken from *Weymouth's New Testament in Modern Speech* by Richard Francis Weymouth. Harper & Row Publishers, Inc., New York, New York.

Scripture quotations marked (NIV) are taken from *The Holy Bible: New International Version®* NIV®.

Healing From Heaven
ISBN 978-0-7394-7905-6

The Great Physician
(Formerly published as *Divine Healing Diamonds*)
ISBN 978-0-7394-7905-6

Balm of Gilead
ISBN 978-0-7394-7905-6

Health and Healing
(Formerly published as *The Royal Road to Health-Ville*)
ISBN 978-0-7394-7905-6

His Healing Power:
Four Classic Books on Healing, Complete in One Volume
ISBN 978-0-7394-7905-6

Published by Harrison House, Inc.
P.O. Box 35035
Tulsa, Oklahoma 74153

CONTENTS

Healing
FROM
Heaven

CONTENTS

FOREWORD

This little book, a reprint of lectures on divine healing delivered to students in the classroom and issued in this form in compliance with numerous requests, is called *Healing From Heaven* because it tells of eternal life brought down to man by the Son of God, which makes all who will accept it as freely as it is given conquerors, here and now, over sin and sickness. The law of the Spirit of life in Christ Jesus hath made me free from the law of sin and death (Rom. 8:2). Disease is death begun, a death process.

I once called on a doctor at his office by invitation to discuss the teaching of the Scriptures on healing, and in taking my seat I accidentally knocked some medicine bottles off a shelf beside me. Laughingly apologizing for the mischance, I said, "Perhaps I shall knock them all down before I get through"; and my words were prophetic, for after taking a few doses of "healing from heaven" out of the Word, the doctor felt no further need of earthly remedies for himself or others but devoted the remainder of his life to presenting the claims of the physician who has never lost a case—Jehovah-Rapha.

Trusting that many others may be induced to taste and see that the Lord is good, this message is prayerfully sent forth.

—Lilian B. Yeomans, M.D.

Chapter 1

HOW I WAS DELIVERED FROM DRUG ADDICTION

**Out of the depths have I cried unto Thee, O Lord.
Lord, hear my voice:
Let Thine ears be attentive
To the voice of my supplications.
If Thou, Lord, shouldest mark iniquities,
O Lord, who shall stand?
But there is forgiveness with Thee,
That Thou mayest be feared.
I wait for the Lord, my soul doth wait,
And in His Word do I hope.
My soul waiteth for the Lord
More than they that watch for the morning:
I say, more than they that watch for the morning.
Let Israel hope in the Lord:
For with the Lord there is mercy,
And with Him there is plenteous redemption.
And He shall redeem Israel
From all his iniquities.**

Psalm 130

Out of the depths He lifted me! Abyss calls to abyss, deep answers to deep. Only those who know what it is to be bound as I was, captive of the mighty, the prey of the terrible, will be able to understand how great was the deliverance which God wrought in me when He set me completely free from the degrading bondage of the morphine and chloral habits to which I had been a slave for years.

Sitting in darkness and in the shadow of death, bound in affliction and iron, I cried unto the Lord in my trouble and He saved me out of my distress, brought me out of darkness and the shadow of death and broke my bands asunder. Do you not think that I have reason to praise God and glorify with every breath our all-conquering Jesus?

My sad story has a glad ending. But if anyone asks me how I contracted the morphine habit and became a drug addict, I can only say, "Through my fault, through my fault, through my most grievous fault."

I had been saved several years before; but like Peter at one stage of his career, I was following afar off when I fell into this snare. It is a dangerous thing to follow afar off; I proved that to my cost.

Of course, it is needless to say that nothing was further from my thought than becoming a drug addict. But I was engaged in very strenuous work, practicing medicine and surgery; and in times of excessive strain from anxiety or overwork, I occasionally resorted to morphine, singly or in combination with other drugs, to steady my nerves and enable me to sleep.

Knowing as I did the awful power of the habit-inducing drug to enslave and destroy its victims and with practical demonstrations of it before my eyes every day among the most brilliant members of the medical profession (I am a graduate of the University of Michigan Department of Medicine, Ann Arbor, Michigan), I was utterly inexcusable for daring to trifle even for a moment with such a destructive agent. And alas, I thought I was toying with the drug; but one day I made the startling discovery that the drug, or rather the demon power in back of the drug, was playing with me. The bloodthirsty tiger that had devoured so many victims had me in his grasp.

Of the anguish of my soul the day I had to acknowledge to myself that morphine was the master and I the slave, I can even now hardly bear to speak.

I have this fault to find with many testimonies to healing: that the individual, in telling of his healing, fails to make it clear that he (the witness) really suffered from the disease of which he professes to have been cured. It may be quite evident that he believes that he so suffered but that is worlds away from the point at issue.

Testimonies of this character are quite valueless from a scientific standpoint; and to avoid falling into this error, I desire to leave no shadow of doubt on the mind of anyone that I was a veritable victim of morphinomania.

My ordinary dose of the drug varied from 10 to 14 grains a day. I thus took regularly about 50 times the normal dose for an adult man. I also took chloral hydrate, a most deadly drug used by criminals in the concoction of the so-called "knock-out drops," taking 120 grains in two doses of 60 grains at an interval of one hour each night at bedtime. The safe dose of chloral (indeed there is no safe dose in my opinion) is only about five grains, so I regularly took about 24 times what would be prescribed by a doctor.

I took the morphine by mouth, in the form of the sulphate, in one-half grain tablets, which I imported wholesale (I was living in Canada at this time) for my personal use.

While some have taken larger doses than this, I find it hard to believe that anyone was ever more completely enthralled by the drug than was I. I could by desperate efforts—only God knows how desperate they were—diminish the dose somewhat, but I always reached a minimum beyond which it was impossible to carry the reduction.

To ask me whether I had taken the drug on any particular day was as needless as to inquire whether I had inhaled atmospheric air; one seemed as necessary to my existence as the other.

When by tremendous exercise of will power I abstained from it for twenty-four hours, my condition was truly pitiable. I trembled with weakness; my whole body was bathed in cold sweat; my heart palpitated and fluttered; my respiration was irregular; my stomach was unable to retain even so much as a drop of water; my intestines were racked with pain and tortured with persistent diarrhea; I was unable to stand erect, to articulate clearly, or even sign my own name; my thoughts were unconnected; my mind was filled with horrid imaginings and awful forebodings. And worst of all, my whole being was possessed with the specific, irresistible, indescribable craving for the drug. Anyone who has not felt it cannot imagine what it is. Every cell of your body seems to be shrieking for it. It established a periodicity for itself in my case, and I found that at five o'clock each afternoon *I had to have it!* The demand for it was imperative and could not be denied. I believe I would have known the time by the call even if I had been in mid-ocean without watch or clock.

Say what you may about will power; for my part I am satisfied that no human determination can withstand the morphine demon when once his rule is established. His diabolical power is superhuman. But thank God! One has said, "I have given you power over all the power of the enemy." (Luke 10:19.) Divine power is to be had for the asking and receiving.

I did not succumb, however, without many fierce struggles. I believe I made at least 57 desperate attempts to rid myself of the horrible incubus. Over and over again I threw away large quantities of the drugs, determined that I would never touch them again even if I died as the result of abstaining from them. I must have wasted a small fortune in this way. I tried all the substitutes recommended by the medical profession. I consulted many physicians, some of them men of national reputation. I can never forget the tender consideration that I received at the hands of some of these, but they were powerless to break my fetters. I got so far away from God that I actually tried Christian Science, falsely so-called. I also took the then famous Keeley Gold Cure. If there is anything I did not try I have yet to learn what it is.

I left the Gold Cure Institute in a crazed condition and was transferred to a sanitorium for nervous diseases and placed under the care of a famous specialist. From this institution I emerged still taking morphine and chloral, as the doctors would not allow me to dispense with them, partly because of my physical condition and more perhaps because of my unbalanced mental state, which always became aggravated when I no longer used them. Of the suffering these efforts to free myself cost me, I would rather not speak.

I was a perfect wreck mentally and physically. "Like a skeleton with a devil inside," one of my nurses said; and I think her description, if not very flattering, was accurate enough. My friends had lost all hope of ever seeing me delivered; and far from urging me to give up the drugs, advised me to take them as the only means of preserving the little reason that remained to me. They expected my wretched life to come to an early close and really could not desire to see so miserable an existence prolonged.

Perhaps many of us know "The Raven," that weird poem of Edgar Allen Poe. The author, though he has been called the prince of American poets, perished miserably at a very early age as the result of addictions such as mine. In this poem he represents himself as opening his door to a black raven, a foul bird of prey. Once admitted, the raven resists all efforts to eject him but perches himself on a marble bust over the entrance and gazes at the poet with the eyes of a demon. Each time he is commanded to depart he croaks out the ominous word, "Nevermore."

"Take thy beak from out my heart,
And thy form from off my door."
Quoth the raven, "Nevermore."

And the Raven, never flitting,
Still is sitting, still is sitting,
On the pallid bust of Pallas
Just above my chamber door;
And his eyes have all the seeming
Of a demon's that is dreaming,
And the lamp-light o'er him streaming
Throws his shadow on the floor;
And my soul from out that shadow
That lies floating on the floor
Shall be lifted
    Nevermore.

The poem is a parable in which the writer tells of his cruel and hopeless bondage to evil habits. It used to haunt me when I, too, was bound, and again and again Satan whispered to my tortured brain the awful word, "Nevermore."

Though I dreamed night and day of freedom, the dream seemed impossible of realization. I said, "It will take something stronger than death to deliver me, for the hold of the hideous thing is far deeper than my physical being." And I was right, for it took the law of the Spirit of Life in Christ Jesus which makes us free from the law of sin and death. (Rom. 8:2.)

Do you ask, "Did you not pray?" Yes, I came to the place where I did nothing else. I prayed and prayed and prayed and prayed. Night after night I walked up and down our long drawing rooms calling on God and sometimes almost literally tearing the hair out of my head. And you say, "And you weren't healed after that?" No, I wasn't healed because I didn't believe the simple statement of the Word of God; rather, my healing could not be manifested because of my unbelief. I shut the door and prevented the power of God from operating unhindered in my body.

"And why did you not have faith?" Simply because I did not have light enough to take it. It is a gift and must be appropriated. And moreover, God's method of bestowing it is through His Word. Faith cometh—note that it cometh—by hearing, and hearing by the word of God (Rom. 10:17).

I was getting very weak and spent hour after hour in bed, and God in His mercy kept me much alone so that He could talk to me. At last I drew my neglected Bible to me and plunged into it with full purpose of heart to get all there was for me, to do all that God told me to do, to believe all He said; and praise God, the insoluble problem was solved, the impossible was achieved, the deliverance was wrought! There is no trouble about it when God can get us to meet His conditions of repentance and faith. When God says faith, He means *faith*. It is well to know that.

If anyone asks by what special Scripture verse I was healed, I feel as though I could almost say I was healed by the whole Book. For it is there in Job, the oldest book of the Bible, that has as clear teaching on healing in the Atonement as the Word contains. (Job 33:24.) In Genesis God made man as He wanted him, in His own image and likeness, even as to his physical being free from every disability. You'll find healing in Exodus when the people of God marched out of Egypt; for in Psalm 105:37 we read that they marched out "with not one feeble person among their tribes." Think of it! What a glorious procession. How did they do it? Through the wonder-working power of the blood of the Passover Lamb. Read about it in Leviticus in the leper-cleansing ceremony where the leper, when he had not a sound spot in his entire body, was healed by the blood of the bird slain over running water in an earthen vessel—which is a picture of Christ, who through the eternal Spirit offered Himself without spot unto God. In Numbers every recorded case of sickness is dealt with by supernatural means, prayer, sacrifice, and atonement. In Deuteronomy God explicitly promised to take away all sickness from His obedient people.

Suffice it to say I found a great number of healing passages in the Bible. And when God's words were found, I "ate" them; and they did their work. They never fail. I knew I was healed, that I couldn't help being healed because God was faithful; and I almost lost interest in my symptoms, I was so certain of the truth. The drugs went—I didn't know for nineteen years after my healing what became of them. I thought maybe God would send an angel to take them away; and I was watching for him, but the first thing I knew they were gone. And that alone wouldn't have helped much, but something else was gone. The specific, irresistible, indescribable craving produced by demon power was gone. The hideous black bird of prey that croaked, "Nevermore," had flown, never to return. I had no more use for morphine and chloral than for rat poison—had no room for them or any other drugs in my physical economy. My appetite became so excellent that I had to eat about seven meals a day, and I had no room for drugs. And needless to say, my soul was filled with His praises: ...My soul doth magnify the Lord, and my spirit hath rejoiced in God my Saviour (Luke 1:46,47).

And the best of all is that this healing was no happy accident, no special miracle on my behalf but the working out in me of God's will for all of us—perfect soundness by faith in the name of Jesus of Nazareth. So far as I know the field, God's work is being done today principally by men and women who have been raised from physical as well as spiritual death, people who were given up to die by the medical profession. I believe I could give offhand the names of one hundred such.

And there are still vacancies in the ranks of the army of the King. If you are afflicted, step out and receive healing and then get to work.

I was in Chicago immediately after my healing and went one day to the Women's Temple to the noon prayer meeting. I don't know how it is now, but it used to be a rallying place for Christian workers; they came from the Moody Bible Institute and many missions and churches. When I walked in, I found the preacher talking of the awful snares in which people who trifle with narcotic drugs, including tobacco, get entangled. He warned them to give them up entirely if they were tampering with them. And then he sat down. I knew from experience that they couldn't give them up unless they took Jesus; and so, prompted by the Holy Spirit, I rose and asked if I might say a word. It was not parliamentary for me to do this, but God was in it; and I got leave. Then I said: "I am glad for the good advice our brother has given us, and I want to tell you how to do it; and I am speaking from the depths of experience." And I told my story. I think many of them didn't believe in divine healing before I told it, but I don't believe there was one who didn't believe in it after I had finished. I was so happy, like some caged thing set free, that they couldn't help rejoicing with me; and spontaneously, they rose to their feet and in one great burst of praise, sang:

All hail the power of Jesus' Name
 Let angels prostrate fall,
Bring forth the royal diadem,
 And crown Him Lord of all.

Chapter 2

GOD'S WILL AS REVEALED IN HIS CREATIVE WORK

And God saw everything that he had made, and, behold, it was very good... (Gen. 1:31).

I believe that one of the greatest hindrances to healing is the absence of certain, definite knowledge as to God's will. There is lurking in most of us a feeling that He may not be willing, that we have to persuade Him to heal us.

People often say, "I know that He is able; He has power if He only will"—like the leper in the eighth chapter of Matthew who said to Jesus, ...if Thou wilt, Thou canst make me clean (v. 2).

Many of us have been taught to pray, "If it be Thy will, heal me." That wasn't the way David prayed: he cried in Psalm 6:2, Have mercy upon me, O Lord; for I am weak: O Lord, heal me; for my bones are vexed. He was evidently very ill indeed; and the excruciating pains in his bones might have been due to his extreme debility, for he goes on in the fourth and fifth verses imploring God to deliver him from impending death and then adds in the ninth verse, The Lord hath heard my supplication; the Lord will receive my prayer.

There were no ifs or buts in that prayer. The prophet Jeremiah, too, had no doubt about God's will as to healing, for he cried, Heal me, O Lord, and I shall be healed; save me, and I shall be saved... (Jer. 17:14).

And we, God's people of this day, should be as free from doubt regarding our Father's will for our bodies as they were, for it is as clearly revealed in the Word as His will concerning the salvation of our souls.

In a sense the whole Bible is a revelation, not only of His willingness to heal our spiritual ailments, but our physical ones also. One of His covenant names is "the Lord that healeth" (Jehovah-Rapha); and He is also the Lord that changeth not, the changeless, healing, health-bestowing, life-giving Lord, undisputed Sovereign over all the powers of the universe.

Jesus is the express image of the Father, the perfect expression of God and His holy will. He could say, "He that hath seen me hath seen my Father also" (John 14:9), and He declared that His works were not His own but the Father's that sent Him. He healed *all* who came to Him, never refusing a single individual. You cannot find a case where He said, "It is not My will to heal you," or "It is necessary for you to suffer for disciplinary purposes." His answer was always, "I will," and this fact forever settles for us God's will in regard to sickness.

Of course, it has to be according to our faith, for faith is the hand that receives the gift, and God can only fill it to overflowing. I once offered a wee child some goodies, and I asked him to hold out his hands; and oh, how sorry I was that they were so tiny. Let us pray for God to enlarge our grasp of faith, for we are not straitened in Him, but in our own bowels, as the apostle puts it.

As the whole Bible is a revelation of God's willingness to heal and keep our bodies, as well as to save and keep our souls and spirits, we will start at the very beginning and ascertain what the first chapter of Genesis has to teach us about the matter.

There we find God's will clearly revealed in His creative work. God created man the way He wanted him, did He not? Did He make him with any disability or disease or tendency thereto? Was he deformed in any way? one leg shorter than the other, for instance? one shoulder higher than the other? or a squint in one eye?

No, we read that God said, "Let us make man in our image, and after our likeness." (Gen. 1:26.) Wasn't that wonderful? Doesn't it thrill you? It ought to.

God had created many beautiful and wonderful things before this—the sun, the moon, the stars, noble trees, exquisitely beautiful plants and blossoms, sea monsters, fish and land animals, some of them of surpassing strength, others models of grace and beauty. But when it came to His masterpiece, man, He did not fashion him after any of these patterns; no, the model after which man was framed was *a divine* one. God said, "Let us make man in *our* image, after *our* likeness"; and after the work was done, God saw it and "behold it was very good." (v. 31.)

Man then, prior to the fall, was in some sense in the image of God, even as to his physical constitution; and there is no doubt that we have not at the present time any adequate idea of what a glorious being he was. Strong, beautiful, perfectly proportioned, magnificent, he stood forth a majestic and worthy head of creation.

Even to this day, though sadly defaced and marred by sin and its results, the human body bears the impress of the divine image and superscription as surely as the coin they handed to Jesus bore that of Caesar. I shall never forget the first time I saw a human brain. I was only a young girl, a medical student, worldly, utterly forgetful of my Creator in the days of my youth. But I can truly say that a feeling akin to holy awe filled me when I beheld it in all its wondrous complexity and beauty. Yes, those pearly gray, glistening convolutions seemed to me the most beautiful things I had ever seen. And when I realized that they were the home of thought parts of the organ through which the most intricate processes of reasoning were carried out, the marvel of it nearly stunned me. I could have fallen on my knees, young heathen though I was, before this mystery and its author, the writing and superscription were so evidently divine.

In studying the anatomy of the human body, there are always two things that impress the careful observer. One is the perfection of the plan on which it is constructed down to the minutest cell: the marvelous adaptation of each part of the organism to its proper function, the wonderful cooperation between different organs and systems of organs, the perfect coordination of all the various parts and tissues to a common end.

The other thing that impresses one is the imperfections that meet you at every point. The trail of disease, or a tendency thereto, is over the whole organism, producing debility and sometimes structural changes resulting in deformity. Evidences of disease of some kind, hereditary or otherwise, are apparent upon close examination of almost any human body, though these are, of course, much more marked in some cases than others.

Yet while this is true, the plan of the whole and the marvelous manner in which it is carried out is so eloquent of infinite and divine wisdom that we instinctively take our shoes from off our feet and veil our faces as we reverently view God's handiwork.

A great scientist once said these words in commenting on the facts that I have just stated:

> I cannot understand how the consummate artist who formed and painted a rose could also create a worm to gnaw at its fragrant heart and cause its pink, flushed, velvet petals to turn the color of decay; neither can I understand how the Creator of such a glorious being as man can bring into existence a foul and voracious thing like a cancer to prey upon that masterpiece of beauty and perfection, the human body.

No, apart from God's Word we are in Egyptian darkness regarding this problem of the ages, but the moment we accept the divine revelation it is as clear as noonday. God created man, the head of a new order of beings, perfect in spirit, soul, and body, free from all deformity and disease, a reflection of the beauty and glories of his Creator. "Whatsoever God doeth it shall be forever." (Eccl. 3:14.) So this is *His eternal purpose concerning us.*

The marring of God's masterpiece, man, in spirit, soul, and body, is the work of that maligned being called Satan, which he affected by leading him to transgress God's law, thus introducing sin into the world with all its disastrous results.

Once a man gets out of line with God's will he is open to all sorts of satanic power which, entering him, defiles, deforms, and ultimately destroys every part of his threefold being. The thief cometh not, but for to steal, and to kill, and to destroy: I am come that they might have life, and that they might have it more abundantly (John 10:10).

But our refuge is in God, and He will not fail us. His eternal purpose that we should be perfect as our heavenly Father is perfect, revealed in His creative work as well as being explicitly stated in the text of the Word, remains unchanged. He has made provision for its fulfillment in you and me; for Jesus Christ was manifested to destroy the works of the devil (1 John 3:8), whether sin, sickness, or death, so that we may be preserved blameless in spirit, soul, and *body* unto His glorious appearing. Faithful is he that calleth you, who also will do it (1 Thess. 5:24).

In closing let me quote a few words on this subject from Dr. F. W. Riale, who has received much illumination on the Word regarding our bodies:

> We are to reckon ourselves dead unto sin and alive unto God, and He will, as in the great faith of Abraham reckon this unto us in a most glorious righteousness. We are to feel that all sickness, like all sin, goes down forever in this great faith conflict. He forgiveth all our sins and healeth all our diseases.

We are to cast all our diseases on the same Lord we cast all our sins upon. His Spirit coming in must banish all as far as the east is from the west. The life of God in the soul of man must mean that the diseases of men go like the sins of men in the fire of the divine life and the divine love...Believe in thy heart that God will most surely accomplish that which He has promised to those who believe, and thou shall be gloriously saved from all the disease that man falls heir to...The Kingdom of Heaven, where sin and sickness are doomed and downed forever, is at hand. It is *now.* Only believe this and thou wilt see the glory of God in thy life.

Chapter 3
THE SOURCE OF SICKNESS

One fine morning I was called by telegram to a certain rural settlement—a beautiful and very rich farming district—where I found a terrible state of affairs. A number of people, including some of their very finest young men, were smitten by an awful scourge, a malignant type of typhoid fever. One magnificent specimen of young manhood, a boy of about seventeen, perfectly proportioned, with an intellectual head and a noble face, the oldest son of his father who was one of the wealthiest men in the vicinity, was in the article of death—perfectly unconscious—when I arrived.

Needless to say, I did what I could, ministered to the sick ones according to the best methods then in vogue, but do you think I stopped with that?

You know I did not. I should have been guilty of criminal negligence if I had not taken steps to have the source of the infection discovered, with the view of shutting it off absolutely and so stamping out the deadly disease.

And the last time I visited that beautiful place I found a great change. The farmers had completely altered their manner of life. The water supply was now free from taint; and the most sanitary methods prevailed in their homes, stables, and dairies so that their connection with the source of the epidemic was shut off; and I never heard of any more typhoid fever in that district. I don't think they ever had any more.

Do you understand the parable? I am sure you do. We have learned from our study of God's creative work that it is His will that His masterpiece, man, should be—as He was created—in the image of God. "Very good," free from all deformity, disability, and disease. This is God's eternal purpose regarding man, for whatsoever "God doeth, it shall be forever." (Eccl. 3:14.) That being the case, let us ask what is the source of all the disease that we see about us, that is working in some of our homes and even in our bodies.

And let us make the inquiry with the view of shutting off our connection with the source of the evil, if it be possible, so that we may stand perfect and complete in all the will of God as it is revealed in His Word, our ...whole spirit and soul and body be preserved blameless unto the coming of our Lord Jesus Christ (1 Thess. 5:23).

It was the best thing that ever happened to those farmers when they discovered that the typhoid was due to dead hogs in the water supply, for they could get rid of them and keep rid of them for all time to come. If they had gone on drinking dead hog soup, they would have gone on having typhoid; but they didn't have to go on drinking it for there was plenty of pure, sparkling water, free from all germs, to be had for the taking. And I believe that God will enable me to point out something important from His Word to all who will listen in faith. First, the source of sickness, and second, how it may be absolutely shut off and how we may drink of the water of life freely, instead of the contaminated wells of earth, which like the water supply in the typhoid infested district, contain the water of death.

Let us go back then to the book of Genesis; and we shall find Satan, the source of sin and sickness, making his initial attack on man in the words addressed to Eve: "Yea, hath God said?" (Gen. 3:1.)

Satan was compelled to attack God's Word, to question the authenticity of the divine revelation; for so long as man rests on the Word of God, he is perfectly invincible, impregnable, immovable. They that trust in the Lord shall be as Mount Zion, which cannot be removed, but abideth forever (Ps. 125:1).

Satan cannot touch them, rather they are the most serious menace to all satanic devices, plans, plots, and schemes, for to them has been given power over all the power of the enemy.

There is not a reinforcement which the prince of darkness can order up from the profoundest depths of his dark domain for which those who believe God's Word are not more than a match; not a poison gas manufactured in hell which the breath of God will not dissipate; not a fiery dart which the shield of faith will not quench; not a pestilence which the precious Blood, boldly displayed on the lintel and doorposts of our dwellings will not avert.

No weapon that is formed against thee shall prosper... (Isa. 54:17). So whether it be shot, or shell, gas, liquid fire, bombs, tanks, submarines, airplanes, artillery, cavalry or infantry, pestilence, famine, earthquake, lightning, or malicious tongues, we are perfectly safe so long as we are abiding in the Word of God.

Satan must dislodge us from our refuge in the secret place of the Most High before he can so much as touch us. Hence, his introductory remark to our mother Eve: "Yea"—he always propitiates, conciliates, agrees with us as much as possible, avoids antagonizing us unnecessarily—"Yea, hath God said?" (Gen. 3:1.)

"Hath God said!" was hatched in hell,
    Hear the serpent speak that word.
Every soul that ever fell
    Entertained that thought of God.
God hath said; Yes, God hath said.
    God hath said; Yes, search the Word,

For what God hath said is all —
    All you need and more and more;
Here is most abundant store —
    God hath said; Yes, God hath said.
God hath said, Lo! It is done.
    What remains for us but praise?
While He conquers in the fight,
    Praise the Holiest in the height.
God hath said; Yes, God hath said."

Yes, God, who at sundry times and in divers manners spake in time past unto the fathers by the prophets, hath in these last days spoken unto us by His Son... (Heb. 1:1,2).

God hath said, and here in the Bible is what He said; and if we will but abide in that Word and treat any suggestion that would cast even the remotest doubt on the authenticity of this revelation or its living truth in every part of it to us at this moment as from the author of lies, continuous victory is ours.

My sister had a fearful physical test some time ago. For hours she coughed almost continuously. I have never heard anyone cough as she did. It was nerve-racking to hear her and constitution-racking to her to do it. She coughed till the whites of her eyes were scarlet from extravasated blood. Her cough was so violent that you would think she would burst in her effort to get her breath. I was kneeling beside her bed in the small hours of the morning taking victory. I reviewed the whole situation in the light of God's Word. Under that illumination, I saw clearly that victory was hers. I took it, as it were, from the hands of God.

It seemed a concrete thing, round in shape and smooth to feel. The rotundity denoted, no doubt, the completeness of our redemption in Christ Jesus; the smoothness, the gentleness of God in all His dealings with us. It was pleasant to the touch. I knew that if she would take it into her hands and hold it there, Satan would flee and that she would breathe as deeply, quietly, and easily as ever in her life.

I so pressed it upon her by prayer and exhortation that twice she took it and held it lightly; but no sooner did she do this than Satan came as a roaring lion and bellowed in her very face; and in her fear, caused by the agonizing sense of suffocation, which the enemy was allowed to put upon her, she let it slip from her nerveless grasp and was at his mercy—and he has none.

The Lord gave her the verse, "Your adversary the devil, as a roaring lion, walketh about, seeking whom he may devour; whom resist, steadfast in the faith" (1 Peter 5:8,9); for he may not devour those who rest on God's Word. If we resist the devil, James tells us, he will flee from us. (James 4:7.) So if he roars, you resist steadfast in faith in the Word. If he roars more, resist him more. If he keeps on roaring, keep on resisting. The louder he roars, the more vigorously you are to resist, and you will have the joy of seeing him flee before you as she did.

But alas, Eve did not resist but allowed Satan to instill doubt, which matured into unbelief and developed into disobedience; and sin, sickness, sorrow, and death entered into the world.

Then God gave them the promise of a Saviour and responded to the faith in that promise by bestowing on them redemption in type. He clothed them with garments not made by themselves, which cost the lives of innocent victims. These were placed on them by God's own hands and enveloped them, spirit, soul, and *body* in a covering of *blood.*

Here we have a beautiful picture of the redemption which is ours in Christ Jesus. Note that it takes in the body. God clothed them and enveloped their physical beings, as well as their souls and spirits, in a righteousness provided by sacrifice.

Jesus took the death penalty, which we had earned, and gave us His life, eternal life, instead. Hence, apprehension of Jesus Christ in all His offices by simple faith brings perfect peace; and thank God! "Tis everlasting peace, sure as Jehovah's throne."

But do you say, "I don't understand how the death of an innocent victim on my behalf can bring me peace"? No, we don't understand, that is true; but fortunately, we don't need to understand but only to believe, and that we can do.

This much we know because God tells us so in His Word, that under His holy law, which will never be altered or diminished in its requirements by so much as a jot or tittle, "the wages of sin is death." (Rom. 6:23.) That death is not only the disintegration and ultimate dissolution of the body by the processes which we call disease or decay but also the separation of the spirit from God; it is something we have justly earned. And God must pay us our wages. Must do so, I say, in conformity with the constitution of His being, which is in its very essence, righteousness and holiness. If I am sovereign of the realm under an absolute form of government and I owe you certain wages and emoluments, I must in common justice pay them. On the other hand, if—under the constitution of the realm—I owe you the death penalty, I must inflict it or cease to be just and right before men and the tribunal of my own conscience.

God owes us something, and that something is death; and He must pay the debt. He will pay it in full—"the soul that sinneth, it *shall die!*" (Ezek. 18:20.) But Jesus Christ, who had no sin laid to His charge, ran in between the human race and the death penalty and bore it for us so that God, having made His Son suffer the full penalty for sin, can justly pardon us.

Now He only requires of us that we acquiesce in this wonderful plan of redemption, that we let ourselves be clothed. Don't come all dressed up in filthy rags of self-righteousness, but be arrayed body, soul, and spirit in the righteousness (rightness) of Christ. This is divine healing and divine health. Never forget that it comes only through the shed Blood.

This teaching is not popular at present; but—what matters a great deal more—it is true, for it is based on God's Word.

A great English artist was once seized with a divine hunger for a clearer vision of the Christ. He said, "If I could see Him in His beauty I could paint Him and make others see Him too." He thought if he could live where Jesus lived while on earth, breathe the same air, look on the same stars that shone upon the Holy One, he might get the vision. So he left everything—friends, home, fellow artists, studios, the applause of the multitude—and lived for years in a tiny tent in the awful solitudes that surround the Dead Sea. He was, like Paul, in peril of robbers, but nothing daunted him as day after day he turned the pages of his Bible. At last the Holy Spirit brought to him the words, ...the Lord hath laid on him the iniquity of us all (Isa. 53:6); and he caught up his brush to paint the crucifixion, the spotless Lamb of God nailed to the tree. No, he could not touch brush to canvas; it seemed too sacred. He turned to the types and shadows of the sacrifice—the high priest robed in garments of glory and beauty, the great Day of Atonement, the priest entering the holiest of all, not without blood, the people outside prostrate on the pavement. No, that was not it.

Again he turned to his Bible and a figure starts out from amidst the shadows, the figure of the scapegoat. It is led forward, and the sins of the people are confessed and laid upon it; the scarlet fillet is tied around its neck ("though your sins be as scarlet"). (Isa. 1:18.) And as the doomed beast beneath its crushing load of guilt is led forth to the wilderness, the high priest turns to the people with words of absolution and comfort, "Ye are clean." And they return to their homes to enjoy the Sabbath rest, free from condemnation and doom; for it is God who has freed them from the burden of sin. But the doomed beast goes its lonely way far from the haunts of men. The moment chosen by the artist for his picture is the sunset hour. The animal is very near its end. Its strength is spent. The white lime soil is blood-marked from its wounded feet. It is crushed beneath its invisible load. Dying of starvation, parched with thirst, tottering with feebleness, eyes glazing, in its dumb distress it bears the curse that the guilty Israelites may go free and rejoice in his glorious liberty. This is a very faint picture of what this great redemption for spirit, soul, and body cost the Lord Jesus Christ. Surely we are bought with a price; therefore let us glorify God in our bodies and in our spirits, which are His.

Art critics were much disappointed in the picture, for the offense of the Cross has not ceased. But while it is foolishness to them that perish (1 Cor. 1:18), to us who believe the cross of Christ is the power of God unto salvation, our only hope and plea, our sole glory.

And in that crushing load our sicknesses, as well as our sins, were borne; and not only that, but the Cross cast into the bitter waters of life, as at Marah, makes them sweet; and we need no longer drink of poisoned springs, for the Lamb will lead us to fountains of living waters.

So we can get rid of sickness and stay rid of it through the law of the Spirit of life in Christ Jesus:

> Banished my sickness, those Stripes did heal,
>   Because the work on Calvary is finished;
> Now in my body His life I feel,
>   Because the work on Calvary is finished.

SAFETY FIRST

Let us go back in thought to the time when the children of Israel were in bondage in the wonderful old land of Egypt. For truly it was a wonderful land, a mighty empire, a surpassing civilization. It is an interesting fact that we really knew very little about that civilization until the beginning of the nineteenth century. Until then the most learned men in the world had utterly failed in their strenuous efforts to read the elaborate system of Egyptian hieroglyphics (the writing of the priests, a sort of sign language).

So we had nothing to go on regarding Egypt except the comparatively meager information in the Bible and the statements of Grecian historians; and the latter cannot be depended upon very much, for the writers themselves did not understand the ancient Egyptians.

But in the year 1799, a French officer discovered at a place in Egypt called Rosetta, a stone, called from the locality where it was found, the "Rosetta Stone." It contains inscriptions in Egyptian hieroglyphics, Greek, and demotic, the language of the Egyptian common people. It was soon discovered that the Greek was a translation of the hieroglyphics and also of the demotic, so the mystery was a mystery no longer.

When it became known that the Egyptian hieroglyphics had been deciphered, interest in everything Egyptian was greatly stimulated. Money was poured out like water for excavation and exploration in Egypt, and the country was filled with people bent on unraveling the long and jealously guarded secrets of the land of the Sphinx and the pyramids. And the results obtained have well repaid the expenditure of money and energy. For it was a wonderful land.

Even now all the great nations of the world have in their official museums collections of Egyptian articles, books, furniture, works of art, tools, ladies' toilet articles, and yes, they had them even way back in the times of the Pharaohs and Ptolemies—games and toys. We know of their religion, with its elaborate ritualistic worship, and their Bible, called most appropriately, *The Book of the Dead.* We have also learned that 4,000 years before Christ they believed in the resurrection of the body and expended tremendous sums in mummifying human bodies because they expected the souls to rejoin them some day.

For my part, I shouldn't want the finest mummy that was ever mummified for a resurrection body. Should you? No. I want one made like unto His glorious body.

The Egyptians must have been engineers of outstanding skill, for I am a witness to the difficulty the best engineers in America encountered in removing the obelisk, which had been brought by ship from Alexandria, Egypt, from the dock to Central Park where it now stands. It is an immense thing, and it certainly made very slow progress along the narrow streets of lower New York.

Now why am I writing so much about Egypt? Why lay such emphasis on its wonders? Simply to bring out clearly that with all its wisdom, learning, glory, and beauty, God had but one use for Egypt so far as His children were concerned and that was to get them out of it. "I loved him and called my son out of Egypt." (Hosea 11:1.)

Egypt is a type of the world, and it is a wonderful old world. It has all sorts of ingenious and beautiful things in it; but like Egypt, it is one vast tomb; its Bible is a *Book of the Dead,* for all who belong to it are dead in trespasses and sins. And so far as we are concerned, there is only one thing for us to do and that is to come out of it—"Come out from among them and be ye separate...touch not the unclean thing." (2 Cor. 6:17.)

In the chapters of Exodus preceding the 11th, we find that God has been dealing with the Egyptians by means of awful judgments to make them let His people go, but all in vain. The heart of Pharaoh is obdurate, and God has come to the end of His longsuffering; and the final, awful judgment, the destruction of all the firstborn of Egypt by means of a pestilence unheard of in virulence and fatality, is impending.

In the first verse of the 11th chapter of Exodus, we find the Lord saying to Moses, "Yet will I bring one plague more upon Pharaoh and upon Egypt." (v. 1.) These terrible words signed the death warrant of Egypt's firstborn, chief of all their strength. And Moses said, Thus saith the Lord, About midnight will I go out into the midst of Egypt: and all the firstborn in the land of Egypt shall die, from the firstborn of Pharaoh that sitteth upon his throne, even unto the firstborn of the maidservant that is behind the mill...And there shall be a great cry throughout all the land of Egypt, such as there was none like it, nor shall be like it any more (Ex. 11:4-6).

This was to be the final plague, death in every house. Truly it was a terrible epidemic!

"But against any of the children of Israel shall not a dog move his tongue, against man or beast: that ye may know that the Lord doth put a difference between the Egyptians and Israel" (Ex. 11:7).

The Lord puts a difference between His people and those who are strangers to Him, as were the Egyptians; and the difference is the difference between life and death.

He draws a line, on one side of which is life—life more abundant, life for spirit, soul, and body, and on the other side of which is death—death for spirit, soul, and body, the second death.

The Egyptians may have been as fair or fairer than the descendants of the Israelites. They may have been as good, from a human standpoint, or better than the offspring of Jacob; nevertheless, throughout the length and breadth of Egypt, from the king on his throne to the menial behind the mill, there was nothing but death. But in the dwellings of the Israelites there was peace and security and the sound of those who kept a holy solemnity unto the Lord as they feasted on the Passover Lamb.

What made the difference? What did the Israelites have that the Egyptians lacked?

Note that before God's clock struck the hour of doom, there was a pause during which absolute safety, perfect immunity from disease and death was provided for all who would avail themselves of it—Israelites and Gentiles too, for there was a "mixed multitude" that went out with the children of Israel by the institution of the Passover, a type of the atoning work of Jesus Christ, the Sacrifice of the spotless Lamb of God.

Further, note that there was one, and only one, protection against this death-dealing epidemic and that was the *blood.* The one thing that the Israelites had that the Egyptians lacked was the *blood* upon their dwellings.

The firstborn of Israel, as well as those of the Egyptians, were secure only through the *blood.* "When I see the *blood,* I will pass over you, and the plague shall not be upon you." (Ex. 12:13.)

All that the Egyptian physician could do—and they could do a great deal—was in vain. The history of medicine shows us that they had a most elaborate system of medicine and surgery. In an ancient graveyard dating back to 1500 B.C., skeletons were exhumed on which all sorts of delicate and difficult surgical work had been performed; and from the Ebers papyrus it is evident that the ancient Egyptians prior to and contemporaneous with Moses performed many surgical operations, including the removal of tumors and operations on the eye—in which department of surgery they were particularly well versed. Skulls on which trephining has been performed have been unearthed dating back as far as 2800 B.C.

Egyptian surgeons, who were also the priests and undertakers, were so skillful in their manipulation of the dead body that they removed the entire brain through the nasal orifices after death, in connection with the process of embalming. In this way they could avoid making the least change in the contour of the face, which might have been occasioned if an incision had been made.

As to medicine, they had an extensive pharmacopoeia, including castor oil and opium. They also used inhalations, potions, snuffs, fumigations, salves, clysters, injections, and poultices. They also seem to have had some quack medicines, or something very like them; for we read of a famous powder called "The Powder of the Three Great Men," while another bore the title, "Powder Recommended by Five Great Physicians." They were enthusiastic about elimination and fasting in the treatment of disease, just as many doctors are today; and they had meat inspected and water boiled if they thought them impure.

Yes, the physicians and surgeons of Egypt were doubtlessly capable and clever; but confronted with the deadly plague which slew the firstborn of Egypt, they were as helpless as infants. No doubt a consultation of the best medical men in the empire was hurriedly called by the royal physician whose business it was to watch over the health of the heir to the throne; but before they could assemble, he had passed forever beyond their reach. A gasp, a gurgle, a convulsive struggle for breath, bulging eyes, a livid hue about the lips, a stiffening of the muscles in the death agony, and the lineal descendant of all the Pharaohs was as dead as the son of the poor servant behind the mill.

Medical science is strictly limited in its possibilities, and the best doctors are the first to confess this. The list of incurable diseases is long, very long, and even in the case of diseases that are classed as curable, the result of treatment is often palliative rather than curative. One of America's foremost physicians, now dead, said, "In back of all disease lies a cause which no remedy can reach."

The cause, we know from the Word of God, is sin; and for sin and its outworkings in the body in disease, debility, and deformity, there is but one remedy. And that remedy is *the blood of Jesus Christ, the Lamb of God.*

To this all-efficacious remedy, and to it alone, the Israelites owed their immunity at the time of the awful visitation in Egypt. And thank God, it has never lost its power.

During the epidemic of Spanish influenza—which baffled our modern physicians almost as much as the plague that destroyed the firstborn of Egypt baffled those of ancient Egypt—thousands of God's people were rendered perfectly immune by getting under the shelter of the blood and staying there.

When the fell destroyer was literally raging in the town in which we lived, my sister said—by faith in the power of the blood to all with whom she came into contact—"Here is one house on which you will never see an influenza placard; for the blood is here, and God will not see it dishonored." And God made her boast in the Lord good; and though we were freely exposed to the disease (I myself never refusing to minister to the afflicted ones), our whole family enjoyed perfect immunity from it.

It was to the blood then, and to the blood alone, that the Israelites were indebted for their deliverance. Carefully note these four essential points with regard to the blood:

1. It had to be *shed.* The lamb must be slain. "Without shedding of blood is no remission." (Heb. 9:22.) For I determined not to know any thing among you, save Jesus Christ, and him crucified (1 Cor. 2:2).

2. The blood had to be *applied.* "Through faith in his blood." (Rom. 3:25.)
3. The blood had to be applied *openly.* "Lintel and door post"; in other words, a public confession of Christ crucified.
4. The blood had to be continually upon them. Ye shall...strike the lintel and the two side posts with the blood...and none of you shall go out at the door of his house until the morning (Ex. 12:22).

The whole man—spirit, soul, and body—was thus continually sheltered behind the blood. So we must ever abide under the shadow of the Cross, and the result will be perfect physical, as well as spiritual, victory.

The lesson, which we are learning from the book of Exodus, is that there is no safety apart from the blood. Would to God that this truth might be burned into our very souls in these days of awful apostasy! So we might cry to those who are prating of "safety" while denying the blood that bought them. "There is no safety, except on the bleeding side of the man of Calvary." We should shun, as we would vipers, all the literature put out by modernists so-called (they are as ancient as the devil himself), or the cults that trample under foot the blood of the Son of God shed for our redemption, if we would really and truly put "Safety First."

The end of this thrilling story we have been reading in Exodus is found in the following words from Psalm 105:37: He brought them forth...and there was not one feeble person among all their tribes.

What a refreshing sight, a mighty nation, including thousands of aged men and women, tiny children, and young mothers, and not one feeble among them all. Every frame erect and stalwart, every skin clear, every eye bright and shining, every man, woman, and child fit for the day's march—their strength as their day.

No wonder the fear and dread of them fell upon the surrounding nations and peoples as they marched along! No wonder Balaam had to confess "God is with him…he hath as it were the strength of an unicorn." (Num. 23:21,22.)

We are told that the things that happened to them were for an example unto us. God has provided "some better thing for us." They dwelt in types and shadows while we have the substance. Theirs were half-lights while we have the full radiance of the outpoured Holy Spirit, who is come to lead us into all truth, to teach us all things. But what kind of a battlefront do we present as compared to theirs?

We are passing in procession down the aisles of the ages as truly as they did; we are being reviewed by a mighty host of witnesses including the heroes of faith of previous dispensations. Does not the thought come to you at times that we present but a sorry spectacle as compared to the Israelites? How many of us are limping along while others actually have to be carried on stretchers? What is the matter with us? Have we one promise less than they? Does not every assurance of physical health and healing, which was made to them, apply equally to us?

No one who believes the Word of God can answer this question other than affirmatively. God says, "I am the Lord that healeth thee" (Ex. 15:26); "My Word shall be health to all your flesh." (Prov. 4:22.) And He also said, "I am the Lord. I change not." (Mal. 3:6.)

The covenant of healing given to them (Ex. 15:26), which secured to them absolute immunity from disease, conditioned upon their obedience to God's statutes, is ours; and the condition need not frighten us, for by the obedience of One many are made righteous. (Rom. 5:19.) And Christ is the end of the law for righteousness to every one that believeth, and the righteousness of the law is fulfilled in us who walk not after the flesh but after the Spirit. (Rom. 8:4.) Therefore, not healing only, but absolute immunity from disease is ours in Christ Jesus as we walk in the obedience of faith.

That is what the world is looking for today. Chinese families are said to pay their doctors to keep them well, and the income of the family doctor ceases from that particular family if any one in the house becomes sick.

Western medical science is involved in the field of preventive medicine also, and I do not desire to belittle anything that may have been accomplished. But this I do say, that immunity from disease which is the dream, the unrealized ideal of medical science, is realizable by any simple child of God who will take his stand on the promises of God and not stagger at them through unbelief.

God wants us to be living epistles. This word is to be written in our very flesh in a language that all can read, for "He is the health of our countenance." (Ps. 42:11.) And the heathen will have to say, "The Lord hath done great things for them" (Ps. 126:2), and they will seek the Lord our God.

A WONDERFUL TREE

The Lord showed him a tree...

Exodus 15:25

The last chapter dealt with the institution of the Passover and of the triumphant march of the Israelites out of the Egyptian bondage under which they had groaned for upwards of 400 years. These events are absolutely without parallel in history, whether sacred or profane. With a high hand, an outstretched arm, and mighty signs and wonders, God delivered them; and they made their exit from the land of the Pharaohs where they had been so long in thraldom, laden down with the treasures of their former masters. For we read in Exodus 12:35 that, according to the word of Moses, they "borrowed" from the Egyptians jewels of gold and silver, as well as raiment.

I once heard a learned Jewish convert to Christianity tell an incident in relation to this text, which I have found most instructive to illustrate how people, who know nothing about it, will venture to criticize the Word of God.

He had dropped into a meeting of socialists in a hall in London, England, just as a speaker was saying: "The God of the Christians! The God of the Christians is a thief, a robber. In the 12th chapter of Exodus, we read that He directed the Israelites on their departure from Egypt to 'borrow' jewels of silver, jewels of gold and raiment, which they could never return. And they obeyed Him and spoiled the Egyptians."

The Jewish convert rose and asked to speak, and when the request was granted, he said: "I think, my friend, that you should know something more about the Bible and its author, God, before you undertake to criticize it. I am a Hebrew; that book is written in my mother tongue. The word in the original is not "borrow" but "ask" (that is the marginal reading in the Bible), and the real meaning of the word is *demand.* Surely you, who profess to be so anxious to see all men righteously dealt with, ought to be the last to object to this. Demand recompense for all your centuries of toil, for your labor, your sweat, your blood, the lives that the cruel lash of the slave master have cost. And this is what they did."

Well, to resume the wonderful tale, the children of Israel were led out and, by God's itinerary, brought to the Red Sea at a point where they were walled in by perpendicular rocks while the horses and chariots of Pharaoh were heard in full pursuit in the rear. At God's command they marched forward, and the Red Sea, which also heard His voice, promptly piled itself up on either side so that they passed dryshod between colossal walls of water. They reached the other side and held a jubilee of triumph. Miriam led in the dance as the maidens played on the timbrels.

> Sound the loud timbrel o'er Egypt's dark sea,
> Jehovah hath triumphed, His people are free.

But alas! Alas! Alas! The echo of these strains of joy have hardly died away before they are replaced by murmuring against God. Can it be possible? Only a short time since these people were doubtless saying: "For my part, after what I have seen with my own eyes and heard with my own ears, I shall never forget the wonder of it! I can never doubt again."

No, not until the next time. Here we find them in Exodus 15:23 murmuring because the waters at Marah were bitter. You would think they would have reflected that the God who had delivered them, who had rolled back the Red Sea at their cry, could also remedy this trouble; but no, they murmured against Moses. When people are not right with God and want to murmur but are afraid to find fault with Him, they are apt to attack His servants. So let us be careful if we find that tendency in our hearts even—much less bitter words on our lips. They had forgotten that it is through our needs that God reveals Himself to us.

Jehovah is distinctively the redemptive name of God; and in His redemptive relation to man, Jehovah has seven compound names which reveal Him as meeting fully every need of man from his lost state to the glorious ending of a completed redemption. Physical healing can be clearly seen in each of the seven.

1. *Jehovah-Jireh.* "The Lord will provide" (Gen. 22:8). Our first need was a perfect sacrifice, and that God provided by giving His Son, the spotless Lamb of God, to bear our sins *and sicknesses* on that cruel tree on the hill of the Skull near Jerusalem.
2. *Jehovah-Rapha.* "The Lord that healeth" (Ex. 15:26).
3. *Jehovah-Nissi.* "The Lord our banner" (Ex. 17:8-15); The Lord who fights our battles for us when Satan would attack us whether in soul or body.
4. *Jehovah-Shalom.* "The Lord, our peace" (Judg. 6:24). Only one who is in perfect health, physically as well as spiritually and mentally, can be kept in perfect peace; and Jesus offers Himself to us as peace for our triune beings, for "He is our peace" (Eph. 2:14).
5. *Jehovah-Ra-ah.* "The Lord our shepherd" (Ps. 23:1). The physical well-being of the sheep is the shepherd's responsibility. He applies the healing balm from his horn of oil to the

sores and bruises. So Jesus, the Good Shepherd, heals those who are His.

6. *Jehovah-Tsidkenu.* "The Lord our righteousness" (Jer. 23:6). Righteousness, or "rightness" for spirit, soul, and body, all three of which God teaches us to pray may be preserved blameless unto the coming of our Lord Jesus Christ.
7. *Jehovah-Shammah.* "The Lord is present" (Ezek. 48:35). The same Jesus who healed all who were oppressed by the devil is with us today.

The bitter waters of Marah reminds us that life, of which water is a type as it forms the great bulk of all living things, is embittered at its very fountain head. The tiny baby is hardly born into the world before the anxious mother is inquiring whether it is strong, or if it shows any evidence of this or that hereditary disease or any tendency thereto; and the saddest thing of all is that every baby has some inherited morbid predisposition, if not an actual disease, when it arrives in this sphere.

And when the Israelites were brought face-to-face with the bitter waters of Marah, God was there to reveal Himself to them under a new name to meet the new need: "The Lord that healeth" [present tense, that always heals—present, continuous healing].

And the Lord showed Moses *a tree!* Oh, for a fresh, God-given vision of that *tree* and the fruit that it bears! Truly as it is put in the Song of Solomon, we can sit down under its shadow with great delight, and its fruit is sweet to our taste.

There is a substance known in chemistry that is about 700 times sweeter than sugar. It was discovered accidentally by a chemist when he was experimenting with coal-tar products. He had been called to dinner; and after washing his hands in the laboratory as usual, changed his coat and sat down at the table. Taking a sip of tea, he was disgusted to find it sweeter than the sweetest syrup he had ever tasted. He was about to remonstrate with his wife but took a bite of bread first to take the cloying taste of the sweetness out of his mouth. To his amazement, the bread tasted like the richest cake. The thought occurred to him, "Is it possible that I am sweet?" He put his thumb in his mouth to suck it like a baby, and it was as though he had a sugarplum in his mouth. To his wife's surprise he jumped and ran to the laboratory where he carefully examined the contents of every test tube and crucible. At last he found the compound he had accidentally produced when boiling some chemicals together, the vapor from which had gotten into his throat, on his lips, and into his lungs, so that he was all sweetness.

When we see this *tree* in the light, which the Holy Ghost sheds upon it through the Word, everything becomes sweet:

> Never further than Thy cross,
>   Never higher than Thy feet;
> There earth's richest things are dross,
>   There, earth's bitterest things are sweet.

Yes, everything is sweet to us for we are ourselves sweet; nay, rather we are sweetness if Jesus, who is the Word of God and who is sweeter than honey and the honeycomb, is dwelling and reigning within us. For "it is no longer I, but Christ who dwelleth in me." (Gal. 2:20.) That was a wonderful tree that God showed Moses, and it bears wonderful fruit.

When Jesus, Moses, and Elias met in the glory of the Mount of Transfiguration, there was no theme so fitting for their discourse as the decease, which Jesus was to accomplish at Jerusalem. For that death was the greatest achievement that this world has ever witnessed, the only act of sacrifice acceptable to God that has been performed by a human being—for Jesus was true man as well as "very God of very God"—since the Fall. For all the righteous acts of the saints are necessarily performed in the power of that one sacrifice of Himself, by which He hath forever perfected them that are sanctified and are, as it were, an integral part of that accomplishment. On that *tree* we find pardon and peace, healing and health, victory over death and hell; for by His death on that *tree* Jesus conquered death and him that hath the power of death. "Bowed to the grave, destroyed it so, and death, by dying, slew."

That *tree* was most fittingly set up on Calvary (Latin, *Calvarium,* the place of the skull), the very zenith of Satan's power. For what more fully shows the depth of man's fall than the transformation of the beautiful human countenance, radiant with intelligence and glowing with emotion, bearing the impress of the divine image upon its lineaments, into a ghastly, grinning, gruesome skull?

This then is the tree that God showed Moses, which when cast into the waters, made them sweet. In a book which I have been reading, it is stated that the waters in the vicinity of Marah are still bitter from an excess of alkali salts but that the fount, which was healed by the branch, can still be distinguished from the others by its comparative sweetness. Notice that the *tree* had to be cast into the waters; that is, the atoning merits of Christ have to be applied to our own particular case of sin, sickness, or both as the case may be, by our own personal faith.

I am told that in the public library at Boston, Massachusetts, Sargent, one of the greatest of modern artists, has brought out most beautifully and clearly in his mural decoration, "The Dogma of Redemption," the truth of our deliverance from sin, sickness, and death through the sacrifice of Christ.

In the picture, Jesus hangs on the cross, and on either side of Him are our first parents, Adam and Eve, each holding in their hands golden chalices in which they are catching drops of the precious blood that flows from His pierced hands. Above the cross are the words, "Dying for the Sins of the World," and beneath the whole, the inscription, "He came to redeem our bodies and to cleanse our hearts." In all the work there is a strong line of demarcation between celestial and terrestrial, but the uplifted cross breaks through this and lets heaven and earth run into one. Praise God! That is what the cross does for us. The cross itself is upheld by angels whose faces are radiant with bliss as though they comprehended the final, fullest, most glorious purpose of God in the Supreme Sacrifice and could not contain their joy. And the instruments of agony, the scourge, the hammer, the spear, are all held in the hands of angels who are bathed with the rest of the scene in unutterable glory.

May God in His mercy show us the *Tree;* and when we see it, may we apply it to our hearts and lives, our spirits, souls, and bodies, so that we may become the very sweetness of Jesus. "There He made for them a statute and an ordinance, and there He proved them!"

The Word of God always proves or tests us. Some people say, "I will try God's promises for healing." No, you won't; they will try you. God's promises are tried, purified seven times, forever settled. *You* are the one that is on trial. God is not on trial. His truth reaches to the heavens and His faithfulness to the clouds. He made this statute and ordinance and they have never been repealed. He sealed them with His covenant, and forevermore He is Jehovah-Rapha, the Lord that healeth. They are conditional upon our diligent hearkening and faithful obedience. But before He made these conditions He showed us the *Tree.*

That Tree cast into our lives will remove every trace of the bitterness of sin and rebellion from our natures and make us sweet with the heavenly sweetness of our Lord. Then we can claim absolute immunity from all the sickness that was brought by God in His righteous judgments on the Egyptians.

The great poet Dante has placed in his poem "Inferno," over the portal of hell, the well-known words, "All hope abandon ye who enter here." But as we enter as little children into the kingdom of heaven through faith in a crucified Saviour, we read in golden letters, "All fear abandon, ye who enter here." For He hath redeemed us from all evil and will preserve us blameless in spirit, soul, and body until His glorious coming.

Chapter 6
THE PRAISE CURE

I have administered a good many cures, seen a good many administered, and heard about a good many more. I remember a friend of mine telling me of one she took. But whatever the results might have been, they were certainly not lasting, as she repeated it every year; and she complained, moreover, that it was very unpleasant.

"It was horribly expensive as well," she continued, "but as I had plenty of money in those days, that didn't matter so much; but the unpleasantness of it, I shall never forget."

"What was there so unpleasant about it?" I inquired.

"Well, to begin with I had to go to Austria for it, for only there is a certain kind of mineral water to be found, which my doctor says my constitution needs. It is horribly nasty, tastes like sulphur matches and rotten eggs would taste, to judge by the smell. When I got there I was put in a little attic room and had to be thankful to get it, the place was so crowded. It was a room such that I should not dare ask anyone in America to sleep in, not even a tramp. Then we were wakened in the morning at five o'clock by a sort of clapper that made a very loud and grating noise. At the very first stroke we had to leap up."

"Why such haste?"

"Because if we didn't get up immediately, we should be late and that meant no breakfast. That was part of the cure!"

"Oh, I understand. I suppose, then, you hastily took your bath and ran down to a well-prepared meal."

"That's all you know about it. There was no bathroom; and already blue with cold, I had to wash in a hand basin in ice water. Honestly, I have sometimes found a thin film of ice on the water in the jug. Then I had to dress as quickly as I could in all my outdoor things, including heavy walking boots, and put on a warm wrap. I then dashed downstairs to join the procession on the way to breakfast."

"Why, where was the breakfast?"

"Oh, miles and miles away. That was part of the cure. The road was very rough; I think that was part of the cure, too, to shake up your liver."

"Well, I suppose you arrived at last and went into a building where they had a huge open fireplace with great logs burning in it and sat down in front of its grateful warmth to a substantial German breakfast, all steaming hot."

"That shows all you know about it. No, when we reached our destination, we were at a sort of fountain surrounded by a platform, which was always slippery and damp, where we formed in line and at last reached the man who dispensed the water. When you gave your name, he turned to a file he had to see how many glasses you had to drink and handed them to you, one by one, watching to see that you consumed the last drop of each. Then, and not till then, he handed you a ticket that entitled you to breakfast; and you made a mad rush with the rest of the patients to a sort of garden, only it had no flowers in it, only some discouraged shrubs. Here there were some small tables (for we always took our meals in the open air if possible, that being part of the cure), on which were rolls of some kind of black bread; but I tell you it tasted good, and the only trouble was the rolls were so small."

"But you could eat plenty of them, I suppose," I interjected.

"Maybe you're a doctor, but it's plain to me that you know nothing about cures," my friend said almost contemptuously. "No, we were allowed only two rolls at the most; some patients got only one all the time they were there. Once in a great while, some of us got an egg each or a very thin slice of cold meat with our roll, but that was only by the doctor's *special* order. Then we had a cup of very weak coffee made with milk. It was hot and was the only warm thing we encountered from the time we got up until dinnertime. They usually had some very thin soup for dinner and two kinds of vegetables—very small helpings—and some days a tiny, tiny bit of meat or fish. No dessert, excepting on gala days, an apple. Supper wasn't worth mentioning, and often I was deprived of it altogether. This ordeal was considered a great cure, and you had to apply months beforehand to be sure of getting in; and counting your traveling expenses, doctors' bills and board, it came to be very high."

That's one kind of a cure, and there have been and are many others; as the grape cure, where patients are allowed to eat all the ripe grapes they can get but nothing else of any kind; the barefoot cure, where they go barefoot; the hot mud cure—no, they didn't have to eat it, only wallow in it. And I am far from saying that nothing is accomplished by these and other kindred methods, but I do say that the cure of which I am going to speak is the only sure cure. It is the most expensive one ever known, but the price was paid by another; for "it was purchased, not with corruptible things, as silver and gold...but with the precious blood of Christ, as of a lamb without blemish and without spot." (1 Peter 1:19.) And the poorest may enjoy its fullest benefits. I call it the praise cure because it is most readily applied by simply singing yourself into it: Enter into his gates with thanksgiving, and into his courts with praise: be thankful unto him, and bless his name (Ps. 100:4). You know you can sing yourself and shout yourself into and through things that you can't get into or through in any other way.

There was an old Presbyterian elder who was terribly opposed to anybody making a noise over his religion. He thought religion should be like the newest style of typewriters, absolutely noiseless and with a guarantee to that effect. He had one daughter, however, a most saintly girl who had so much glory in her soul that she occasionally boiled over. He labored with her to no effect; for it seemed as though she could not help it, though she hated to grieve her old father. At last one day the old man came to the end of his well-spent life; and as he felt himself entering the valley of the shadow of death, he had a glimpse of the glory that is to be revealed. And to the amazement of all his family, he gave one shout of great joy and cried for his shouting girl, "Come along, daughter, and help me shout my way through clear home to glory." And that is exactly what she did, though the tears were streaming down her face all the while.

And we can stand on God's Word for salvation and healing after we have met God's conditions and grounded every weapon of rebellion. We can praise our way through to perfect manifested victory. This I call the praise cure, and it never fails when the praise is the outflow of a heart resting on God's unchanging Word.

There was a missionary to China staying at Mrs. Carrie Judd Montgomery's Beulah Heights in Oakland, California. She had the most wonderful healing of smallpox while on the field by the application of the praise cure.

She fearlessly nursed a sister missionary who had the disease though she had not been vaccinated, standing on God's promise that no plague should come nigh her dwelling. Then a very bad case of confluent smallpox—that was what it looked like to the doctors—came out on her, and she did not know what to do; so she asked the Lord, and He told her to sing and praise Him for His faithfulness to His Word. They isolated her and told her to lie quiet; but she said if she didn't praise God, the very stones would cry out. So she sang and sang and praised and praised. The doctor said he feared for her life, that the case was serious and awful complications threatened. But she praised and praised and sang and sang.

He said she was evidently delirious but that he had so little help that he couldn't restrain her—and she sang and sang and praised and praised. They told her that if by any chance she recovered, she would be disfigured for life—and she sang and praised louder than ever. They asked, "Why do you praise so much?" She answered, "Because I have so many pox on me. God shows me I must praise Him for each one separately." And she kept right at it.

The Lord had shown her a vision of two baskets, one containing her praising—half full—and the other, in which was her testing—full. He told her that the praise basket must be filled so that it would out balance the other, so she kept at it. Her songs and shouts were so Spirit-filled that they were contagious, and the Christian nurses couldn't resist joining in; so they kept the place ringing. At last the Lord showed her that the praise basket was full and overflowing. She saw it sink and the testing basket rise in the air; and in a moment, as it seemed, the eruption and all attendant symptoms vanished, leaving no trace in the way of so much as a single scar.

Perhaps that may seem almost too much to believe to some, but I can furnish from my own personal experience a case where the smallpox eruption disappeared instantaneously in answer to believing prayer and the application of the praise cure.

One evening we were about to open the meeting at a mission where I was then working when a man rushed into the hall and asked to have a few moments of private conversation with me. After I led him to the prayer room, he said, "Dr. Yeomans, my wife has just broken out all over with smallpox!"

"How do you know that it is smallpox?" I inquired.

"Why, we had a doctor who said so and told us not to stir from the house as he was going down to get the health doctor and have the place quarantined without a moment's delay. But as soon as he had left the house, my wife said, 'Run down to the mission. Ask Dr. Yeomans to pray, and I am sure God will clear this plague off my skin and out of my blood.'"

So right on the spot we applied the praise cure, and the brother ran home to find his wife without a single trace of the disease. A little later the doctor returned with the health doctor and was unmercifully teased by the latter for reporting a case of smallpox when there wasn't a pock in sight, nor any symptom of disease.

"Where is your smallpox?" the health officer inquired.

"Well, where is it? It was here when I left."

"Well, where is it now?" inquired the health doctor; and with some jokes as to the probable character of the beverages, which his colleague had been indulging in, he left the place without any further comment.

Yes, the praise cure works every time. It is not unpleasant; rather it is delightful; the cost of it has been met for us by another, and it is available this moment to each of us.

Are you ready to begin it? The last clause of 1 Peter 1:8 tells us exactly how to begin: "*Believing,* ye rejoice with joy unspeakable and full of glory."

Just believe what God says that Jesus has done for you, body, soul, and spirit—think about it, talk about it, sing about it, shout about it, and the praise cure has begun. You are not to take it once a year but all the time. I will bless the Lord at all times: his praise shall continually be in my mouth (Ps. 34:1). The Psalms—the book of praise inspired by the Holy Spirit, which has been used by the people of God in all ages and which Jesus Himself used—are full of this praise cure. Just observe the first five verses of Psalm 103: Bless the Lord, O my soul: and all that is within me, bless His holy name. Bless the Lord, O my soul, and forget not all his benefits: who forgiveth all thine iniquities; who healeth all thy diseases; who redeemeth thy life from destruction; who crowneth thee with lovingkindness and tender mercies; who satisfieth thy mouth with good things; so that thy youth is renewed like the eagle's.

I personally knew a man who was dying of acute tuberculosis of the lungs who praised himself into perfect, rugged health that lasted a lifetime. His remarkable recovery and good health was the result of following the words of this Psalm. Begin now. You can't afford to postpone it by so much as a moment. Tread the young lions under your feet by the praise of faith. It has never failed and never will.

Sometimes people say, "That's true and I feel better already. But when Jesus spoke the word when He was here in person, the symptoms always disappeared instantly; and mine haven't disappeared or have only partly disappeared; so I can't be healed."

The scriptural answer to this difficulty is that the symptoms did not always disappear immediately, even when Jesus was here in person.

The nobleman's son, referred to in John 4:49-53, "began to amend," or get better, improve, convalesce, at the seventh hour when the fever left him.

The healing of the blind man at Bethsaida, related in Mark 8:22-25, is not only markedly gradual but in three distinct, separate stages.

First, Jesus took him by the hand and led him out of Bethsaida, which city He had abandoned to judgment. (Mark 8:23; Matt. 11:21-24.)

Second, Jesus began the healing with an anointing of spittle, after which He asked the man if he saw aught (anything). And the man replied that he saw men as trees walking; or in other words, that he had a degree of distorted vision.

If the man who now possessed enough sight to enable him to blunder around had departed and told people that Jesus had healed him but that he could only see to get around and had no use of his eyes for work that required clear vision, I believe he would have done just what many thousands of people who come for prayer for healing are doing today. Those to whom he told his story would have said, "Well, that's the kind of work Jesus of Nazareth does, is it? It's a wonder He wouldn't have made a good job of it while He was at it." But that wouldn't have been Jesus' fault, would it? And it isn't His fault if you have not perfect soundness. If you are in the second stage, press through to the third one. For in it the man received perfect sight and saw every man clearly. Notice that Jesus made him look up (v. 25), and that one look of faith to the Lamb of God brought perfect restoration of his sight. Let us look into His face and praise Him for the fullness of the redemption He has purchased for us, for it is a wonderful cure—the praise cure—and the only unfailing one that has ever been discovered or ever will be discovered.

Chapter 7
TIMOTHY'S WINE AND HEZEKIAH'S POULTICE

Drink no longer water [or "water only," marginal translation], but use a little wine for thy stomach's sake and thine often infirmities (1 Tim. 5:23). It is wonderful how many people can quote this verse more or less correctly. I remember hearing a preacher say that he had met those who couldn't quote another verse from the Bible but who were quite familiar with this one. I once had a seeker at the altar with whom I was dealing whose greatest weakness was a love for strong drink. He said, "But doesn't the Bible say that Timothy was told by the apostle Paul to use a little wine for his stomach's sake?"

"Yes, to be sure, Paul told Timothy to use a little wine for his stomach's sake, but that does not warrant you in using a *great deal* of whiskey to destroy your stomach and all the rest of your organs," I replied.

And then I have had people quote it as their authority for using all sorts of drugs. Because Paul told Timothy to take a *little* wine, they felt clear to take a *great deal* of quinine or some laxative or favorite tonic or aspirin or Tanlac or other patent medicine.

Of course, this matter is only part of a much larger question; namely, "What is the attitude of the Word of God toward man-made systems of healing?" But let us look into this question of Timothy's wine. In studying this passage, I do not feel free to omit what the eminent Bible scholar, Moffatt, says of this verse that it is "either a marginal gloss, or misplaced." But as it occurs in the King James and other versions in use among us, I shall consider it as belonging to the original text. I believe that in it Paul advised Timothy in regard to his diet, suggesting the substitution of the juice of the grape—which is most valuable from the standpoint of nutrition—for water as a beverage, just as though I should counsel one of you to take cocoa or other nourishing drinks with your meals instead of water only. In the New Testament we are left perfectly free, under God, as to our diet. And so long as we eat and drink to His glory, we may consult our preferences as to the selection we make. Indeed, with a perfectly healthy person—and God makes us perfectly healthy if we trust Him—the tastes are an index of the requirements of the system and should be regarded as such. That God desires us to enjoy a variety of foods is evident from the fact that He has provided so many different kinds, each possessing some special property peculiar to itself and valuable to us. I believe that we should show our gratitude to Him; first by thanking Him for His lavish kindness in this regard; and second, by furnishing our tables with a varied diet, so far as our means will permit. There is no doubt that such a diet makes for health and efficiency. Children should be trained from their earliest days to eat and enjoy a varied diet, comprising as many different kinds of vegetables and fruits as are obtainable, as well as nuts, a little meat, milk, eggs, butter, cheese, cereals, whole wheat bread, etc.

With reference to Hezekiah's poultice, we note from careful study that his case was a perfectly hopeless one. God Himself had told him to set his house in order, for he was going to die. The case has been analyzed by a distinguished Christian physician, author of a treatise on Bible diseases, and pronounced one of carbuncle, followed by general blood poisoning. A carbuncle is like a gigantic boil, which involves the deeper tissues of the body. Hezekiah prayed and received God's promise of healing and was told that fifteen years would be added to his life. Isaiah then directed him to place a poultice of figs on the boil, but such an application could have no effect on the course of such a hopeless disease as carbuncle and general blood poisoning. It might have been used as a cleansing application. It used to be customary to cleanse ulcerating and discharging surfaces by applying large moist poultices of soft pultaceous material, such as bread and milk, linseed and charcoal, etc.; but they had no curative properties. On the other hand, the order to place a lump of boiled figs on the boil or carbuncle may have been merely a test of Hezekiah's obedience, just as Naaman was ordered to dip seven times in the Jordan. While on this point, allow me to quote the following from the *Sword of the Spirit*.

> Any means ever used in the Bible had no healing virtue in them whatever; and as we have already said in this article, were used only as a test of faith and obedience.... When the children of Israel were bitten by the serpents in the wilderness, God told them the means by which they might be healed, which was for Moses to make a polished brass serpent and put it on a pole. One look at this serpent would bring pardon, cleansing and healing to the bitten and dying Israelites. The serpent was preserved as a memorial of what God had done. A long time afterwards in Hezekiah's time, they began to depend on the virtue supposed to be in the serpent. This brought a stem rebuke from Hezekiah, who ground the serpent to pieces and threw it away.

Now let us consider the question referred to earlier in this chapter: What is the attitude of the Word of God toward man-made systems of healing?

Of the futility of turning to human physicians instead of to Him in sickness, God has given us three examples in the Bible. First, the illness and death of Ahaziah, king of Israel and son of Ahab, who enquired regarding his case of Baalzebub, god of Ekron, instead of the Lord God of Israel. (2 Kings 1:2-4.) Second, the illness and death of Asa who sought not the Lord but the physicians and "slept with his fathers." (2 Chron. 16:12,13.) I once talked with a doctor about different schools of medicine—allopaths, homeopaths, naturopaths, and others. He said, "*All* the 'paths' lead but to the grave, so it doesn't matter much which 'path' you take." That was where Asa's physicians led him, that is certain. And third, the woman who suffered many things of many physicians, spending all she had and was nothing better but rather grew worse. (Mark 5:25,26; Luke 8:43.) It is worthy of note that Luke, himself a physician, does not speak of the woman having suffered many things of the medical fraternity and being rather worse than better as the result of their ministrations, though he mentions that she had spent all she had upon them. But the most striking thing about the attitude of the Word of God toward human systems of healing is that they are ignored therein as though they were nonexistent. In view of the fact that elaborate systems of medical science flourished during the periods covered by the Sacred Record, it seems that no words could be more eloquent than the divine silence regarding them.

The distinguished scientist, Dr. Albert T. Buck, in his exhaustive work on the history of medical science, after writing of the skill of ancient Egyptian physicians and surgeons, the many remedies including powders, inhalations, potions, snuffs, salves, fumigations, injections, etc., employed by them, their dietetic measures, eliminative treatment, and other therapies, adds a note about the Israelites. "The Israelites made small use of medicinal agents, dietetic measures and external applications. They placed their chief reliance on prayers, sacrifices and offerings."

No, the Israelites had no need for Egyptian remedies, efficacious though they may have been. Their God had promised that He would bring on them none of the diseases which He brought upon the Egyptians, for He is the Lord who heals His people. (Ex. 15:26.) The history of medical science reveals the fact that from prehistoric times men have fought with all the powers of intellect they possess against sickness, but noble as have been their efforts—for science has its martyrs as well as religion, and many have actually laid down their lives in the battle against disease—they have yielded very unsatisfactory results, scientific men themselves being the witnesses. Note these words from the pen of H. A. Rowland, in the *American Journal of Science,* quoted by Dr. Fielding H. Garrison in his *History of Medicine.*

> An only child, a beloved wife; lies on a bed of sickness. The physician says the disease is mortal; a minute plant called a microbe has obtained entrance into the body and is growing at the expense of the tissues, forming deadly poisons in the blood or destroying some vital organ. The physician looks on without being able to do anything. Daily he comes and notes the failing strength of the patient; daily the patient goes downward until she rests in her grave. But why has the physician allowed this? Can we doubt that there is a remedy that will kill the microbe? Why then has he not used it? He is employed to cure but has failed. His bill we cheerfully pay, because he has done his best and has given a chance of a cure. The reason for his failure to cure is ignorance. The remedy is yet unknown. The physician is waiting for others to discover it, or is perhaps experimenting in a crude and unscientific manner to find it.

And this sad confession is made after centuries and centuries of investigation, research, and effort, during which the animal, vegetable, and mineral kingdoms have literally been ransacked for remedial agents. In the 16th century A.D., a Chinese doctor published a work on medicine in 52 volumes, and at that time the Chinese had 1800 drugs in their regular pharmacopoeia.

Some people go so far as to say that medical science is God's way of healing His people, that He enables men to discover remedies in order that we may utilize them. If that were the case, Moses—who was versed in all the learning of the Egyptians, including medical science—would have so taught the children of Israel instead of pointing them always and only to God, the Lord, as their physician. If medical science were God's chosen way of meeting our need in sickness, it would not be so uncertain, unreliable, fluctuating, and changing, nor so diverse in its teaching.

In all periods of the world there have been conflicting and rival schools of medicine as there are today. If the physician is God's way for me, I shall have to ascertain which physician, the regular, the homeopath, the eclectic, the osteopath, the chiropractor, the drugless, etc. No, God's way of healing is one, even Christ Jesus the Lord, who is not only the Way, but who is the Truth and the Life of spirit, soul, and body.

While we know that God always blesses men just as much as they will let Him bless them and meets them just where they are, we have the plain statement of the Scriptures that the Lord Himself is the healer of His people, and His glory He will not give to another.

The great French physician, Charcot, says, "The best inspirer of hope is the best physician." Our physician is the God of hope, for the Lord Jesus Christ is Himself our hope. (1 Tim. 1:1.) So in order to be true to God and His Word, it seems to me that we have to do as did His people of old and trust our bodies, as well as our souls, to Him alone.

The Bible teaches that sin, sickness, and suffering actually exist, are real and not illusions of mortal mind as the Christian Scientists would have us believe. But it also teaches that they are completely removed by God in answer to believing prayer offered in the name of Jesus Christ, who Himself bore the full penalty of our sins in His body on the cross of Calvary. This truth, which was fully and simply accepted in apostolic times and for hundreds of years afterward, was later so mixed with prayers at the tombs of saints and the veneration of their relics, bones, clothing, and things of the kind, as to be almost lost to the church. But at the time of the Reformation it again came to light with the unearthing of the Scriptures and their diffusion among the people when many notable healings took place. With every subsequent revival the tide of divine healing has risen higher. Remarkable healings took place in the Quaker revival and the meetings led by the Wesleys, under Simpson, Dowie, Cullis of Boston, and others; and now in connection with the last great outpouring of the Holy Spirit, the mighty tide of healing is rolling in with an irresistible flood of blessing.

In this connection I shall quote some statements regarding a case of organic disease, tuberculosis of the lungs and spine, which was cured by the prayer of faith and anointing according to James 5:14. This healing came after all human means had been applied unsuccessfully, according to certificates furnished by the attending physicians, men eminent in the profession. The quotes are from the *Elim Evangel,* published in Belfast, Ireland, by Pentecostal leaders in Great Britain, among whom are Pastors George and Stephen Jeffreys.

Sister Edith Cuffley, the person who was healed, gave her testimony at a meeting at Elim Tabernacle, London.

> I am led by God to let others know, especially those who are seeking divine healing, how very miraculously I was cured after being ill for four years and nine months.... I was a sewing-machine operator by trade, consequently my work was very heavy, especially so when the war broke out, and I had to do soldiers' coats, tents, etc.... One day I collapsed while at work and had to be taken to the hospital. Two weeks later I had a very bad hemorrhage of the lungs; and for two years I lay in my own home in Kennington, having a nurse daily to attend to me, and the doctor coming three times a week. During this time, the doctor tried to get me into a hospital or sanatorium, but admission was not obtainable, as by this time I had become a bedridden case; so then I began to lose all use of my limbs and endured dreadful pain in my spine. The doctor found that the disease had traveled to the spine, and I was put under X-rays to make sure; and to my great sorrow, it was found to be true. The pain became so great that my husband asked the

> doctor to try and get me away, and the only place that was available was the Home for Incurables and Dying, at Thames Ditton, where I lay from April 1919, till August 1920. Here my condition became very critical and a spinal jacket was made, with the hope that it might prove to be a support and enable me to sit up in bed. This, however, was quite useless; and when I was put into it, the pain only increased. I got much worse, was put on a waterbed, and was given hypodermic injections, twice a day for eight months.

In August, 1920, she left the hospital in an apparently dying condition, her relatives yielding to her wishes to be at home, though those in charge of the institution warned them that she would probably die on her way there. However, she did not die but lived to declare the wonderful works of God. When in awful agony and almost departing this life, the Lord appeared to her in a most wonderful vision. She says:

> It was as though the roof lifted and a most wonderful beam of light shone into my room. Then I saw the Lord in all His glory and this is what I heard, "Fear thou not, for I am with thee; be not dismayed, for I am thy God." (Isa. 41:10.) Then I felt His touch on my arm and heard His voice saying, "These are my words, take them, and believe them, and act upon them." The verses were James 5:14-15. Three times I heard these words repeated to me.

In response to her call, seven Christian brothers and sisters gathered in her room; and after prayer and reading of the Word, carried out implicitly every command in James 5:14-15, anointing her with oil in the name of the Lord and praying the prayer of faith over her. Jesus again visited her in glory; she felt His hand on her head, her limbs were straightened out, and she felt a tingling, starting at her toes and reaching to her fingertips. The Lord spoke, saying, "Arise and get up." She said, "O Lord, I cannot." He spoke the second time, "Arise and get up—now or never!" She said, "O Lord, I will have it *now.*" Then she received power to obey His command, jumped out of bed, and walked around the room. Immediately she was perfectly restored to health and said, "Give me something to eat." Her deformed body was absolutely straight, and she ate two eggs and bread and butter and drank some tea with enjoyment. The next evening she walked one mile to a meeting.

The following certificate was signed by her attending physician, P. Eugene Giuseppe, M.D., C.M., J.P., formerly Government Medical Officer, Trinidad, British West Indies:

> 180 Kinnington Park Road, S.E.
> April 15, 1921
>
> I hereby certify that Edith May Cuffley has been under my professional care since December 1917, and before that date under my predecessor, the late Dr. R. Foster Owen, for several years. She was rendered unfit for work in June 1916, by reason of pulmonary tuberculosis, which was followed by spinal tuberculosis. She was more or less prostrated from that time until the 4th of April last, when she appears to have mysteriously recovered, having received no systematic treatment since her removal from a sanatorium in August 1920. For the last two years she has been crippled, bed-ridden and believed to be incurable. In my opinion she is now recovered and will soon be quite fit for work, and her cure can only be ascribed to her wonderful faith in prayer. (Signed.)

The following notes are from the pen of Dr. A. T. Scoffield, specialist, of Harley Street, London:

> To my great pleasure I can record the case of Mrs. Cuffley, of 40 Denmark Road, Camberwell, S.E. After careful examination, I must consider it a supernatural cure of organic disease. Mrs. Cuffley developed tubercle of the lung, had hemorrhaged, and lay in her bed for two years. X-rays showed advanced tubercle, and she was removed to the Home for Incurables and Dying at Thames Ditton. She lay in a spinal jacket and later on a waterbed.... She has been nearly eight months perfectly well, walking about all day, visiting the sick and poor. I examined her chest and spine and there was certainly no active disease.

Chapter 8
THE CONQUERED CURSE

Christ redeemed me from the curse of the law,
    As He hung on that shameful tree,
And all that is worse is contained in the curse,
    And Jesus has set me free.

Refrain:
Not under the curse, not under the curse,
    Jesus has set me free;
For sickness, I've health; for poverty, wealth,
    Since Jesus has ransomed me.

Christ paid the price of the broken law,
    He paid the whole price for me;
God saw not one spot, one blemish or blot,
    In the Lamb that was slain for me.

Do not abide in the ancient days,
    Ere ever the Lamb was slain;
Take that which was given as freely as heaven,
    And joined in the glad refrain.

From Deuteronomy 28, it is evident that disease, all disease, is included in the curse of the broken law. The following eleven diseases are specified as part of the penalty for disobedience to God's holy commands:

Blindness

Botch (perhaps leprosy)

Consumption

Hemorrhoids

Extreme burning (acute inflammation) Fever

Inflammation

Itch (incurable form)

Madness

Pestilence

Scab

The Word further states: Moreover he will bring upon thee all the diseases of Egypt, which thou wast afraid of; and they shall cleave unto thee. Also every sickness, and every plague, which is not written in the book of this law, them will the Lord bring upon thee, until thou be destroyed. And ye shall be left few in number, whereas ye were as the stars of heaven for multitude; because thou wouldest not obey the voice of the Lord thy God (Deut. 28:60-62).

It is related that Frederick the Great of Prussia once said to his chaplain: "Prove to me in one word that the Bible is a divine revelation." The chaplain replied, "The Jew, Your Majesty."

And surely nothing could be more stimulating to faith than a consideration of the unchanging faithfulness of God in fulfilling to His chosen people Israel every promise, whether of blessing or cursing. In a certain town in which I resided for some time, there was a synagogue. It was located in an obscure district, amidst unattractive surroundings, but was nevertheless a favorite place of pilgrimage for me. Not that I ever entered it or took part in the worship that was held there or even became acquainted with the worshipers. No, I only stood and gazed and gazed at the building, noted the date of its erection—given in accordance with Jewish chronology—its name, House of Jacob: O house of Jacob, come ye, and let us walk in the light of the Lord (Isa. 2:5). And I noticed the strongly marked Hebrew characteristics of the faces of the attendants at the services. Once I caught a glimpse of a man robed in a tallit, or prayer shawl. And as I looked, God's Word, found in the chapter we are studying, words uttered through human lips thousands of years ago, would chant itself in sad, solemn strains in the very depths of my spirit: ...because thou wouldest not obey...ye shall be plucked from off the land whither thou goest to possess it. And the Lord shall scatter thee among all people, from the one end of the earth even unto the other...And among these nations shalt thou find no ease, neither shall the sole of thy foot have rest: but the Lord shall give thee there a trembling heart, and failing of eyes, and sorrow of mind: and thy life shall hang in doubt before thee; and thou shalt fear day and night, and shalt have none assurance of thy life (Deut. 28:62-66).

And the reason I loved to gaze at the synagogue and the poor exiles from the Promised Land who worshiped there, was that I learned from their condition—scattered among strangers who despised them—the exactitude with which God fulfills His Word, whether of blessing or doom. He permits us to see with our eyes and hear with our ears, the literal fulfillment of many portions of this 28th chapter of Deuteronomy; and history records the fulfillment with the most marvelous accuracy of many other portions. Take for instance verse 32: Thy sons and thy daughters shall be given unto another people, and thine eyes shall look, and fail with longing for them all the day long; and there shall be no might in thy hand.

In Portugal and Spain there were actually laws in force at one time that enabled anybody who was so minded to seize Jewish children and bring them up Catholics, which was esteemed a very meritorious action and one not infrequently performed by believers in Roman Catholicism. In such cases the Jewish parents were without recourse, had "no might" in their hands, as the Bible foretold. Look also at verses 49 and 50: The Lord shall bring a nation against thee from far...as swift as the eagle flieth; a nation whose tongue thou shalt not understand; a nation of fierce countenance, which shall not regard the person of the old, nor shew favor to the young.

Perhaps the Roman standard, which bore the eagle, is referred to here; no two languages could be more unlike than the Hebrew and Latin, and the typical Roman countenance of the Caesar era is cruel and stern. Note verses 52 and 64: And He shall besiege thee in all thy gates.... "He," being first Nebuchadnezzar and later Titus. And the Lord shall scatter thee among all people, from the one end of the earth even unto the other.... This has been literally fulfilled.

A converted Hebrew, the Rev. Mr. Schor, recently traveled extensively showing the present condition of the Hebrew race by means of exhibits, which I carefully examined, finding among them photographs of Jews taken in all parts of the world: Chinese Jews wearing robes and queues, African Jews (many of whom were almost if not quite black in color), Russian Jews, Polish Jews, English Jews, etc., all partaking more or less of the characteristics peculiar to the countries where they resided.

If you ever have any doubts as to whether God always means *exactly* what He says, read with me verse 68: And the Lord shall bring thee into Egypt again with ships...and there ye shall be sold unto your enemies for bondmen and bondwomen, and no man shall buy you.

This actually happened after the taking of Jerusalem by Titus. After the Jews had filled the measure of their rebellion against God by crucifying His Son, their Messiah and our blessed Saviour, their young men were shipped to the Roman works in Egypt and there sold as slaves; for so despicable were the Jews deemed at this time that Romans were actually ashamed to have them working for them as slaves, which was doubtless one reason for their transportation to Egypt.

I wonder how many of us feel that these instances are sufficiently numerous to convince us that God means just what He says in this 28th chapter of Deuteronomy. How many think so? Well, then we may feel sure that every other promise we find here, whether of blessing or of cursing, will be as exactly fulfilled as the ones that we have examined. So we shall consider more, especially the ones relating to sickness and deliverance therefrom.

The Children of Israel, whom we have followed in their exodus from Egyptian bondage, Red Sea crossing, and wilderness wanderings, have now entered the Promised Land where they are immediately confronted with two alternatives: the blessing or the curse. The blessing would come by following obedience to God's commandments, which embraced every part of their beings and possessions—spirit, soul, body, children (fruit of their bodies), cattle, crops, and other possessions. It guaranteed them immunity from all disease. Blessed shalt thou be in the city, and blessed shalt thou be in the field (v. 3). Blessed everywhere, whether they went out or came in: "In all that thou settest thy hand unto...the Lord shall command the blessing upon thee...The Lord shall establish thee...and all the people of the earth...shall be afraid of thee. The Lord shall make thee plenteous in goods, in the fruit of thy body, and in the fruit of thy cattle, and in the fruit of thy ground...The Lord shall open unto thee his good treasure...the Lord shall make thee the head, and not the tail."(vv. 8-13.)

And the *curse* was consequent upon failure to obey, which included every form of sickness and disease that can attack humanity. In other words, disobedience to God's law *puts* men under the curse, which includes every form of disease. God is the Lord who changeth not. A life of holiness is essential to a life of physical wholeness; and both are ours through faith in the Lamb of God (who was made a curse for us) and can be obtained in no other way. While I am far from depreciating the efforts that are being made to stamp out sickness by scientific research, I say on the authority of God's Word that such efforts can only be attended with a very limited measure of success; for so long as sin exists, it will—when it is finished—bring forth death, and disease is death begun. The latest statistics show a greater mortality from cancer than ever before in the history of the human race in spite of all the work that has been done in millionaire-endowed laboratories.

Perhaps no more determined effort has ever been made by leaders among men than that which has been directed against the white plague, tuberculosis. I myself knew personally a most able man who spent eighteen years of his life in research work on this one disease alone. The results of his labors were contained in locked books, the contents of which were written in cipher. He was only one of an army of scientific explorers and investigators doing research on this disease. But in spite of their labors, tuberculosis still claims its annual quota of victims. And even if it could be completely stamped out, so long as sin still remains, it would inevitably be followed by sickness of some sort or other; for, as has already been said, "Sin, when it is finished, bringeth forth death." (James 1:15.) And disease is death begun.

So to be delivered from disease we must come to the One who settled the sin-and-sickness question for us on the cross of Calvary by being made a curse for us, and looking to the Lamb of God, sing with grateful hearts:

> Not under the curse, not under the curse, Jesus has set me free,
>
> For sickness, I've health, for poverty, wealth, Since Jesus has ransomed me.

At one time I wondered that God saw fit to *specify* so many diseases in Deuteronomy 28 as part of the penalty for breaking His holy law, when it plainly states that all sickness— "every sickness, and every plague, which is not written in the book of this law" (v. 61)—is included in the curse. But the Holy Spirit gave great light to me on this point when dealing with persons afflicted with some of the diseases so specified. Take tuberculosis of the lungs, for instance, commonly called consumption. I thank God that I have personal knowledge of many marvelous healings of this disease, which is so hopeless. I use the word advisedly, for while modern methods have undoubtedly done a great deal toward arresting its course in the earlier stages, there is still practically no prospect of recovery for advanced cases, excepting by faith in the work accomplished for soul and body on Calvary. And I know no better way of dealing with them than giving them the Word of God in the 28th chapter of Deuteronomy, along with some New Testament verses, more particularly Galatians 3:13: Christ hath redeemed us from the curse of the law....

"There's no hope for me, doctor; I have consumption; three physicians have pronounced it tuberculosis of the lungs. I have been X-rayed and all the rest. They say it is quite advanced and the utmost I can expect is that my life may be prolonged somewhat if I am very faithful in following the instructions they have given me and in taking their remedies."

To which my answer is, "Do you believe that the Bible is the Word of God and absolutely true in every particular?"

"Oh, yes; I know it is."

"Well, then, the Word of God explicitly states that Christ Jesus healed you of consumption, mentioning the name of the very disease from which the doctors tell you you are dying at this moment."

"Oh, where is it? I have never seen it in the Bible."

And then turning to Deuteronomy 28, I point out that consumption is part of the curse of the broken law, from which curse Galatians 3:13 tells us that Christ has redeemed us by being made a curse for us, or in our stead.

"Now repeat with me, 'Christ hath redeemed me from the curse of the law, of which curse consumption is a part, so Christ hath redeemed me from consumption.'" And the seeker obeys; and repeatedly, with the Bible open before us at Deuteronomy 28:22 and Galatians 3:13, we say together, "Christ hath redeemed me from consumption." And faith cometh by hearing the Word of God, and the mountain is cast into the sea.

How thankful I am that God in His mercy and wisdom saw fit to include consumption, the great white plague, among the diseases specially mentioned in this category in the twenty-eighth chapter of Deuteronomy!

Let me relate in brief the history of a woman who was healed by the Word of God in my sister's ministry in our own home in Calgary, Alberta, Canada. I may say that later the sister received the baptism in the Holy Spirit and has been a true witness for Jesus on all lines since her deliverance.

She is a trained nurse, and upon being pronounced tuberculous and made to live in a separate bungalow from the rest of the family and eat off marked dishes, she became very interested in the things of God. She had been saved some years before and came to our house in the hope of getting nearer to Jesus in her spiritual life. She had no hope of being cured of the disease from which she was suffering and wanted to be ready for the home call.

My sister was alone in the house when she called. After a little conversation, which served to reveal the needs of the seeker, the Bible—in which the sick one implicitly believed—was searched, especially regarding healing. The twenty-eighth chapter of Deuteronomy and other verses were brought to her notice, with the result that she saw full salvation for her whole being, including her body, perfectly secured when Jesus was made a curse for her on Calvary. And she was immediately healed.

Some time afterward she was staying at the home of a prominent doctor who had a great esteem for her. He had not known her prior to her healing. One day, just for fun, my sister called him up and asked him if he saw any signs of tuberculosis of the lungs about the nurse he had in his family.

"Certainly *not,*" he replied rather testily, and then he was told the wonderful story.

We are in constant touch with this nurse, hear from her at regular intervals and know her life ever since her healing. It has been one of continual effort and sacrifice for others, a "poured out life," and there is never a hint of any recurrence of the dread disease from which she suffered.

It is noteworthy that among the diseases enumerated as part of the curse of the broken law are found some of the most malignant and virulent from which humanity suffers. Botch, for instance, is said to mean leprosy. Fevers are among the most dreadful scourges, especially in hot countries, such as typhus, typhoid, scarlet fever, smallpox, and other eruptive fevers. Blindness is one of the most awful afflictions from which any one can suffer, being only surpassed by madness, or insanity. The scab, an incurable form of itch, evidently refers to some of those awful and intractable forms of skin disease with which we sometimes come in contact.

How delightful to be able to say, on the authority of God's Word, Christ has redeemed you from *fever,* whether it be typhus, typhoid, scarlet fever, or smallpox; I can give you chapter and verse for it. Christ has redeemed you from *blindness;* for Deuteronomy 28:28 says it is included in the curse of the broken law, and Galatians 3:13 says that Christ redeemed you from the whole curse. Christ has redeemed you from that hopeless skin disease. The Bible says so.

I remember going out to a rather remote settlement with an evangelistic party comprising several workers. The girls were given a little house to live in, but the poor boy was taken to sleep with a game warden, who had a terrible skin disease from which he was seeking healing.

He told us the next day how sorely tempted he had been to refuse to sleep with the man. But how could he allow himself to be afraid of contracting a disease that he was telling the other fellow was part of the curse from which Christ had redeemed him? The devil said, "If you have to get into bed with him, keep all your clothes on, and you may escape contagion, though even then you will be taking terrible risks."

At first he was going to accept this suggestion, but the Holy Spirit lifted up a standard and said, "Can't you trust Jesus?"

And with that he said, "Yes, I can and do trust Him." And peeling off his clothes, he jumped into bed and slept as peacefully as an infant on its mother's breast. And the brother with the skin disease was perfectly healed. He always called his trouble itch, though it wasn't itch at all but something far more serious. I suppose it *itched*—it looked as though it would—and that was the reason he gave it the un-poetical name.

And it seemed as though we would never hear the last of his healing. Sometime a little later we were holding meetings in a fine Methodist church, where the large congregation contained many prosperous and refined persons.

In opening the service one evening I called for testimonies. Of course, I meant nice, polite testimonies; but who should jump up but Johnnie Hourie, the game warden. I didn't even know he was there, as it was far from his home; and he simply convulsed the audience by his testimony.

"Well, praise the Lord! He healed me of the itch!"

You should have heard them laugh! And you couldn't doubt his testimony. He made it very plain that he had suffered tortures, of which God had completely relieved him, in consequence of which he was bubbling over with gratitude.

And how glorious to be able to tell each sick one, no matter what the disease from which they are suffering, that Christ has redeemed them from it, even if it is not specified by name in this wonderful twenty-eighth chapter of Deuteronomy; for we are told in verses 60-61 that all diseases, without a single exception, are included in the curse.

Chapter 9

THE BIBLE OR CHRISTIAN SCIENCE

The Bible or Christian Science, which shall it be? You cannot have both, for they are opposed to one another on all essential points.

"But I thought that Christian Scientists recognized the Bible and are diligent students of it," someone says.

They may read the text, especially portions of it, and carry a copy of it, along with *Science and Health with Key to the Scriptures,* but they do not receive it as the Word of God in truth, eternal, immutable, forever settled in heaven. For on page 139, lines 20 and 21, of their official textbook, we read: "A mortal and material sense stole into the divine record, with its own hue darkening to some extent the inspired pages." And of a statement of the Holy Ghost, in Genesis 2:7, "The Lord God formed man of the dust of the ground," Mrs. Eddy does not hesitate to say (you will find it in the third paragraph of page 524 of the *Key to the Scriptures:* "*How* then could a material organization become the basis of man?...Is this...real or unreal? Is it the truth, or is it a lie?...It must be a lie...." (All quotations are from the edition of 1917.)

Much of Christian Science literature is vague and difficult to understand, but whenever anything essential is stated clearly, it is found to be absolutely antagonistic to the Scriptures.

Sometimes people ask, "What is the difference between Christian Science and divine healing, as taught in the Bible?" They have *nothing* in common. The false philosophy on which Christian Science is founded denies that Jesus Christ is come in the flesh and that His body was a real body, and it is therefore anti-Christian.

The Bible teaches healing as coming to us through the atoning work of Christ on Calvary, with which Christian Science does away altogether; for according to Mrs. Eddy's teaching, since there is no sin, there can be no redemption.

"But do they not have healings?" I believe, from the Bible, that they do; for we are taught to expect to see miracles wrought by satanic power, especially toward the end of the age. But the infidelity with which they teach is so fatal that I feel about their healings like a woman who sent a request for prayer for her son to a meeting I was holding in a Methodist church in Oakland. "My son is terribly sick," she wrote. "There is no human hope, but I ask you to pray for his healing to the God with whom all things are possible. But let none but those who believe in the precious blood of the Lamb as our only approach to God pray for my boy. Let no one who does not honor the blood touch my suffering boy by so much as a thought."

Dr. A. B. Simpson was one of the most well-balanced men spiritually I have ever met; and he says of Christian Science, "I would rather be sick all my life with every form of physical torment, than be healed by such a lie."

"Open confession is good for the soul," and I feel impelled to relate just here a bit of my personal experience (which I much prefer to keep to myself) and to say that if anyone ever *tried* to believe Christian Science, I was that person.

As I have already told you in an earlier chapter, I wakened one morning to the realization that I was in a hopeless quagmire of drug addiction, from which nothing human could extricate me.

I had tried everything that medical science could suggest, had been discharged from the hospital as a patient they could not help and had taken the Gold Cure. After spending practically all I had, impoverishing my poor mother and other relatives as well by my ceaseless efforts to find relief from some source, I turned to my neglected Bible and my interrupted prayer life. And very soon the light on healing began to dawn upon me from the cross of Calvary.

As I felt a faint flutter of hope in my breast—where all had been for so long the stillness of despair—I turned to older Christians for encouragement and not one crumb of comfort did they give me. Remember this was over twenty-six years ago. As I read and re-read the Bible, I saw more and more clearly that not only was provision made for our healing but that we were ourselves commanded to go forth and in the name of Jesus lay hands on the sick and heal them. I said, "I will go to some of the believers I know and point these verses out to them, and ask them to pray with me that I may be healed." And I started on my weary rounds.

I was so desperate that I knew no shame in presenting my petition. No rebuff was stinging enough to make me desist. Some said, because they were ashamed to confess that they did not believe the Word of God: "We are too busy to deal with your case today. Some other time, at the prayer meeting perhaps, you might ask for prayer."

And I would reply, "Nothing you can possibly be doing is as important as complying with Jesus' last command to you to lay hands on the sick that they may recover. Pray with me right here and now, and I believe God will heal me."

But they would not, and at last I said, "The Bible says, 'These signs shall follow them that believe' (Mark 16:17); and as they don't follow these professed Christians, evidently they are not believers. It is said that they follow Christian Scientists, that they heal the sick; so they must be believers, and I will appeal to them." I went to New York City and got in touch with the leaders of the work there.

Through the influence of a friend who stood very high in Christian Science circles (she was afterwards a prominent practitioner in Berlin),

I secured treatments from a most eminent scientist, then practicing in New York. Of course, I paid a goodly sum for them; but it was a great favor to get them at any price, and I was made to feel that I was under the greatest obligations to all who had assisted me to do so.

Of course, I purchased all their literature; and at the command of my practitioner plunged up to the neck in *Science and Health,* reading it every waking moment, or nearly so, very rarely allowing myself a dip into Mrs. Eddy's *Miscellaneous Writings.* I was told that there was absolutely no trouble about my morphine addiction and the awful physical conditions which had resulted therefrom; that it did not really exist and would vanish like snow wreaths before the sun as soon as I freed my thoughts from its "self-imposed materiality and bondage" by absorbing enough of *Science and Health.*

I had a fall, I broke my arm, wherever should I go?
  A Christian Science doctor shall dissipate my woe.
I found the lady calm and sweet, for it was office hours,
  And she on absent treatments must concentrate her powers;
You think she felt the broken bone? No, nothing half so tame,
  She looked into the distance and just denied the claim;
"In mortal error you are swamped but truth you now shall see,
  For as you have no arm to break, no arm can broken be.
Since all is good, and good is all, just voice the truth and say,
  'My arm is strong, and sound, and whole.' Ten dollars,
    please. Good-day!"
I said, "Because in light and truth you're plunged up to the neck,
  Just say, 'I have ten dollars now, and thank you for
    your check.'"

That sounded good to me, you may believe, and I simply devoured Mrs. Eddy's book. Although I did not know the Bible then as I do now, I felt something like the man whose experience I read some time ago. He was told by a woman friend that what he needed was to study *Science and Health with Key to the Scriptures,* by Mrs. Mary Baker Eddy.

"Why, I didn't know the Scriptures were locked; but if they are, it is a mighty lucky thing the lady found the key," he replied.

"Yes, it is the greatest blessing that has ever befallen humanity," said his friend.

And she was so enthusiastic that he finally consented to read the Bible with her. She obligingly opened it with the wonderful "key."

"Mother used to teach me the Bible," he said, "and it seems as if I would enjoy visiting some of the old rooms in it. Take me to the one where we learn about how God created man and man disobeyed God and fell."

"Oh, this is a very wonderful book. And you must be prepared for some surprises, delightful ones all of them. That room you speak of is closed, for Mrs. Eddy has discovered that God did not create man, for 'God and man co-exist and are eternal' (page 336, line 30, *Science and Health*), and also that 'Whatever indicates the fall of man...is the Adam-dream...it is not begotten of the Father'" (page 282, lines 28-31).

"Lead me to the incarnation room where we are brought face-to-face with the ineffable mystery of the Word made *flesh,* the Holy Spirit coming upon the virgin, the power of the highest overshadowing her, so that the holy thing that was born of her, Christ Jesus, was true God and true man."

"Well, I must prepare you for changes there, for 'Those instructed in Christian Science have reached the glorious perception that...the virgin-mother conceived this idea of God and gave to her ideal the name of Jesus'" (page 29, lines 14-18, *Science and Health*).

"But if Jesus was only an 'idea' how could He say to His disciples after the resurrection—you will find it in Luke 24:39—Behold my hands and my feet, that it is I myself: handle me, and see; for a spirit hath not flesh and bones, as ye see me have?"

"Oh, don't let that trouble you at all. Mrs. Eddy explains it away beautifully. Just listen to these marvelous words of wisdom; you will find them on page 313, lines 26-29, of *Science and Health:* 'To accommodate Himself to immature ideas of spiritual power...Jesus called the body, which by spiritual power He raised from the grave, flesh and bones.'"

"Well, if you don't mind, I think I will keep out of that room for there is a verse that says, Every spirit that confesseth not that Jesus Christ is come in the flesh is not of God: and this is that spirit of anti-christ.... Receive him not into your house, neither bid him God speed: for he that biddeth him God speed is partaker of his evil deeds (1 John 4:3; 2 John 10,11). Take me to the room where Jesus Christ is evidently set forth crucified, His own self bearing our sins in His own body on the tree, by whose stripes we were healed, where the Blood, which cleanses from all sin, and brings us nigh to God, by which we have boldness to enter into the holiest, is extolled."

"I cannot, for that room is closed forever to all believers in Christian Science."

"Closed? What do you mean? The Bible says in Hebrews 9:22, ...without shedding of blood is no remission."

"Yes, but Mrs. Eddy has made the glorious discovery, which has much to do with the wonderfully rapid increase in our membership; that there is no need for remission of sin because there is none to be remitted. She has taught us the 'nothingness of sickness and sin' (page 347, line 28), that 'sin, sickness and death' are 'a dream' (page 188, line 12). Isn't that a blessed release? Just believe it and see how comfortable you will feel!"

"I don't seem to get much comfort out of it for a scripture that Mother taught me, If we say we have no sin, we deceive ourselves, and the truth is not in us (1 John 1:8), will keep floating through my consciousness, try as I may to drown it. Perhaps I had better pray for light. The Bible says, 'Ask and ye shall receive.' (Matt. 7:7.)"

"To what purpose? We are taught in *Science and Health* that prayer to a personal God is a hindrance. On page 3 (lines 7-9), we find this question: 'Shall we ask the divine Principle...to do His own work?'"

"So you are taught to think of God as a principle merely. Well, it seems to me that there isn't much left of the Book after the lady that found the 'key' gets through with it."

And that was the way I felt as I studied the textbook, but I was so determined to be *healed* that I tried to shut my eyes to its blasphemous heresies and to swallow it holus-bolus.

My practitioner was a lady with exquisitely beautiful hair, which was always so artistically puffed that it seemed there was not so much as a single hair out of place. She was placid as a summer sea and assured me in the sweetest, calmest way possible that my sin and sickness were only bad dreams from which I should shortly awaken to find everything all right. And at last I really began to half believe it. Like Jonah, I was sinking, down, down, down, down; and like Jonah, I was saved by the direct intervention of God.

I made up my mind to go on with the thing and see what it could do for me. But God had other plans for me, and He sent a whale—it was a big one—to swallow me.

One morning I awakened to find that complete paralysis of the right arm had come on me during the night; and as I am not in the least ambidextrous, it would be hard to find anyone in a worse predicament than mine.

Of course, I rushed to my practitioner to find her wholly undisturbed by the catastrophe. How could she be disturbed when she knew that not only had I no paralysis of the arm but no arm to be paralyzed? She never turned so much as a silver hair but assured me that "There is no life, truth, intelligence, nor substance in matter. All is infinite Mind and its infinite manifestation, for God is ALL in ALL. Spirit is immortal truth; matter is mortal error. Spirit is real and eternal; matter is unreal and temporal. Spirit is God and man is His image and likeness. Therefore, man is not material; He is spiritual." This clearly proved, as you will no doubt perceive, that I had no arm and, therefore, could not have paralysis in it.

Whether or not I had an arm, there was one thing that I didn't have: money. And I was so sure of it that I didn't need to resort to Christian Science to tell me that I didn't have it. I couldn't stay in New York in my helpless condition without money. There was room rent in a very expensive house just off Central Park. There was the high fee charged for treatments. Living in the area was extremely high, so I had no alternative but to return to my home in Winnipeg, Canada.

Indeed, I thought it advisable to leave immediately before any of my other limbs went out of business. So I said a farewell to my practitioner, who was still floating on a summer sea up to the last glimpse I had of her; and having fortified myself with Christian Science literature to enable me to continue my treatment after I reached home, I left.

And there God provided just what I needed. An old friend, an aged minister of the gospel whom I deeply reverenced, was sent from a far land to minister to me. His heart went out in Christ-like sympathy when he beheld the havoc Satan had made in me, the utter destruction of everything that could make life worth living. He did not chide me when he saw me clinging to *Science and Health;* but he did say, and most solemnly, "Sister, that book is straight from hell, and the first step you must take to get deliverance is to burn it."

He did not argue, but he prayed—prayed, I believe, without ceasing; I know of one whole night he spent in prayer for me. And at last one day I staggered down to the kitchen; I was almost too weak to stand upright, but I deposited my copy of *Science and Health* on the glowing coals. It is the only proper place in the universe for it.

Not very long afterwards the light of the glorious gospel of Christ for soul and body shone into my heart. And the drugs with the resultant diseased conditions vanished like snow wreaths, not because they had not been real but because Jesus Christ who died and rose again to deliver me from them is real. They were *real* sin and *sickness,* but in Him I found a *real* Saviour able to save to the uttermost.

To recapitulate, the Word of God, which "endureth forever," and *Science and Health,* produced by Mrs. Mary Baker Glover Eddy, are diametrically opposed on all essential points; so we have to choose between them. Which shall it be then, the Bible or Christian Science?

FOREVER SETTLED

For ever, O Lord, thy word is settled in heaven (Ps. 119:89). "My word...that goeth forth out of my mouth...shall not return unto me void, but it shall accomplish...." (Isa. 55:11.)

Ralph Waldo Emerson said, "No accent of the Holy Ghost this heedless world hath ever lost," which is true; not that the heedless world has safeguarded the priceless treasure, but that the Word of God can't be lost. "It abideth forever." (1 Peter 1:23.) It is incorruptible seed; frost will not kill it; the sun cannot scorch it. It liveth, and behold! it is alive forevermore. It is not only true; it is truth: "Thy word is truth." (John 17:17.)

"Where the word of a king is, there is power" (Eccl. 8:4), and where the Word of the King of Kings is, there is omnipotence. In order to make that almighty Word operative in us and for us, one thing only is necessary and that is to believe it.

The Word of God is with us today, for it cannot be lost. It is just as omnipotent as it always has been and always will be. It is incorruptible, so it cannot suffer change of any kind. We have but to make connection with the batteries of heaven by pressing the button of faith to have the exceeding greatness of God's power revealed in our lives.

It is possible we have all read the story of the blowing up of Hell Gate in New York harbor, an engineering feat that was considered very remarkable at the time of its performance a number of years ago.

When it was decided to remove the dangerous rocks, which had caused the loss of many ships and precious lives, large gangs of men were set to work to honeycomb them with drills. When the drilling was completed, powerful explosives were placed in position, and the whole was wired and connected with batteries located many miles away.

When the hour announced for the explosion arrived, the chief engineer was in his office in New York City with some officials and his staff of assistants. On his knee sat his tiny granddaughter and in front of him on his desk was an insignificant looking key, or button, by means of which little Mary was to blow up Hell Gate.

How it was to be accomplished she had not the remotest idea; that was Grandpa's business, but that it would be done she could not doubt, for had not Grandpa said so; and with perfect confidence that, as she did it, those gigantic rock masses were splintered into fragments and scattered to the four winds, just as Grandpa had told her, she pressed the button with all her might. Far away in the distance a dull booming sound was heard, and in a moment the message was flashed over the wire, "Hell Gate is no more."

The touch of a child's finger in obedient faith in her grandfather's word unlocked the forces that his wisdom had provided for the demolition of the frowning obstacles; but the touch, feeble as it was, was requisite. Though everything necessary to the clearing of the channel was finished, the child's finger had to release the power.

Do you understand the allegory? God's Word of full salvation for spirit, soul, and body, eternal and glorious deliverance for the entire man has been spoken; nay, is being spoken, for *it liveth* and back of it is Omnipotence; but we, children as we are, must press the button with our tiny fingers. When God's people do this in its fullest sense, the message will be flashed to heaven, "Hell's Gate is no more." And the day is coming when this will happen, for we are told that the gates of hell shall not prevail against the church. (Matt. 16:18.) This does not mean that we are merely to defend ourselves against Satan's aggressions but that we shall march against his gates and demolish them.

In Luther's time the enemy had the harbor of peace with God so blocked with dangerous rocks that many were lost in their attempts to make it. With all their penances, fastings, pilgrimages, scourgings, and grovelings before popes and priests, perhaps comparatively few in his day knew what it was to be free from condemnation before God; the way was a veritable "Hell's Gate." But by believing the Word, ...The just shall live by faith, "To him that worketh not, but believeth on Him that justifieth the ungodly, his faith is counted for righteousness" (Rom. 1:17; 4:5), Luther pressed the button. Omnipotence was brought into action, the channel was cleared, and countless myriads sailed safely into port and proved for themselves that ...being justified by faith, we have peace with God through our Lord Jesus Christ (Rom. 5:1).

The Word regarding our bodies is just as expressed as that concerning our souls. Jesus healed the sick and said, "Thy faith hath made thee whole, go in peace." (Luke 8:48.) And the way into healing and wholeness is just the same today, for He is the same; and if anyone will be small enough and humble enough and trustful enough to obey Jesus as exactly and simply as little Mary obeyed her grandfather, we shall have an explosion of divine power one of these days that will shatter the rocks and clear the channel into the harbor of perfect soundness through faith in His name.

Thank God for what He has done, but "there's more to follow," as the old hymn says.

God's Word regarding healing is "forever settled" and it has always been made living and real in exact proportion to the degree of faith exercised by His people. To show that this statement is amply borne out by recorded facts, let us briefly review the history of divine healing from the earliest ages to the present time, dwelling a little on the work of some of the more modern exponents of this truth.

It is a noteworthy fact that there is in every religion that has ever existed some belief, either clearly expressed or tacitly implied, that the healing of the human body is part of the function of the god or gods worshiped by the followers of that creed. One writer, the president of a university, says that the fact that the healing of the sick has been mixed up from time immemorial with religion has most seriously hindered the development of medical science.

I believe that the widespread existence of this belief is due to the common origin of mankind, and the retention—to some extent at least—by all peoples and races, of the original revelation of God to our first parents. This includes the fact that sickness is the result of sin and that the Supreme Being, whose law has been violated, is the only one who can effectively deal with it. I further believe that the healing of disease is "mixed up with religion," as the writer I have quoted puts it, because God has joined them; and what God hath joined together man may not put asunder. (Mark 10:9.)

History shows us the ancient Babylonians, Chinese, Egyptians, East Indians, Greeks, Romans, as well as other races, having recourse to religious observances, sacrificed to their demon deities prayers and various other ceremonies in case of sickness; but writing about the Jews, one historian states, "Disease was considered a punishment for sin, and hence the cure was religious rather than medical."

From the foregoing it is evident that it has been the general conviction of mankind in all ages that sickness has a spiritual origin and requires divine power for the remedy; even the heathen in their benighted way bear witness to this truth. So far from being a modern fad, as it has sometimes been called, divine healing is the ancient and original method of dealing with our inherited ills, even among heathen peoples. Among God's chosen people, the Jews, nothing else seems to even have been thought of until after the reign of Solomon during which so much of what was idolatrous was introduced.

It was prophesied of the Christ some 700 years before His first advent by the prophet Isaiah that He would bear not only the sins of the world but their infirmities and sicknesses as well on the cross, which word He fulfilled, healing all that were oppressed of the devil and commissioning His followers to carry on the work after His ascension, promising to be with them until the end of the age.

In the book of the Acts of the Apostles, we learn how literally they understood and how faithfully they executed this command; and at least for the first three centuries of the church's history their example was closely followed by believers of the Lord Jesus Christ.

Listen to the following quotation from one of the best-known fathers of the early church, Irenaeus, dated about A.D. 180, as he draws a comparison between heretics and true believers on the Lord Jesus Christ.

> They [the heretics], can neither confer sight on the blind, nor hearing on the deaf, nor chase away all sorts of demons...nor can they cure the weak, or the lame, or the paralytic or those who are distressed in any other part of the body. Nor can they furnish effective remedies for those external accidents which may occur, and so far are they from being able to raise the dead, as the Lord raised them, and the apostles and as has frequently been done in the brotherhood, the entire church in that particular locality entreating with much fasting and prayer the spirit of the dead man has returned in answer to the prayers of the saints—that they do not even believe that this could possibly be done.

In another place he says: "Others again heal the sick by laying their hands upon them, and they are made whole. Yea, moreover, as

I have said, the dead even have been raised up and remained among us for many years."

The great Christian father, Origen, wrote in the third century of the Christians of his day: "They expel evil spirits and perform many cures...Miracles are still found among Christians, and some of them more remarkable than have ever existed among the Jews; and these we have ourselves witnessed." These statements would have been challenged by Origen's opponents if they had admitted of being disputed.

It would appear that praying for the sick and anointing them with oil never ceased to be practiced for the first seven centuries of the Christian era, though after that it began to decline as the result of the changed attitude and apostasy of the church. But in spite of this, many notable healings took place after that date; and the fact that as superstition became rife, it was usual to connect these with the name of some saint or other instead of giving all the glory to Him to whom it rightfully belongs—our blessed Jesus—does not invalidate the fact that the healings, which were prayed for in the name of Jesus, actually occurred.

Perhaps these people did not grieve the Lord any more when they connected their healings with the prayers of Saint Solemundygundus or some other saint or a relic of Saint Ann or a piece from the Virgin's robe than we do when we think that if this brother or that sister prays with us, we shall be healed, instead of placing all our confidence in Jesus alone.

That the healings actually occurred, all historians are agreed; and as one of them, not a religious writer, says, if we refuse to believe it we may as well decline to accept the whole historical record, for they are as well attested as any part of it.

In the beginning of the 12th century we find Bernard of Clairvaux (France), author of the famous hymn, "Jerusalem, the Golden," a leader of Christian thought in his day. He was a man eminent for holiness of life, mightily used in healing the sick; 36 miraculous cures being reported as taking place under his ministry in a single day—the halt, the blind, the deaf, the dumb being perfectly restored in answer to his prayer in the name of Jesus. On one occasion a dying man was brought to him who was so emaciated that his legs were no larger than a child's arms; and when Bernard prayed, "Behold, O Lord, they seek for a sign, and our words avail nothing, unless they be confirmed with the signs following," and laid hands on the living skeleton in the name of Jesus, the sick man arose from his couch healed.

Toward the close of the 13th century, an Englishman, called Thomas of Hereford, was much used in healing; documentary evidence, which is still extant, shows that no fewer than 429 miracles of healing were performed by him through laying on of hands in the name of the Lord Jesus Christ. Though it occurred long after his death, his faith and teaching seem to have inspired the trust in the Word of God that brought the following miracle to pass at the beginning of the 14th century. I quote from the original account of the occurrence:

> On the 6th of September, 1303, Roger, aged two years and three months, the son of Gervase, one of the warders of Conway Castle, managed to crawl out of bed in the night and tumble off a bridge, a distance of twenty-eight feet; he was not discovered until the next morning when his mother found him half naked and quite dead upon a hard stone at the bottom of the ditch, where there was no water, or earth, but simply the rock that had been quarried to build the castle. Simon Waterford, the vicar who had christened the child, John de Bois, and John Guffe, all sworn witnesses, took their oaths on the Gospel that they saw and handled the child dead. The King's Crowners [coroners], Stephen Ganny and William Nottingham, were presently called and went down into the moat. They found the child's body cold and stiff, and white with boar frost, stark dead. While the Crowners, as their office required, began to write what they had seen, one John Syward, a

> near neighbor, came down and gently handled the child's body all over and finding it as dead as ever any, prayed earnestly, when the child began to move his head and right arm a little, and forthwith life and vigor came back into every part of his body...That same day the child, feeling no pain at all, walked as he was wont to do up and down in the house, though a little scar continued in one cheek, which after a few days, quite vanished away.

I used to be very much puzzled at the reports I read in the course of my studies in history of the healings of hopeless cases of tuberculosis, then called "scrofula" or "king's evil" (some of them signed by eminent doctors of the age in which they were stated to have occurred), as the result of the king's touch. These patients were carefully examined by court physicians before being allowed to present themselves for the king's touch. The screening was necessary because some who were not grievously afflicted were anxious to be touched and to receive the small gold coin, which was the custom for the king to give to those to whom he ministered in this way and which was worth far more than its intrinsic value; and in some instances these very doctors solemnly attested that the people had been perfectly cured. When I came to look into the matter, I found to my great surprise that the ceremony was a solemn religious one based on the words in the last verses of Mark's Gospel. "In my name...they shall lay hands on the sick and they shall recover" (Mark 16:17,18), and that this verse, among others, was read aloud to each person who sought healing; also that the king prayed as he touched the sufferer, in which prayer his chaplains and all bystanders were supposed to join. In view of these circumstances it is no wonder that real healings took place in some instances, through the power of the Word operating on souls and bodies.

Indeed, the reports of some of these healings are so convincing that I cannot doubt for my part that the boundless grace of God found a way to honor the Word and magnify the glorious name of

Jesus, even though the instruments employed were not always all that might have been desired.

King Edward the Confessor, who was a real Christian, prayed for a young woman whose case is very striking. The woman was afflicted with large abscesses in the neck. The king placed his hands gently on the diseased tissues, stroking it as he prayed for her recovery. The abscesses opened, discharging tremendous quantities of putrid matter filled with maggots. Within a week no trace of the disease could be found.

With the Protestant Reformation came a revival of faith for healing, and the tide has been gradually rising ever since that time. These believers are just a few God has used in the healing ministry: Martin Luther; George Fox, founder of the Quakers; John Wesley; Charles G. Finney; Dorethea Trudel, whose work became so extensive that it was investigated and finally in some sense licensed by the Swiss government; Dr. Charles Cullis of Boston; A. J. Gordon; Dr. A. B. Simpson of New York; Mrs. Carrie Judd Montgomery, formerly of Buffalo, New York, later of Oakland, California; Mrs. Elizabeth Mix of Connecticut, a black woman through whom Mrs. Montgomery was healed; John Alexander Dowie of Zion City, Illinois; Dr. William Gentry of Chicago and Mrs. Aimee Semple McPherson. Many other names stand out in this connection as we pass the centuries in review.

It has been my privilege to know personally some of these men and women. And in passing I should like to dwell for a few moments on recollections of two of them who have passed to their reward, Dr. John Alexander Dowie and Dr. A. B. Simpson.

I met Dr. Dowie in about 1900. He introduced himself to us and dwelt on the meaning of his name: "John," by the grace of God, "Alexander," a helper of men. As for the "Doctor," it had been bestowed upon him by grateful people who were healed in answer to his prayers. While I could never fully follow Dr. Dowie in all of his teachings, I could not doubt the truth of his statement that God had conferred upon him gifts of healing. The Holy Spirit answered to it in my soul, and he was approved of God by miracles and wonders and signs, which God did by him, and which the very man in the street could neither gainsay nor resist.

For instance, I once asked one of the very best dentists in Chicago what he thought of Dr. Dowie. He did not know that I had any acquaintance with him. He replied, "Well, it is impossible to deny the genuineness of his healings; how he does them I cannot explain, but he does them without the shadow of a doubt. I myself know a young lady who had her leg lengthened three inches and who now stands on even feet. You can see her any Sunday in Dr. Dowie's choir."

When Dr. Dowie began his work in Chicago in 1893, I think it was, he set up a wooden hut at the World's Fair and rang a dinner bell to get the people to the meetings. This is history. He had some wonderful healings, among others that of Ethel Post, a little girl of about 13 years of age whose mouth was so full of a bloody, spongy cancer that she could not close it day or night. The surgeons would not touch it for fear she would bleed to death, for the blood vessels in it were so infiltrated with cancer cells that they would not hold ligatures. As Dr. Dowie drove across Lincoln Park to pray with her, the Lord gave him the verse that He is God to kill and make alive (2 Kings 5:7), and he prayed, "O Lord, kill the cancer and heal the child."

The malignant growth withered away and fell out of her mouth and throat, and she was completely and permanently healed. When I alluded to her case in a meeting quite recently, a lady rose and stated that Miss Post is alive and well and actively engaged in some branch of commercial art. She used to sell her photographs, "Before and After the Lord's Healing Touch," for the benefit of the Lord's work, and they in themselves constituted a wonderful testimony to the faithfulness of God toward those who trust Him.

I visited at Dr. Dowie's Divine Healing Home in 1898; it was then on Michigan Boulevard, Chicago, and was a most luxurious hotel fitted up in approved modern style. But it had something I had never seen in any other hotel: a staff of helpers all of whom were filled with faith in the Word of God. Their faces shone, and any one of them—from the furnace man to the elevator boy—was ready to preach you a sermon at a moment's notice if you dared to doubt that Jesus Christ is the same yesterday, today, and forever.

Dr. Dowie's devotion to the Word of God was beautiful; he would read it to his sick folks for hours on end, sometimes not even stopping for dinner; and as he read they would visibly lift up their heads like flowers after a gracious shower. I have known him to put dinner back when it was served and the waitresses waiting to attend the tables because he said we needed the Word so much more. He simply brought you right up against the Word, ...I am the Lord that healeth thee (Ex. 15:26), and expected you to believe it then and there without any regard to symptoms.

One of his favorite hymns, which we sang very frequently, was a sort of keynote to his character and work. I will quote part of it here; and if you are familiar with it, you will notice that he altered it to suit himself:

Have God's own faith
    And trust His might,
That He will conquer as you fight,
    And give the triumph to the right,
Have faith, have God's own faith.

Have God's own faith
    What can there be
Too hard for Him to do for thee?

He gave His Son, now all is free,
Have faith, have God's own faith.

Dr. Dowie had invincible, God-given faith in the Word of God as being the same today as it ever has been and ever will be, "forever settled," absolutely supreme and unconquerable, "whose faith follow." If there was anything in his life or teaching that you do not see to be in accordance with God's Word, you are not called upon to follow it; but his faith in God's Word you are exhorted to imitate.

It was a hopeless, organic disease of the heart that threatened to end Dr. A. B. Simpson's life in the very midst of his career of usefulness as a minister of the Gospel that brought him to a knowledge of the truth of divine healing. When he was in such a condition that there was constant danger of his falling from the pulpit or into the open grave as he officiated at funerals, Dr. Simpson was ordered by his physician to stop work and take a prolonged rest. He was given but little hope that he would survive long, no matter what precautions he took. He was earnestly looking to God when the truth was revealed to him through the Word.

Without the faintest improvement of any kind in his symptoms, he took God at His Word and believed himself healed, ever after acting on this through a long and most arduous life of service. God never failed to meet his physical need; and eternity alone will tell the story of the work accomplished in practically every country of the world by this faithful soldier of the Cross, for the great burden of his soul was world evangelization in preparation for the coming of the King.

In a little verse he wrote, which I shall quote, is found the explanation of the great work, which by divine grace, he was able to perform:

I am crucified with Jesus,
And He lives and dwells in me;

I have ceased from all my strugglings,
'Tis no longer I but He.
All my will is yielded to Him,
And His Spirit reigns within;
And His precious Blood each moment,
Keeps me cleansed and free from sin.
I'm abiding in the Lord,
And confiding in His Word,
And I'm hiding, sweetly hiding,
In the bosom of His love.

All my sicknesses I bring Him,
And He bears them all away,
All my fears and griefs I tell Him,
All my cares from day to day.
All my strength I draw from Jesus,
By His breath I live and move,
E'en His very mind He gives me,
And His faith, and life and love.

Dr. Simpson had some wonderful healings in his ministry. Only a few days after he accepted Christ as his physician, his little daughter, their only child, was taken with malignant diphtheria. Her throat was filled with an awful membrane and her condition was most critical. He took her out of her mother's arms and into a room where he was alone with God and there anointed her with trembling hand. She was only the second or third person he had ever anointed. He knew that unless God manifested His power quickly there was going to be a crisis in the family, for his wife was not at that time one with him on the subject of healing.

All night he knelt beside the child in prayer. And when with the first streak of dawn the mother entered the room with haggard face and eyes heavy with weeping, the little one opened her eyes and smiled at her, the smile of health and happiness; and not one vestige of the dread disease remained. "All hail the power of Jesus' name!"

Chapter 11

SIGNS FOLLOWING

Now when Jesus was risen early the first day of the week, he appeared first to Mary Magdalene, out of whom he had cast seven devils. And she went and told them that had been with him, as they mourned and wept...Afterward he appeared unto the eleven as they sat at meat, and upbraided them for their unbelief and hardness of heart, because they believed not them which had seen him after he was risen. And he said unto them, Go ye into all the world, and preach the gospel to every creature. He that believeth and is baptized shall be saved; but he that believeth not shall be damned. And these signs shall follow them that believe; In my name shall they cast out devils; they shall speak with new tongues; they shall take up serpents; and if they drink any deadly thing, it shall not hurt them; they shall lay hands on the sick, and they shall recover. So then after the Lord had spoken unto them, he was received up into heaven, and sat on the right hand of God. And they went forth, and preached every where, the Lord working with them, and confirming the word with signs following

Mark 16:9,10,14-20

Here we have in the plainest possible words God's program for the age in which we are living—a program in which every believer has his or her appointed part to play. It is not too much to say that we are here simply and solely for this purpose, for we are ambassadors for Christ, as though God did beseech by us, "be reconciled to God." (2 Cor. 5:20.) As faithful ambassadors, we have all the resources of heaven to draw upon and Omnipotence to empower and protect us.

I have worked under the government and know what it is to receive instructions, often by telegram, directing that certain changes be made and new regulations promulgated and enforced; and as these were complied with, the government invariably confirmed them by official letters bearing the great seal and by such action as might be necessary to ensure the discharge of all governmental obligations in connection therewith. I do not remember that they ever failed to confirm their word; perhaps they did. But the government of heaven never fails to make the Word of God good in every respect, to fulfill every promise contained therein and to inflict every penalty threatened for disobedience thereto; for the Lord Himself is working with us, confirming the Word with signs following. So we can be absolutely certain that if we speak as the oracles of God, as we are directed to, He will not let any of our words fall to the ground but will confirm them with signs following, setting the seal of heaven on our utterances.

As we proclaim salvation from sin and deliverance from its guilt and power through the cross of Calvary, men and women will have their shackles struck off before our eyes; and as we preach a Saviour who bore our pains and sicknesses as well as our sins, the sick will be healed, the deaf will hear, blind eyes will be opened, the lame man will leap as a hart, and the tongue of the dumb sing.

If the puny governments of earth cannot afford to let their utterances go unconfirmed, is it likely that the King of Kings will allow His eternal Word to be unfulfilled? It is unthinkable.

I am going to relate a few instances which have come under my personal observation of the confirmation of the Word of God by the signs following—with the view first of glorifying Jesus, and second of inspiring faith in the hearts of those who hear them, or of increasing and strengthening it if it has already been inspired.

People sometimes speak as though the healing of the body through faith in the sacrifice of Calvary were something quite distinct from salvation, instead of part and parcel of it. Let us look for a moment at the case of the paralytic who was brought to Jesus by four, in the fifth chapter of Luke. Here Jesus first speaks the word of pardon—first things first: "Man, thy sins are forgiven thee" (v. 20), after which follows his physical healing as a visible sign of his forgiveness and as evidence before the eyes of all of the power on earth of the Son of man to forgive sins.

Jesus desires to convince the unbelieving world of the reality of His gospel by His healing miracles on the bodies of the sick who come to Him for deliverance. Often in this way a door of utterance is opened for the heralds of the Cross, which would otherwise remain closed; and the first incident that I shall relate is an illustration of this.

Just before leaving Canada for California, my sister and I received an urgent call to hold meetings in a rural part of Alberta. We had to drive a long way in a car to get there—it was a considerable distance from the railway—and the roads are not like the ones in California. We seemed to have to pray the car along almost every foot of the way, partly because the roads were bad and partly because the car was none too good. However, we got there at last and were soon hard at work holding meetings in schoolhouses and homes, visiting the sick, tarrying with seekers for the baptism in the Holy Spirit, and doing other work that came to hand; and we had the joy of seeing God move in a blessed way.

Finally we felt that we were free to return to complete our arrangements for going south, so we bade them all a loving farewell and told them to have the famous car ready for an early departure the following day. Quite late the last evening we expected to spend there, a man called to see us, bringing his wife and family. He was an unbeliever; and I noticed that one of his children, a little boy, had a marked squint in one eye. I told the parents that it was not God's will that the little thing should be so deformed and afflicted and that we would pray for him if they wished. As they replied in the affirmative, we laid hands on the child in the name of Jesus, and then they went home. I cannot remember that I noticed any change in the eye directly after we prayed, but as we were very busy seeing people who came to say goodbye, it may have escaped our notice; in any case, early the next morning before we had finished breakfast the man returned and reported that the child was so improved that they were all amazed and recognized God's hand in the healing. He implored us to stay a while longer and promised to come and bring his family to the meetings if we would do so, which meant something as he lived a long distance from the place where we held them.

As he added that he and his family were ready to make an unconditional surrender to the Saviour who had healed the child, we decided that the happening was a token from the Lord that He still had work for us to do there. We announced that we would continue the meetings, inviting all who were really seeking the baptism in the Holy Spirit, but *no others,* to come to a tarry meeting in the upper story of our host's barn that very evening. It was a wonderful barn, the finest one in the whole district. And I certainly shall never forget that meeting; it was in some respects the most wonderful one I ever attended.

As I was on my way to the meeting, I saw a man with a most unhappy expression on his face, skulking in the distance but casting longing glances all the same toward the huge, gray barn. I called to him and asked him if he wanted to come to the meeting.

"Yes," he said, "I want to come but I am too bad a man. I am known all over this district as a bad man. My wife is at the meeting; she is a godly woman, and I have led her an awful life. I am a bad man."

"Well," I said, "you are the kind the meeting is for, for the worse you are the more you need Jesus; and we are going to seek Him there tonight as Saviour, Healer, Baptizer, and All in All. Come along."

So the "bad man" (we'll call him John) accompanied me to the meeting. Maybe the people were astonished to see him come in, but that was as nothing to the astonishment that was to fill them a little later.

The people knew almost nothing about the Baptism; and as they were from various churches and societies, I explained the way of full salvation in the simplest manner possible, including the baptism in the Holy Spirit as in Acts 2:4 and told them to look to the Lamb of God and praise Him for all He had procured for them. And they began. Everybody expected John's wife to receive the Baptism first. I found that she was considered the best person in the district.

I can see those people now if I close my eyes. It was a beautiful loft, a real "upper room," the floor covered with new mown hay and the whole place lighted by lanterns hung round the walls. The faces of the seekers looked so earnest in the flickering lantern light. There was a spirit of love and harmony, for all who were not seeking the Baptism were asked to stay at home.

John knelt on the outside of the ring where the shadows were deep as the lantern light hardly penetrated to that distance. I wondered how he was getting along and intended going to pray with him; but before we had been on our knees many minutes, the power fell and a sister—not John's wife—received her Baptism. As she was kneeling next to me, she fell over on me; and I could not get away.

When John's wife actually heard this sister praising in other tongues, she seemed to grow desperate in her longing and began with all her might to call upon God for the Baptism.

I was encouraging her when suddenly, as a flash of lightning, the power of God struck John where he was kneeling, bolted him upright at the edge of the group and felled him to the floor with a crash so mighty that it seemed as though it must pull the building down. And he lay there under the power, which moved and manipulated every part of his body with such force and lightning-like rapidity that the people thought he was having an awful attack of convulsions. Indeed it was with great difficulty that I calmed their fears. At last the Spirit began to speak through him, first in English, describing the vision he was having of Calvary. Would to God that every sinner in the world could have heard him! It would have melted a heart of stone. And after that, he spoke with awful power and majesty in a new tongue.

His wife was so dumbfounded when she heard him that she said to me: "He's got the Baptism before me, and he was so bad. Perhaps I need to be saved from my goodness more than he needed to be saved from his badness."

And I said, "Perhaps you do. Just repent of everything and cast yourself on Jesus."

And just then, to the amazement of all, John raised himself to his knees and came along to us, and placing himself in front of his wife, he preached the most wonderful sermon on Calvary I ever heard.

"Oh, look away from yourself, bad or good," he cried. "See where *He* hangs, bearing your sins away forever and making your peace with God—everlasting peace, sure as Jehovah's throne!"

It was thrilling. He seemed to see Jesus and to be able, through the power of the Spirit, to make us see Him, too.

As he kept pointing her to Calvary, the power caught another sister up as though on a whirlwind; and she danced all round the loft lighter than a feather—she had never seen dancing in the Spirit—praising and singing meantime in Gaelic. Later the language changed to High German, which I had studied for years and understood a little; and she was unable to speak anything else for a couple of days. When spoken to in English, she replied in German. She had no knowledge of the language.

A sister who was taking charge of her baby—he had awakened by this time—asked for his bottle, and she danced all round the loft looking for it but unable to stop dancing and singing.

Meantime the power was falling on others and there were days of heaven on earth, and the salvations and baptisms came about through the healing of the child's eye. It is pretty hard to separate healing from salvation, isn't it? For my part I have given up trying.

I am now going to relate another healing, which we always called, "the man borne of four," because he came in the light of that verse in Luke 5, which was referred to earlier in this chapter.

He was an old man between 70 and 80 years of age with a cancer on his face, on the temple near his eye. Sometimes people say that the diseases of which we claim to be healed are imaginary, but they could not say that about this case; for he had a face and he had a cancer on that face. He was not at all a good-looking old man and with this hideous growth he presented a most repulsive appearance. As far as you could see him, you would notice it; and unless you were very careful, you were likely to exclaim, "Isn't that awful!"

The old man was genuinely saved and was quite willing to bear the affliction until he was called home, if God so willed. But as he listened to the teaching from the Word, he became more and more certain that Jesus had purchased his full deliverance on the cross of Calvary and more and more determined to have that deliverance manifested in his mortal body.

As he considered himself weak in the faith, he asked God to give him some special help and was directed to request four sisters, whose prayer joints were kept well oiled, to carry him to the feet of Jesus as the bearers carried the paralytic. Nothing loath, they accepted the task and performed it so faithfully that the cancer simply dropped off and vanished forever.

It seemed to me that it went so quickly that it was there one day and gone the next; but I know there was an interval between the prayer and his manifested deliverance, though I cannot say exactly how long it was. God enabled them to fight the good fight of faith during it anyway, and the disappearance of the cancer was a grand testimony for Jesus in that town; for no one could deny that Grandpa had had cancer, and no one could find a trace of it after his healing. I have heard him preach an eloquent sermon on the Lord's healing with the cancer for a text more than once, and I have never heard anyone attempt to dispute his statements.

The next case of which I shall speak was one of blood poisoning following childbirth, and the woman who was healed was actually dying when the miracle occurred. I mean that she was in the very article of death. Indeed, I could not find the faintest trace of a pulse when I laid my hand upon her. I had taken a long drive to reach her; and as it was raining and we were in an open vehicle, rivers of water were pouring from my slicker; but her husband insisted on my going in without a moment's delay, saying when he met us at the door with a face as white as chalk that she was just passing away.

As I felt the immediate presence of death and the power of darkness rolling like a flood over the woman, who was perfectly unconscious, the Spirit of the Lord within me raised up a standard against the enemy. I could not have done it; I was too scared, and through my lips came the words, "The prayer of faith shall save the sick, and the Lord shall raise him up, and UP YOU COME"; and at the same instant she opened her eyes and spoke to her husband (who was bending over her weeping, never expecting to hear her voice in this world again). "Don't cry, sweetheart; Jesus is here" — she had a vision of Him — "and has healed me." She was so occupied with Jesus and His beauty and sweetness that she did not even know that I had been there until after I left. I met her some little time afterwards on the main street of the town on a shopping trip with a flock of curly-headed little ones after her; and she was certainly very much alive.

The last case I call "the story of Samuel," not the Samuel of the Bible but another Samuel who was named after the Samuel of the Bible because he was, like him, a child of faith.

This husband and wife were godly people who had a good, comfortable home with the benediction of God resting upon it but no children to brighten it and inherit the blessing promised to the seed of the righteous. This was a great grief to them, especially as the woman suffered a great deal at the hands of physicians who endeavored unsuccessfully to remove, by means of painful operations, the trouble that prevented her from bearing a child. But, alas! Like the woman in the Gospels, she grew worse rather than better; and the only results attained were physical debility and suffering and large doctors' bills. She was getting well on in years when she and her husband received the baptism in the Holy Spirit and a fresh illumination on the sacred page. With this came a conviction that barrenness and disease were not God's will for her but part of the curse of the broken law which Jesus had borne in her stead when He was made a curse for her. She prayed that the blessing of Abraham, which includes fruitfulness, might come upon her and was determined to prove God and see if He would not open the windows of heaven and pour out upon her the blessing of motherhood.

So we gathered around her, a little praying band of earnest people, and with her took our stand on the unchanging Word. So real was our part in the matter that when the child arrived (he had to arrive, for the Scripture cannot be broken), we with one accord named him Samuel, saying with Hannah, the mother of the Bible Samuel, "For this child I prayed." (1 Sam. 1:27.) All of us felt that he belonged to us quite as much as to his father and mother. We used to set him in our midst and gloat over him; and when a year and a half later the Lord graciously sent him a little sister just for good measure, she was called Ruth (completeness); and our cup of rejoicing was full.

But what shall I say more? Space would fail me to tell of the sick I have seen healed of almost every disease that flesh is heir to: the goiters that have melted away; the blind that have been made to see; the deaf to hear; the lame to walk; the cases of tuberculosis; heart disease; kidney disease; indigestion; gall stones (one Roman Catholic woman who had pulmonary consumption and gall stones was instantly healed on her deathbed after receiving Extreme Unction, and then the Holy Spirit fell upon her at the same time so that she praised God for her deliverance in a new tongue); tumors of various kinds (including cancer, which have been perfectly cured, sometimes instantly when hands were laid on and prayer made in the name of Jesus).

A woman who was healed of cancer of the breast in our home in answer to prayer seemed to constitute herself a publicity agent for the Lord's healing. Every now and then our phone would ring and somebody would say when we answered it, "Do you remember Mrs. Campbell who was healed of cancer in your house? She told me that if I would ask for prayer in Jesus' name, I would be healed, too."

Yes, the signs follow. God always confirms His Word. Step out upon it this minute, whether for yourself or others, without a tremor. It has never failed; and it never will fail, for they that trust in the Lord shall never be confounded.

Chapter 12

TEACHING, PREACHING, AND HEALING

Among the last words uttered before the closing of the Old Testament canon, before the sad, silent centuries which intervened between Malachi and the first coming of the Lord Jesus Christ (by whom God hath spoken to us in these last days), we find predicted the rising of the Sun of Righteousness with healing in His wings (Mal. 4:2). This prediction was fulfilled when Jesus, the dayspring from on high, visited us; and as He was manifested to destroy the works of the devil—including sickness as well as sin—He healed *all* that came unto Him, *all* that was oppressed of the devil.

And, thank God, He is still the Sun of Righteousness with healing in His wings and is beaming love, forgiveness, cleansing, and healing on all who will let the blessed Sunshine—the life which is the light—into our hearts and lives. "Clear the darkened windows, open wide the door, let the blessed sunshine *in.*"

It is hard to keep sunshine out. Even when you have drawn every curtain closed, pulled down the blinds, locked the shutters, and shut every avenue of approach, it has a way of stealing in and making a spot of glory in the midst of the gloom. And God is not willing that any should perish; and even when the doors are barred against Him, He loves us so much that He is always sending some ray of divine light through the prayers of His people or their testimonies or their loving smiles or some Word of God dropped into our minds by the Holy Spirit to lighten our darkness and to invite us to throw our whole beings wide open to the illuminating, warming, electrifying, healing, energizing, vitalizing, magnetizing rays of the Sun of Righteousness.

I saw some little children once who were the very incarnation of health. They were nut-brown from head to foot, and they radiated physical vigor and well-being from every pore. I asked their mother, "What have you been doing to them?" And she replied, "I had them at the seaside; and it was beautiful weather, just sunshine all the time. And I stripped off their clothes and put tiny bathing trunks on them so there wasn't a thing between them and the sunshine, and the sun did all the rest. Dr. Sun is my doctor from henceforth."

Yes, the sun is a wonderful doctor, but even he sometimes fails; but the Sun of Righteousness never fails to illuminate the darkest heart that is opened wide to receive Him and to heal the most hopeless case that comes to Him. Only we must be like the tiny children; we must have nothing between us and the Sun, not so much as a cloud to arise and darken our skies or hide for a moment our Lord from our eyes, nothing of sin or self that could separate us from Jesus.

Shall we open wide the doors and windows? If they are already open, throw them wider; or better still, step right out of ourselves into Christ. As a song in the Spirit, which the Lord gave to my sister, says:

Step out into the light, and stay there,
    Walk there, sit down there;
Step out into the light, and grow there,
    Praise the living Word;
In Jesus all is bright, so live there,
    Rest there, abide there;
Step out into the light,
    Pass on through faith, to sight,
        The light of God.

Now let us take a look at the work of Jesus, the Saviour and Healer, as described in the New Testament. Note first of all that He followed a definite method and order in its performance: (1) teaching, (2) preaching, and (3) healing. (Matt. 4:23.) "First things first," so Jesus first teaches; He reveals to man God's will for him and shows him how far he has wandered from it. Second, He preaches, or proclaims, to man the salvation provided for him through Christ Jesus, which, accepted by faith, brings him into perfect harmony with the divine will. And third, heals; He removes from human bodies the results of sin. This is God's order, and it is well to remember that it is unchanging.

Sometimes people who come to be healed of some distressing complaint are likely to feel rather impatient when—instead of at once praying for their immediate deliverance—we deliberately, prayerfully, and reverently, read to them from the Word (even for hours if the Spirit so leads). They forget that the words themselves are "Spirit and life" (John 6:63) and that "He sent his word and healed them." (Ps. 107:20.)

I have seen patients who were so completely drained of vitality that, from a medical standpoint, I should have thought it necessary to administer powerful heart stimulants at frequent intervals to prevent collapse. But they listened to the Word of God for hours continuously and lifted their heads under the distillation of its heavenly dews like a parched garden after a gracious shower.

The Word *teaches,* reveals God to man, so that man abhors himself in dust and ashes. As Job says, ...now mine eye seeth *thee.* Wherefore I abhor myself, and repent in dust and ashes (Job 42:5,6). *It also preaches,* shows him the way out of defilement and into holiness, by the blood of Jesus. Having therefore, brethren, boldness to enter into the *holiest* by the blood of Jesus (Heb. 10:19), and *heals all* who will through the boundless grace that flows from Calvary, accept God's perfect will for spirit, soul, and body, that they may

...be preserved *blameless* unto the coming of our Lord Jesus Christ (1 Thess. 5:23).

When Jesus said to the impotent man in the fifth chapter of John's gospel, "Wilt thou be made whole?"(v. 6), He meant nothing short of this. Not only that his poor atrophied body should rise from its supineness but that the whole man should rise to walk in heaven's own light, above the world and sin; for in the 14th verse of the same chapter we find Him telling the man to sin no more. It is God's revealed will toward us not only to remove all sin and disease but to also lift us far above the realm in which sin and disease operate, even into the resurrection life of Christ: For the law of the Spirit of life in Christ Jesus hath made me free from the law of sin and death (Rom. 8:2). And He is saying to each one, "Wilt thou be made whole? Not *half,* not 60 percent or even 90 percent, but 100 percent, whole!"

So much for a general consideration of the teaching of the New Testament regarding healing. Now we will study some particular cases found in the eighth chapter of Matthew.

The first thing that strikes us as we begin is the fact that each case in the New Testament has certain features peculiar to itself, not to be found in connection with others. I believe that this is to show us how inexhaustible are God's resources and how perfectly able He is to meet the need in each case that is unreservedly placed in His hands.

The first patient in the eighth chapter of Matthew is the leper who believed implicitly in the power of the Lord to heal him but doubted His *willingness.* ...Lord, *if thou wilt,* thou canst make me clean (Matt. 8:2). Jesus, the author and finisher of faith, completes the supplicant's faith by His "I will," (v. 3) and the result is the man's immediate healing.

The Bible, from Genesis to Revelation, is God's "I WILL" to every seeker for full salvation for soul and body. Jesus, the only begotten Son of God, hanging on the cross in agony and blood, is

God's "*I have* delivered you, and this is what it cost me. Can you doubt My willingness?"

Jesus speaks of healing as "the children's bread" in the 15th chapter of Matthew, verse 26; and no earthly father worthy of the name will withhold bread from his children, much less our heavenly Father.

We are taught to pray, "Thy will be done on earth as it is in heaven" (Matt. 6:10); and there is no sin or sickness in heaven, for nothing that defileth can enter there.

God desires our bodily healing just as He desires our spiritual well-being, for the apostle John prayed for the well-beloved Gaius, Beloved, I wish above all things that thou mayest prosper and be in health, even as thy soul prospereth (3 John 2).

Some say that this leper was told not to testify, but that is a mistake. Rather, he was directed just how, when, where, and to whom he was to testify. He was to testify to the priest, the official appointed to examine lepers and pronounce them clean in the event of their healing; and he was to bring the required offering. One reason for this was that leprosy is a type as well as a result of sin, and the righteousness that is by faith in Jesus Christ is to be witnessed by both the law and the prophets. (Rom. 3:21.) After I was healed of the morphine habit, some of my Christian friends begged me never to mention the fact that I had been a drug addict. But the Lord told me to show what great things He had done for me, even if it humiliated me to do so; and He told me just when, where, and how I should testify. Shortly after I was delivered, I went to a church in Chicago, a Methodist church; and as soon as opportunity was afforded for testimony, I rose and told what a marvelous deliverance God had wrought in me.

After I sat down a young man stood up in the back of the church and said that he praised God for my testimony, for it gave him courage to tell what God had done for him. He had been a hopeless drunkard and had been completely delivered and gloriously saved. His friends had begged him to keep quiet about it (he belonged to a wealthy family), but my example so inspired him that he declared he was going to testify for Jesus every chance he got and preach for Him too, for he felt called to preach. And I heard him give a splendid sermon that very evening at the hall of the Volunteers of America.

After the service in the Methodist church, a gentleman walked up to me and introduced himself as Dr. William Gentry. He was in medical practice in Chicago then. He told me how impressed he was with what I had said, the truth of which he could not doubt. Later he gave up the practice of medicine and devoted himself to the Lord's work from that time.

The next case in this chapter in Matthew is that of the Roman centurion who sought healing for his servant who was delivered in answer to his master's great faith. Note that the centurion asked for nothing but the word: "Speak the word only" (Matt. 8:8); and also observe that he did not base his request on any merit in himself. "Lord, I am not worthy...speak the word." I believe that if we could and would divest ourselves of every vestige of self-righteousness and settle it once and for all that we in ourselves are worthy of nothing but eternal doom (but that the Lamb of God who was slain for us, Christ Jesus, in whose name we come, is worthy to receive "power, and riches, and wisdom, and strength, and honor, and glory, and blessing"), we would witness signs and wonders such as have not as yet gladdened the eyes of men.

One of the most prompt deliverances I ever witnessed was that of a young ballet dancer who had an awful attack of appendicitis and had been ordered to the hospital for an operation. And I believe that one secret of her instantaneous healing was the fact that she knew, as did everybody else, that she had nothing in herself to recommend to God. It had to be "all Jesus."

She was just a wicked, flirting, swearing, smoking sinner who had to cast herself in self-despair at the feet of Jesus; and He taught her that way and brought her that way, "Lord, I am NOT worthy...speak the healing word." And He spoke it, and in one minute after that she had no more need of an operation for appendicitis than I have this moment. She was a perfect little heathen when I first met her, and she was transformed into the most earnest advocate of the Lord Jesus as the healer of His people that I have ever known.

The next case in this chapter is the healing of Peter's mother-in-law (Matt. 8:14,15), in which I call Jesus the *family* Physician.

Here there does not seem to have been any special question to settle prior to the healing, as in some other healings recorded in the Word. Peter, the head of the family, had accorded to Jesus the rightful place of preeminence, and He enters the home and banishes the works of Satan from the premises. Luke tells us (he was a physician, remember) in correct medical phraseology that she was suffering from a "great fever," following the teaching of the famous ancient Greek physician, Galen, who divided fevers into lesser and greater. But as the sufferer, with flushed face and aching head, tossed uneasily on her bed of pain, Jesus drew near and touched her hand and the fever left her; for vital contact with Christ banishes disease. "Some one hath touched me," and by vital continuity with Him we are delivered from the power of sin and sickness and quickened by resurrection life (Rom. 8:2,11). As the result of her healing, Peter's mother-in-law arose, took higher ground—every one who is healed by faith in Jesus does that—and ministered unto Him (Matt. 8:15, margin). We are saved and healed to serve Him.

It is a glorious thing to have Jesus as our family Physician, and no one is too poor to secure His services; for they are "without money, and without price." Let me tell you a true story of what He did for a little girl whose father and mother placed their home under His almighty care and keeping.

At a tent meeting in western Canada at which I was one of the workers, a sweet little five-year-old girl, whose ears had been destroyed by the ravages of scarlet fever, was brought to the altar by her mother to be healed of deafness.

The child was so deaf that it was impossible for her to hear any sound, no matter how loud; and there was no prospect, humanly speaking, of any improvement in her condition. I asked the mother, who led the child to the altar, if the father was saved; and on receiving a reply in the affirmative, I asked him to come with his wife and child and definitely receive Jesus as the family Physician, claiming perfect spiritual and physical deliverance for all under the rooftree through the power of the blood upon the door.

> I'll sing it, yes, and I'll shout it!
> The blood! the blood!
> There was never a soul saved without it,
> THE BLOOD OF CALVARY.

After they had unitedly and publicly taken this stand, the child was anointed and prayed for in accordance with James 5:14-15, and left in the hands of the family Physician. The meeting was a very large one, and I never happened to see her again. But some months after returning to our home, we received a beautiful feather pillow (I really think it is the finest one I ever saw in my life) as a thank offering from the mother for the child's complete recovery, with the statement that she could hear a pin fall. We handed the pillow over to my own little adopted daughter; and as she laid her head on it every night for years, the fact that it was an offering from a little girl who had been healed of deafness was a constant inspiration to her faith in Jesus as the family Physician.

Well, perhaps you say, "But my case is quite different from any of those you have cited. It is not like the leper's, nor that of the centurion's servant, nor Peter's mother-in-law. How can I be sure from this verse that there is healing for *me?*"

If that is your feeling, turn to the 16th verse of this same chapter where we read, "...they brought unto him many...and he cast out the spirits with his word, and healed all that were sick." "All that were sick." He healed all that were *sick*. How many did He heal? All, no matter what kind of people they were or what the nature of the diseases from which they were suffering, whether acute, sub-acute, chronic, functional, or organic. He healed all that were sick. All. You cannot get outside of that, can you? So bring your case to Him now, singing:

> Just as I am without one plea,
>   But that Thy blood was shed for me,
> And that Thou bidst me come to Thee,
>   O Lamb of God, I come.

And you will go away not only healed in body but in soul also; for Jesus removes not only symptoms but also the deep-seated cause of symptoms, sin in the heart, which no remedy but the Blood can reach.

THE
Great Physician

CONTENTS

FOREWORD

That the ministry of healing played a very important part in the growth of the early church is abundantly evidenced by the New Testament, especially the book of Acts, and the first centuries of church history.

On their way to the temple to pray, Peter and John were appealed to by a lame man, crippled from birth, and therefore a perfectly hopeless case. Undaunted by his condition, they obeyed literally the instructions given them in Mark 16:18 and laid their hands on him in the name of the living Christ, who was working with them. As a result, the man leaped up, stood and walked, and leaping and praising God, followed them into the temple.

"And all the people saw him." (Acts 3:9.) "And all the people ran together unto them." (Acts 3:11.)

"And though persecution arose, many believed, and the number of the men were about five thousand." (Acts 4:4.)

The heart cry of people today is still, "Sir, we would *see Jesus.*" (John 12:21.) Jesus saving, Jesus healing, Jesus baptizing, Jesus coming in the clouds in great glory. When they *see Him* they will run toward Him.

That this little book may be used to help them to see Him as the "Healer of every sickness," the Great Physician, is the earnest prayer of the writer.

—Lilian B. Yeomans, M.D.

[illegible]

[illegible]

[illegible]

[illegible]

[illegible]

[illegible]

[illegible]

[illegible]

Chapter 1
THIRTY-FIVE YEARS OF DIVINE HEALTH

At the conclusion of a Bible reading I gave some time ago, a number of people crowded around me to ask for prayer, counsel, and so forth; and I dealt with them, according to their various needs, as the Lord enabled.

All the time that I was doing this I was aware of the presence of a silver-haired lady, a stranger, who was gazing intently at me from the very edge of the group. She made no move to approach until the others had dispersed. Then she came up to me, and looking right into my eyes said, "Can you tell me where I can see Dr. Lilian B. Yeomans?"

I said, "*Look* at me."

Her eyes seemed to try to pierce my very soul as she further inquired, "Are you that dope woman that I saw one day, years ago, clinging to any support within your reach to keep you from falling; and in spite of it you did fall on the floor from very weakness?"

"Yes, I am that woman," I replied.

And when I had convinced her of my identity, she related to me the story of meeting me in the most deplorable condition while I was still "hurt with fetters" and "laid in iron" before the King sent and loosed me on that glorious and never-to-be-forgotten day, the 12th of January, 1898.

The dear woman's incredulity made me realize as never before how marvelous was the miracle God wrought in me when all those years ago, He delivered me from the last stages of narcotic addiction, into which I had fallen through overwork in the practice of medicine and surgery.

It was almost impossible for her to credit the evidence of her senses when she saw "that dope woman," after thirty-five years, not only rejoicing in health, strength, vigor, and tireless energy, but actually engaged in confidently pointing others to the source of these, the river of the water of life, clear as crystal, proceeding out of the throne of God and of the Lamb, for "everything shall live whither the river cometh."

Yet, such has been my occupation for thirty-five years, and praise God, such is my delightful task today!

Thirty-five years of divine health, life more abundant, superabounding vitality! For though I was strong and robust before my constitution was wrecked and my whole system poisoned by the large quantities of lethal drugs, sulphate of morphine, and chloral hydrate (my steady diet, though I toyed with a number of others), which I took daily in the dark period of my abject slavery to narcotics, I can truly say that there is a sense in which I never knew before I accepted Christ as my physical life, what it means to *live*.

Let me try to tell some of the things it means to me. First, victorious life for the body. Not that I have always been exempt from Satan's attacks on my physical being, but through the continuous inflow of a river of life from the indwelling Christ, these have been repelled.

Second, the promises of God turned into facts in bones, muscles, nerves, organs, and tissues.

Third, it means, at times, the most delightful buoyancy and all-around sense of physical well-being imaginable, far exceeding the "joy of life," which used to make me want to hop, skip, and jump incessantly as a child.

Fourth, it means that when I am not mounting up on wings like an eagle, or running without resultant weariness, I can walk and not faint. "Jog trot, jog trot, jog trot." That is the pace that kills by its ceaseless continuance and awful monotony. It brings me to the very end of myself, but we which live are always delivered unto death for Jesus' sake, that the life also of Jesus might be made manifest in our mortal flesh. (2 Cor. 4:11.)

And now the flesh must daily die
Beneath the chastening rod,
Yet see the inner man renewed
By hidden bread from God.

O bruised meal that wasteth not;
O oil that cannot fail!
And thus I see that mighty hand
Here in my flesh prevail.

I find my strength assured by boarding at Elijah's boarding-house, the home of the widow of Zarephath. "The barrel of meal shall not waste, neither shall the cruse of oil fail"(1 Kings 17:14), for they symbolize the "life also of Jesus" manifested in our bodies. When you come to the end of your strength you find Omnipotence.

These thirty-five years have not been spent wrapped up in cotton wool or reclining on flowery beds of ease. God forbid! I shall praise Him throughout eternity for the privileges He has accorded me in traveling thousands of miles, on the King's business, addressing thousands in His name, and praying for thousands of unsaved, sick, and burdened ones; also for the exalted privilege of feeding His sheep.

And all of this is a tiny fragment of what thirty-five years of divine health have meant to a one-time "dope woman"!

This story "will be continued" in eternity.

Chapter 2

A WOMAN OF CANAAN

Jesus...departed into the coasts of Tyre and Sidon. And, behold, a woman of Canaan came out of the same coasts, and cried unto him, saying, Have mercy on me, O Lord, thou son of David; my daughter is grievously vexed with a devil. But he answered her not a word. And his disciples came and besought him, saying, Send her away; for she crieth after us. But he answered and said, I am not sent but unto the lost sheep of the house of Israel. Then came she and worshipped him, saying, Lord, help me. But he answered and said, It is not meet to take the children's bread, and to cast it to dogs. And she said, Truth, Lord: yet the dogs eat of the crumbs which fall from their masters' table. Then Jesus answered and said unto her, O woman, great is thy faith: be it unto thee even as thou wilt. And her daughter was made whole from that very hour

Matthew 15:21-28

Do you not love to plunge your hands into the Bible, that casket of rarest gems, and bring them up dripping with sapphires of eternal truth, emeralds of undying hope, and flashing faith diamonds? God's throne rests on a pavement of sapphire, "a rainbow...like unto an emerald" encircles it. (Rev. 4:3.)

Out of what darkness these diamonds are mined oftentimes. Here is one, a Kohi-noor, Great Mogul, and Eastern Star, all in one blazing, flashing, gleaming, glittering, glowing, sparkling, scintillating, a star of the first magnitude in the gospel firmament, a "treasure of darkness," mined out of the broken heart of a "woman of Canaan."

A woman of Canaan! An alien from the commonwealth of Israel, a stranger from the covenants of promise, without Christ, having no hope, and without God in the world. (Eph. 2:12.)

A woman of Canaan! A devotee of the most ferocious and licentious forms of heathenism that ever blotted the pages of history with crime and tears and blood.

A woman of Canaan! Yet destined to wear forever on her bosom, placed there by the Son of God Himself, an order of merit beside which all earthly decorations and distinctions are but tinsel, and the very stars of heaven fade into dimness! "O woman, great is thy faith!" (Matt. 15:28.)

Everything was against her. There was absolutely nothing in her favor. Very possibly she had never met a follower of the Lord Jesus Christ or heard a Scripture passage read. But somehow a word of God had been borne to her by the "wind (that) bloweth where it listeth."(John 3:8.)

Maybe a neighbor said, as he returned from a trip to Galilee, "I saw the man of Galilee yesterday."

"You saw Him? What was He doing?"

"Healing sick children. A mother laid a little, pale, puny baby in His arms; and He just patted it gently and looked up; and the baby laughed and crowed with glee and began to play with Him. He surely loves children."

"Did He say anything?"

"Yes, He stretched out His arms and said, 'Come unto me, all ye that labor and are heavy laden, and I will give you rest.'" (Matt. 11:28.)

"Are you sure that He said that? Just that exactly?"

"Just that."

"He didn't say, 'Come unto me all Jews that labor and are heavy laden'?"

"No, He said 'all.' But where are you going?"

"To Him. He said for me to come, didn't He? If anybody is heavy laden, I am sure I am with that poor, tortured, writhing girl of mine."

But when she comes to Jesus she is met with silence! How can He refuse to answer her when He bade her come? When the disciples beg Him to get rid of her—they are ashamed to be in her company—He answers in a way that seems to close the door of hope to her forever: ...I am not sent but unto the lost sheep of the house of Israel (Matt. 15:24). He was only teaching the baby to walk by faith.

But when she presses to His very feet He uses language so apparently harsh that one would think she would flee, affrighted and affronted—...It is not meet to take the children's bread, and to cast it to dogs (v. 26). He called her "a dog," a type to the Oriental mind of everything unclean and loathsome, to bring her to a realizing sense of her exceeding sinfulness.

Her path was beset with difficulties, but difficulties are the food on which real faith thrives best. It must be tried as gold is tried in the fire. The Lord Jesus saw in her true metal that would stand the fire and come out gleaming brighter than ever. So He plunged her into the furnace because He loved her and longed to see her shine as the stars, forever and ever.

The way up is down, and before honor is humility. Jesus brought her to a sense of sin; and when she had taken her place as a poor, wretched sinner, a vile dog, He was able to exalt her to the place of highest privilege and put the key of His treasure house into her hands.

Nobly she met the test. See the faith-gold gleam in her simple answer! "Truth, Lord" (v. 27)...Thy Word is truth. And may we not imagine her saying to her own heart, "I take the place it assigns to me. Yet I will not despair. A dog, but even a dog has provision made for him." And then to the Master: "Thou wilt not deny to me the dog's portion, the crumb that falls from the Master's table. It is all I crave. Thou canst not deny it!"

And He could not. He places in her outstretched hand an unlimited order on His unsearchable riches.

"Be it unto thee even as thou wilt," and with it bestows an encomium worth more than all the plaudits ever received by earth's greatest ones: ...O woman, great is thy faith: be it unto thee even as thou wilt. And her daughter was made whole from that very hour (v. 28).

Chapter 3

THE MAN WITH THE WITHERED HAND

It is only by faith that we can please God and fulfill His will. To believe on Jesus Christ is the work of God, that is, the work that He requires of us, from which all lesser works necessarily flow (John 6:28,29). They, the lesser works, are inevitable, however, for ...faith without works is dead (James 2:20).

> You can't get to heaven in a rocking chair,
> The Lord won't have no lazy folks there.

This is the work of God that you believe, and it is *work* and not play.

If ever a man was certain of numerous progeny, Isaac—to whom offspring as the dust of the earth and the stars of heaven had been promised, and upon whose betrothed wife, Rebecca, the blessing "Be thou the mother of thousands of millions" (Gen. 24:60) had been invoked—was that man. Yet, it was not till the Lord was "intreated of him" (Gen. 25:21) for his wife, who was barren for twenty years, that Esau and Jacob made their appearance upon the stage of human history. Isaac had to take the blessing by faith.

Yes, to "turn promises into facts," as Dr. Northcote Deck puts it, you have got to work the work of God, walk the walk of faith, and it takes two feet to walk it, to "pray and take." You may hop around forever on one foot, praying, praying, praying, and get nowhere. If that is your case, put down your "take" foot this moment and march on to victory. Even Isaac had to do it; it is the only way through.

In Luke 6:6-11 we find a flashing faith diamond, a "gem of purest ray serene," a man who "took," though his right hand was withered and he had nothing to take with. Jesus was teaching in a synagogue and saw him with his withered hand, powerless, no grasp to appropriate, no grip to retain, no punch to fight.

Dr. A. B. Simpson commented on this passage: "So many Christians have no hands! They have no grip in their fingers, no stamina in their will, no hold in their faith." If that be so with any of us, let us not forget that there is healing for spiritual, as well as physical, paralysis with the Great Physician.

To return to the scene in the synagogue, we note that there was a powerful opposition present. There always is; look out for it! That is always the case when God manifests His power.

The scribes and Pharisees were doing the work of their master, the accuser of the brethren, and though they were silent, Jesus knew their thoughts.

He knows yours and mine too. It is not enough to keep our faces smug and our tones honed. Let us pray, "Let *the meditation of my heart* as well as the words of my mouth, be acceptable in thy sight, O Lord, my strength and my Redeemer!" (Ps. 19:14.)

The Lord Jesus began dealing with this man by commanding him to do what he could: "Rise up, and stand forth in the midst." (Luke 6:8.) In other words, He made him take higher ground and publicly confess his abject helplessness and utter dependence upon divine power for deliverance.

People would rather conceal their deficiencies if possible. A German emperor who had an atrophied arm exhausted the ingenuity of artists, who painted and photographed him, in their efforts to provide poses that would hide the deformity.

This man, however, met the test. Faith always does what *it can.* But it never stops there. It wouldn't be faith if it did. It goes further and does what *it can't do.* Faith is the work of God, and He demands the impossible. ...Ye must be born again (John 3:7). You can't do it, but you must do it. No choice about it.

"Be ye holy." (1 Peter 1:16.) You can't do it, but you must do it. No choice about it. "Be ye clean...." (As disease pollutes every drop of blood it is essentially unclean, and this Scripture involves a command to be whole, as well as holy.) You can't do it, but you must. No choice about it.

To return to the man with the withered hand, Jesus has told him to do what he can do; and he has obeyed. Now comes the command to perform the impossible.

...Stretch forth thy hand! And he did so: and his hand was restored whole as the other (Luke 6:10).

How did he do it? The only way it can be done. He worked the work of God, believed on Him whom God hath sent (John 6:29), knew that Jesus never fails and that His commands are enablings.

With God all things are possible, and all things are possible to him that believeth, for faith makes room for God to work and thus releases omnipotence.

Sometimes the simplest things serve to make the sublimest ones clear to our understandings. Nothing has ever helped me to realize just what faith is so well as my youthful experience in learning how to mount a horse when I was only a chunky child, with little length of limb and no spring in me.

My father was a surgeon in the U.S. Army; and we were stationed at a frontier post in northwestern Texas, where an officer kindly undertook to teach me to ride.

I was wild with delight and perfectly fearless, so I was soon prancing around like a regular cavalryman. When my teacher arrived, he always found me mounted and ready for my lesson. There was a reason for this, which he never suspected. The only way I could mount the animal—a huge mettlesome charger belonging to my father, which seemed to me as high as a battleship—was to lead him round to the chicken coop and roll off the roof onto his back.

One day my teacher was expressing his satisfaction with my progress in equestrianship to another officer, when the latter replied, "Oh, she rides well enough when once she is mounted, but it's a scream to see her mount. Did you teach her to roll off the roof onto the horse's back?"

The next time my teacher came I met him, ready mounted as usual, when to my horror, he said with the voice he used when he was drilling the troops, "Dismount."

"Oh, please don't make me dismount. I don't want to."

With a dangerous glint in his eye he said once more, "Dismount," as though I was a regiment of cavalry, and I was on the ground in a moment. Then he said, "Now you will mount properly."

"No, thank you. I don't want to go riding today."

"You will go riding today, after you have mounted properly."

He held out his hand and made me touch it with the tips of my toes—of course, it was all sidesaddles and long skirts in those days—and then said, "Spring." And *I couldn't, but I did.* And the next thing I knew I lighted in the saddle as easily as a bird flies. For I only tried to spring, and my instructor's strong right arm did all the rest.

That is the way you can "take" that precious thing for which you are longing and praying. Take it *now.*

Then stand upon His Word, which endures for aye,
For God will bring it to pass;
The elements will melt in your sight some day,
But His Word will God bring to pass.

Yes, God will bring it to pass,
Yes, God will bring it to pass;
It does not depend on you, or it never would come true,
But God will bring it to pass.

Chapter 4

THE MAN BORNE OF FOUR

> It came to pass on a certain day, as he was teaching, that there were Pharisees and doctors of the law sitting by, which were come out of every town of Galilee, and Judaea, and Jerusalem: and the power of the Lord was present to heal them. And, behold, men brought in a bed a man which was taken with a palsy: and they sought means to bring him in, and to lay him before him. And when they could not find by what way they might bring him in because of the multitude, they went upon the housetop, and let him down through the tiling with his couch into the midst before Jesus. And when he saw their faith, he said unto him, Man, thy sins are forgiven thee. And the scribes and the Pharisees began to reason, saying, Who is this which speaketh blasphemies? Who can forgive sins, but God alone? But when Jesus perceived their thoughts, he answering said unto them, What reason ye in your hearts? Whether is easier, to say, Thy sins be forgiven thee; or to say, Rise up and walk? But that ye may know that the Son of man hath power upon earth to forgive sins (he said unto the sick of the palsy), I say unto thee, Arise, and take up thy couch, and go into thine house. And immediately he rose up before them, and took up that whereon he lay, and departed to his own house, glorifying God. And they were all amazed, and they glorified God, and were filled with fear, saying, We have seen strange things today.
>
> Luke 5:17-26

There is a beauty about a cluster of gems that oftentimes surpasses even the exquisite loveliness of a solitaire. I was looking at some single stones the other day, blue, yellow, green, and pure white ones; then I gazed at some clusters, and they seemed fairly ablaze with every conceivable color of flame. Here in this scripture passage we have a splendid cluster, a magnificent group of five great blazing gems. Faith diamonds!

Please note the setting carefully. You have noticed that diamonds are often placed on black onyx to enhance their brilliance. Or they are worn over black velvet. So this cluster of faith diamonds is surrounded by the blackest, most determined, most persistent unbelief recorded in the New Testament.

It was not a matter of individual unbelief, but of corporate, national unbelief. For this occurrence took place at a regular convention, a concerted gathering at which were assembled Pharisees—the acknowledged spiritual leaders of the Jews, respected, nay revered, by all the people—and doctors of the law, learned men versed in the Scriptures and esteemed as authorities in all matters relating thereto. These were assembled from every town "of Galilee, and Judea, and Jerusalem."

There can be no shadow of doubt that they had come for the express purpose of investigating the claims of Jesus as the expected One, the Messiah who was promised to Israel. To investigate, nay to carp and criticize, to criticize God incarnate, Immanuel, God with us! And yet the sacred record adds, ...and the power of the Lord was present to *heal them* (Luke 5:17).

Grace, grace, marvelous grace,
    Grace that will pardon and cleanse within,
Grace, grace, infinite grace!
    Grace that is greater than all my sin!

And it was not God's fault if any of them went away unhealed.

There is never a person who comes to a healing meeting, I care not how sinful or how sick he may be, but that the power of the Lord is present to heal him. God is not willing that any should perish. He wants to save and heal all. Even if they are carping and criticizing He desires to bring them to repentance and faith and to heal them. It is said of our Lord Jesus Christ that He ...went about doing good, and healing *all* that were oppressed of the devil; for God was with Him (Acts 10:38).

Now these magnates filled the house where Jesus was teaching so that there was no room for real seekers. There they sat occupying every inch of space, listening with ears that were deaf to the divine power of the message; gazing with eyes blinded lest the light of the glorious gospel should shine into them; refusing to enter themselves and preventing others from entering. There are people today who are regarded as spiritual leaders who are doing that very thing.

Into this darkness enters the cluster of flashing faith diamonds. The man borne of four.

How do we know that the paralytic exercised faith?

Because he allowed the four bearers to carry him, helpless, palsied creature that he was, into a struggling mass of humanity. I spent years in hospitals and I can assure you that it took faith on his part. Many and many a time I have known paralytics refuse absolutely to permit themselves to be moved. If it were done, in spite of their protestations, they would rend the air with their cries and groans.

It is hazardous enough to go into a mob like that if you are possessed of all your physical powers, but to allow yourself to be thrust into it when you are a perfectly inert mass of impotence takes faith.

Try as they might the courageous four could not find by what way they might bring him in because of the multitude.

Did they give up? Did he cry and whimper, “Boys, you shouldn’t have brought me. Take me home. I only hope I may live to get there.” No: he had *faith*. Faith doesn’t know how to give up. Do you remember when Elijah was praying on the top of Mount Carmel and sent his servant to look towards the sea to see if there was any sign of the rain for which he was praying?

The servant came back and said, “There is nothing.” And Elijah said, “Go again.” And he returned with the same message and received the same instruction. And again, and again and again it was repeated. There could be no giving up. *God had promised.*

So, to return to the paralyzed man and his four bearers, may we not imagine this conversation?

“We are going to hoist you up the side of the house and let you down through the roof.”

And his replying, “I don’t care what you do with me as long as you lay me at the feet of Jesus. That’s the place for me.”

He must have been not only willing but also anxious, or they would never have attempted such a difficult and dangerous procedure. I have directed the transfer of too many helpless patients not to know that.

Nothing would stop them, the fearless five; faith knows no fear. They tear up the roof; doubtless the owner of the house expostulates, and we may imagine the conversation continuing:

“Never mind, Neuben; we will make you a new roof that will beat this all to pieces, when he is healed.”

“I’ll mend it with my own hands,” adds the paralytic.

“Easy there, boys,” as they begin to lower him.

“All right, down you go; you’ll walk home,” from the faithful four.

And with indignant gazes the dignified rabbis behold this ignorant man, unversed in the Law of Moses, actually about to tumble on their reverend heads. To avert this catastrophe they hastily take them out of the way. And the paralytic reposes restfully at the feet of his Redeemer.

Those who have reached that haven of rest after battling midst the fierce waves of physical anguish and mental torture know what blessed quietness fills the entire being there. To alter the dear old hymn a little:

From every stormy wind that blows,
From every swelling tide of woes,
There is a safe, a sure retreat,
'Tis found at Jesus' sacred feet.

Chapter 5

AT THE BEAUTIFUL GATE

Apparently the friends of this unfortunate man had done all in their power to aid him. Day after day they washed him, dressed him, fed him, and carried him to the Beautiful gate of the temple where his pitiful plight was sure to appeal to the sympathies of worshipers in that sacred place. And they had persevered in this benevolent work for years, for we are told that the man was "about forty years old" at the time of his healing. But let us note that all that human effort could accomplish left him *outside* of everything worthwhile.

It was a beautiful gate but he was on the wrong side of it. A gate is something through which to pass to something beyond: an entrance, a portal, to the supply of your needs, the satisfaction of your longings and desires, the fulfillment of your aspirations.

How perfectly the condition of this sufferer typifies the state of unregenerate humanity!

By nature we are outside the Beautiful gate, "far off," without God and without hope; "strangers from the covenants of promise." (Eph. 2:12.)

It doesn't matter how people may cleanse us by reform methods, or how resolutely we may endeavor to cleanse ourselves, how we may be dressed up in culture, morality, and refinement, we are still outside the Beautiful gate.

We may be borne along on our own native resolution, or the will power of others, to the very portal; but we cannot enter; for Jesus has said, ...no man cometh unto the Father, but by me (John 14:6). *It takes Jesus to bring you in.* And how ready He is to do it! See where He comes, in the persons of two of His representatives, Peter and John, and of them the lame man "asked an alms." (Acts 3:3.)

What a poor, imperfect prayer! But a prayer nevertheless, and oh, the power of prayer! He *asked,* and One has said, Ask, and it shall be given you; seek, and ye shall find; knock, and it shall be opened unto you: for everyone that asketh receiveth... (Matt. 7:7,8). Everyone that asketh, no matter how imperfectly, receiveth.

Many years ago I heard a woman address an audience of thousands in one of the great cities of the world. She has been in the homeland for a long time now, and it is not necessary to mention the name by which she was known on this earth. Suffice it to say that she bore a title of nobility and had been closely associated with royalty. She was educated, cultivated, accomplished, graceful, and beautiful. She lived in a splendidly appointed house and had been brought up in a most dignified church where she was accustomed to sit in cathedrals, with the light pouring from windows of amethyst, ruby, and topaz stained glass, and to listen to the sobbing of great organs and the oratory of famous ecclesiastics and murmur responses out of a prayer book to the prayers prescribed by the ritual.

She didn't realize that she was outside the Beautiful gate till one day when stark, staring, shameful tragedy stalked into her home, and she had to find a living Christ to help her bear her unsupportable burden. Under the shadows of the trees of her ancestral woods, at evening when the dusk was falling and the stars were beginning to shine, she cried: "Oh, God, let me know that You are!" For truly she was outside everything. Quick as a flash came the answer. "Act as though I was and thou shalt know that I am."

So real was the message that she replied, "I'll do it." Into the house she went to pick up her Bible, to fall upon her knees; and in a few moments she found herself inside the Beautiful gate, brought nigh by the blood of Christ. How astonished people were! I could not begin to tell you how wines were banished from her home, how prayer meetings took the place of balls and dinner parties, how she forgot to send cards to the dukes and duchesses and instead invited the poor and lowly. Yes, prayer, even a poor, imperfect prayer, if heartfelt, will work wonders.

Now to return to the lame man who is still outside the Beautiful gate. In answer to his prayer Peter says, "Look on me." (Acts 3:4.) It matters everything where you look. The power of a look! It brings what you look for right into your soul and body. It changes you into what you look at.

"We...beholding as in a glass the glory of the Lord, are changed into the same image."(2 Cor. 3:18.) Beholding the glory of the Lord, we *are changed into the same image*. God says so. There is life, spiritual life, physical life—for a look at the crucified One.

And the lame man obeyed, gave heed to them, expecting to receive something of them. Looking and expecting, he could not be disappointed. Neither can you. Look *and expect* this moment. Those who do this are never disappointed.

But right here Peter carefully explains to the man just what he may expect from *Peter and John* and that is exactly and precisely nothing. No more and no less.

"Silver and gold have I none." (Acts 3:6.)

"We're bankrupt, so far as I go. Personally, I couldn't heal you of a wart on your finger or the smallest corn on your little toe." That is what Peter would tell us if he were here this moment, and by actions, if not words, he said further: "Nevertheless look on us and see through us; and in us, another, who is Almighty; whose will it is to heal all who call upon Him! 'Such as I have give I thee.'" (v. 6.)

"Then you have something?"

"Yes," he could have answered, "I have the Name, which conveys the power of Jesus the Son of God. Utterly bankrupt and perfectly helpless in ourselves, we are nevertheless the accredited agents of Omnipotence. ...In the name of Jesus Christ of Nazareth rise up and walk." (v. 6.)

And the lame man, looking steadfastly with the eye of faith, saw no longer feeble human beings but ambassadors for God, plenipotentiaries, through whom God is operating. He yields to the kind, warm grasp and lets himself be lifted up. And immediately—the response to immediate faith is instantaneous—his feet and ankle bones receive strength, "and he leaping up (Oh, the buoyancy, the ecstasy of newborn faith!), stood, and walked, and *entered with them into the temple.*" (v. 8.)

Blessed moment of fruition! He passed through the Beautiful gate, at which he had gazed longingly for so many weary years, and entered "with them," the apostles of the Lamb, with the redeemed of all ages, into the temple, the house of God! There he is, where no human hand could ever have led him, where no self effort could have placed him; and he is quite at home, for he leaps, and walks, and praises God.

This is the first recorded miracle of healing in the Holy Ghost dispensation. As that is the era in which we are living, we have a right to expect that God will work, in answer to implicit faith, just as mightily today. And we shall not be disappointed if we cast ourselves upon Him and trust Him wholly.

Are you outside the Beautiful gate? Don't stay there. Yield to the kind, strong arm that is held out to lift you up. It is the arm of Omnipotence, though it looks no larger than a man's hand. The Beautiful gate will swing open for you, and you will enter into the fullness of the blessing of the gospel of Christ.

Chapter 6

A COVENANT AND THE CONTRADICTION

God made a covenant with Abraham. He said to him, ...my covenant is with thee, and thou shalt be a father of many nations. Neither shall thy name any more be called Abram, but thy name shall be Abraham (father of many nations) for a father of many nations have I made thee (Gen. 17:4,5).

Abraham had a covenant with God, who is ever mindful of His covenant, who remembereth it forever, who confirmed it with an oath, swearing by Himself because He could swear by no greater. Abraham also had, in his bodily condition as revealed by the evidence of his senses, an absolute contradiction to the provisions of the covenant God had made with him.

God's Word pronounced Abraham fruitful, with progeny as the stars of heaven, and as the sand upon the seashore for multitude. Common sense pronounced him, so far as possible paternity was concerned, as dead as the rods of the rebellious princes of the children of Israel when Aaron's rod budded, and produced blossoms and yielded almonds before their startled gaze.

The whole world sided, and sides, with the common sense view, that is, judging after the sight of the eyes and the hearing of the ears. Let us not forget that, while we are in the world, we are not of the world.

Let us not, after singing lustily, "Do not look for me way down in Egypt's sand, For I have pitched my tent far up in Canaan's land," be found walking in the "counsel of the ungodly" (Ps. 1:1), who refuse to believe the promises of God and...to ...calleth those things which be not as though they were (Rom. 4:17).

Athanasius, the intrepid champion of the true deity of our Lord Jesus Christ against the attacks of the Unitarians, Arius, at the Council of Nicaea, A.D. 325, was warned by a wishy-washy well wisher, "Have a care, Athanasius; the *world* is against you."

"Then I am against the world," he replied.

Athanasius against the world! Believers are necessarily "against the world." They cannot for one moment accept worldly beliefs and standards, for "all that is in the world...is not of the Father." (1 John 2:16.) Thank God, like Abraham and Athanasius, they are also overcomers of the world, for ...this is the victory that overcometh the world, even our faith (1 John 5:4).

But to resume the thread of our meditation, Abraham, the covenant and the contradiction. How did he reconcile these two irreconcilables? You remember what they were: God's Word which declared him the father of nations, and the deduction of human reason, based upon the evident physical impossibility of his begetting offspring.

Now get your mouth ready for a delicious morsel, a luscious tidbit, a spiritual feast. Abraham *didn't reconcile the two*. He didn't even attempt to reconcile them. There could be no necessity for such reconciliation, for as Abraham well knew, "What *God's Word says is...is*."

Having *divine light* upon conditions, why give a moment's thought to deceptive appearances? Under such circumstances they are to be *ignored utterly.* This is the only course a believer can consistently and safely pursue, ...for whatsoever is not of faith is sin (Rom. 14:23).

"Considered *not* his own body, now dead...and it was imputed to him for righteousness.... It was not written for his sake alone...but for *us* also." (Rom. 4:19,22,23.)

Yes, God has given us a covenant, ...I am the Lord that healeth thee (Ex. 15:26). Claim it; meet the annexed conditions by the power of the indwelling Christ. If you fail, fly like a bird to your mountain:

"Death and despair, like the sea waves cold,
    Threaten the soul with infinite loss;
Grace that is greater; yes, grace untold
    Points to the refuge, the mighty cross."

Then, stand fast in the liberty, physical as well as spiritual, wherewith Christ hath made you free.

When Satan comes along with some bodily appearance or sensation that contradicts the covenant God has made with you covering healing and immunity from disease, what are you to do? Consider not your body. Consider the covenant. Consider the Apostle and High Priest of your profession whose precious blood seals the everlasting covenant.

Consider not. Blessed words! Unfailing refuge from all the fiery darts of the wicked one: consider not. Heavenly atmosphere in which no disease germ can survive for a fraction of a second! Consider not. Do not accord to physical symptoms a passing thought: ignore them. Refuse to take them into your calculations. Would that I had some medium, other than cold ink and dry paper, in which to convey to you the blessedness of the relief from distressing symptoms of all kinds that *invariably* attends this Abrahamic method of meeting contradictions. Invariably? Yes, I repeat it, "*invariably.*" Jesus never fails. ...According to your faith *be it unto you* (Matt. 9:29) stands, though heaven and earth pass away.

"O why don't these distressing symptoms disappear? I was prayed for by the elders according to James 5:14!" Your speech betrayeth you. You are considering your own body and that is why they persist.

"But," someone asks, "is it possible to 'consider not your own body' when it so unpleasantly, even painfully, obtrudes itself upon your notice?"

Yes, it is *gloriously* possible, for the God of Abraham is our God. As we unflinchingly take our stand on the naked promise, there springs up within us the "faith of God" (Mark 11:22, margin), which makes walking on the water a delight and swinging out over the aching void with nothing beneath us but His Word, heavenly bliss. Hallelujah!

Chapter 7

A BIBLE BIRTHDAY PARTY

Everybody has a birthday; and most of us have sometimes enjoyed celebrating it by giving a party and feasting our friends at a table adorned with a beautiful birthday cake, all ablaze with lighted candles, receiving appropriate gifts, and in various other pleasant ways.

That being the case, I think we cannot fail to be interested in studying a Bible birthday party, especially that of such a mighty man of God as Caleb, the Son of Jephunneh, the Kenezite, of the tribe of praise (Judah).

Oh, how they would make the very heavens ring with the praises of God, and the atmosphere vibrate with His power, for we read that God inhabiteth the praises of Israel. (Ps. 22:3.) There is no party in all the world that is so ecstatically blissful as one where everyone belongs to the tribe of Judah (Praise). I remember such a gathering at which a very solemn Scotchman was present. At least, he was very solemn when he came in, and I feared that he did not belong to the tribe of Judah. But if not, he changed his tribal allegiance, for as we were lifted into the very presence of God on great waves of adoration and wings of praise, his face shone; and he murmured to me, "It's heavenly revelry."

I believe that was what Caleb's birthday party was like. I don't know if he had a birthday cake; but if so, they had to put 85 candles on it. But was he downhearted? No, No, No! Was he wrapped up in cotton and hot-water bottles? By no means. He was interested in one thing only and that was his *birthday present.*

It was this way: forty-five years before God had promised it to him, and after waiting all that time without a doubt or a fear, he boldly comes to claim it on his eighty-fifth birthday.

Isn't it a wonder that he didn't get discouraged and give up and die long before that? Oh, no, that was the farthest from his thoughts. He couldn't think about dying, hadn't time to die in fact, for there was that promise to be claimed and proved upon first.

The very thought of that birthday present had kept him alive. Now you are all aquiver with curiosity to know what this wonderful present was. If you will read Joshua 14:6-14, you will learn that the birthday present was a mountain full of giants, the Anakims (Num. 13:33). It was his tonic, his stimulant.

The thought of that mountain had kept him alive. But what about the giants on it that he had to overcome before he could take possession? Why, he tells us in Numbers 14:9 that they were his "bread." He fed on them in thought continually and waxed stronger and stronger. People often asked me if I believe in dieting. Yes, I believe in dieting on giants. Just devour, eat up every difficulty and trial that comes your way. You will wax stronger and stronger. A diet of giants will keep you fresh and youthful. Just appropriate, masticate, digest, and assimilate one giant difficulty after another. That diet, steadily persisted in, will make *men,* nay *overcomers.*

Caleb wasn't afraid of "that which is high" like the old man in Ecclesiastes 12:5, who lived on human strength alone. No, he asked for a mountain:

> See the mountain tower high, frowning almost to the sky,
> And on its peak those cities fenced and great;
> Lo, the people cover in fear, for the Anakims live there,
> And each day with dread their coming they await.

> Oh, give me this mountain, for I am of the tribe of Praise,
> And, through the victory of Israel, the Jubilee I'll raise.
> See the giants, how they flee! for our Lord, He fights for me,
> Lo, I drive them out for our Lord has said that I am able.

It is said concerning Billy Bray, the Cornish miner, that at one time when he was praying, God promised him a certain mountain and everyone upon it. At that time there were three cottages on the mountainside. He went into the first and led the people in it to the Lord. Then he went into the second and there was a miniature revival in that cottage as all its inhabitants found Christ. Then he went into the third with like results.

But that was not enough for Billy. He immediately began to pray that the Lord would put some more cottages on that mountain. Some time after this the whole estate of which this mountain was a portion was sold and a new village was erected. An Episcopal church was built, but to Billy's great disgust the vicar of this church was a ritualist, an unsaved man. But Billy remembered God's promise to him and continued to beseech the throne. And William Haslam, the Episcopal rector in that church, was marvelously saved. Billy was delighted and went over to the vicar's home and caught up this very reverend gentleman and carried him around the house like a sack of potatoes crying, "Parson's saved, parson's saved!"

There followed a gracious revival in that village in which Billy had his share. God gave him that mountain and every soul upon it.

But let us note especially two things about Caleb: First, he was of the tribe of Praise. Faith is the victory that overcometh, and praise is the voice of living faith. When the Israelites entered the Promised Land the Lord said, Judah shall go up: behold, I have delivered the land into his hand (Judg. 1:2). Second, his name, Caleb, means "dog." He says that God kept him alive because he *wholly* followed the Lord (Josh. 14:9). A dog asks no questions, has no suggestions to make. He simply follows his master whithersoever he goes.

The great Scotch philosopher, Thomas Carlyle, had a tiny Scotch terrier that was devoted to him. One night he sat by the fireside in his Highland cabin in the mountains, and a terrible storm raged without. Carlyle was suffering from one of the awful periods of depression to which he was liable; and he felt so in tune with the shrieking tempest, rolling thunders, and flashing lightnings that he threw his plaid about him and went out into the storm bidding the tiny dog stay at home. But the faithful animal so besought him by whines and cries to be permitted to accompany him that he had not the heart to refuse, though he feared the little frail thing might perish on the mountain. As he walked along in the well-nigh impenetrable gloom, he noticed the tiny speck of white fluff keeping close to his feet in every step. No peril could daunt, no darkness affright that living little heart. He had but one desire—to follow wholly.

If we will do that like Caleb, we too can ask for and obtain a mountain. Mountain dwellers see sunrise before those in the valleys; and the sun lingers longer with them at night. The air is clearer and purer there. The eagle gives one shriek when the clouds gather and rises above them to the mountain.

Flee as a bird to your mountain.

What mountain will you have?

Arrant: Rest in a finished redemption for body, soul, and spirit.

Calvary: Dying with Jesus, His death reckoned mine.

Carmel: Where the fire falls from heaven and consumes the sacrifice.

Hermon: Transfiguration. Beholding as in a glass the glory of the Lord we are changed into His image. (2 Cor. 3:18.)

Olivet: Behold He cometh!

Chapter 8

HIS FACE TO THE WALL

In Isaiah 38 we read that Hezekiah was "sick unto death" and that Isaiah the prophet came unto him and said: ...Thus saith the Lord, Set thine house in order: for thou shalt die, and not live (Isa. 38:1).

So the case was an absolutely hopeless one. Not only was the patient incurable by any remedies known to medical science, but God Himself had pronounced the death sentence upon him. "Thou shalt die and not live."

Yet, amazing fact: Hezekiah did not die! He did not even set his house in order! What did he do? He turned his face to the wall. To *the wall;* away from man, even from Isaiah, the greatest of the prophets; away from his own sensations, symptoms, and sufferings; away from sympathizing friends and relatives; away from surgical skill (his case was a surgical one), to the wall.

What did he see there?

I read that when the famous English preacher, Dr. Joseph Parker, when pastor of City Temple, London, crossed the ocean to minister in America, some young men who were most anxious to talk with him were sorely disappointed because he sat hour after hour gazing at the vast expanse of water as though unconscious of all else.

At last one of the group, more venturesome than the rest, said to him:

"What do you see there, Dr. Parker?"

"Nothing but God," he replied without turning his head.

Face to the wall! Blessed place where you see nothing but God! With face steadfastly turned to the wall, seeing nothing but God, with every faculty of his being concentrated on the beatific vision, there was imparted to Hezekiah the faith to which nothing is impossible (When God says "nothing" He means NOTHING), and the courage to go to God Himself to pour out his heart before Him and petition Him with tears for a prolongation of his life.

Because ...all things are possible to him that believeth (Mark 9:23), Isaiah received a command, before he had reached the middle court of the palace on his way out, to return to the king and announce the glad tidings that God had graciously acceded to his request and had added to his life fifteen years.

In all ages those who have done exploits for God have had to turn their faces resolutely to the wall, away from the human and everything connected therewith, to the divine.

Noah saved the human race from extinction by turning his face to the wall, where he found grace and an ark, type of Christ, as the refuge of His people from judgment.

When everything human, Aaron included, failed Moses and the people worshiped the golden calf, we read that he "returned to the Lord" who was ready to destroy the Israelite nation if Moses, His chosen, had not stood before Him in the breach to turn away His wrath. (Ex. 32:30-32.) But Moses had to turn his face to the wall.

David at Ziklag, when his possessions were in ashes, his loved ones taken into captivity, his followers, who had been so noted for their loyalty to him, ready to stone him, turned his face to the wall, and ...encouraged himself in the Lord his God (1 Sam. 30:6). The result was a great victory and much spoil.

Augustine, Bishop of Hippo, in the fifth century, tells us of a Carthage man of high rank, Innocentius by name, who was hopelessly ill of a malady for the cure of which he had endured a number of fearful operations without any improvement in his condition. At last the surgeons, while plainly stating that they feared it would cost his life, advised a final operative procedure as his only faint hope of surviving.

Augustine relates how the man with whom he had been asked to pray, "prostrated himself as if someone had forcibly thrust him down and began to pray, with what earnestness, with what emotion, with what a flood of tears, with what agitation of his whole body, I might almost say with what suspension of his respiration by his groans and sobs, who shall attempt to describe? For my part I could not pray. This alone, inwardly and briefly, I said: 'Lord, what prayers of Thy children wilt Thou ever grant if Thou grant not these?' For nothing seemed more probable than that he should die praying."

He goes on to tell us that when the surgeons came and removed the dressings, they found the diseased tissues perfectly healed and normal in every respect. Innocentius, in short, turned to the wall and found there a God for whom nothing is too hard.

Martin Luther knew what it was to turn his face to the wall in utter despair of all human aid. When he found Philip Melancthon, his God-given helper in the Protestant Reformation, in the very act and article of death, eyes set, speech gone, consciousness almost gone, face fallen; Luther turned away from the awful scene to the window and there called on God, urging upon Him all the promises he could repeat from the Scriptures, and adding, with incredible boldness, that God must hear and answer now if He would ever have the petitioner trust Him again.

Melancthon, writing to a friend, said, "I should have been a dead man had I not been recalled from death itself by the coming of

Luther." Luther wrote as follows to friends: "Philip is very well.... I found him dead; but by an evident miracle of God, he lives."

I am associated in the Lord's work with a dear sister who had seven major operations performed on her by some of the best surgeons in this or any other country. Her friends jokingly say that everything was removed except her brains. I can testify that they are intact and fertile of many splendid expedients for advancing the kingdom of our Lord and Saviour Jesus Christ.

After all this surgery, adhesive inflammation set in; and she was simply "glued together inside," to quote her own words. Every effort was made to relieve this condition but all in vain. Lying on her hospital cot dying, she, like Hezekiah, turned her face to the wall. There she saw Jesus only. Such childlike confidence and unclouded trust came with the sight that she knew the work was done. She was prayed with for healing and saw herself submerged in depths of burning white light. In Him was life; and the life was the light of men (John 1:4). From the day, nine years ago, she has done two days' work every day of her life. I am a constant witness of her unceasing activity.

I had thirty-five blessed years added to my life because I dared, when dying from the abuse of narcotics, to turn my face to the wall and cast myself upon God. I said to myself as I drew a sigh of utmost relief, "It can't fail now because it's ALL GOD." It didn't fail, and I don't know how many more blessed years He is going to grant me, if the Lord should tarry.

I feel it to be a priceless privilege to live at this period of history when we have golden opportunities of turning our faces to the wall and taking victory over all the power of hell through faith in our all-conquering Christ.

We are co-workers together with God, and our work is to *believe* on Him whom God hath sent. If we don't believe, we are not workers but ciphers, and worse. God has made man's cooperation necessary in the plan of redemption. If thou canst believe, all things are possible to him that believeth (Mark 9:23).

The Lord Jesus awaits the trembling, tearful cry of the father of the demon-possessed boy, ...Lord, I believe; help thou my unbelief (v. 24), before He speaks the word of power: ...I charge thee, come out of him, and enter no more into him" (v. 25).

The eyes of the Lord are running to and fro throughout the whole earth to show Himself strong on the behalf of them whose heart is perfect toward Him, that is, those who fully trust Him.

I am sure God is *sufficient* for "these things," the things that He allows to come into your life and mine, the tests spiritual, mental, physical, financial. If we will but turn our faces to the wall and see nothing but God, we shall find ourselves more than conquerors in all of them.

Nay, more. I believe that God will use us, if we will look away from all else to Him alone, to mitigate the awful conditions that surround us, to heal the broken-hearted, to proclaim liberty to the captives and the opening of the prison to them that are bound. But He has made man's *faith* a determining factor in the execution of the divine purposes; and the indispensable prerequisite to being so used is that we turn our faces to the wall and see nothing but God.

Chapter 9
A SONG OF RESURRECTION

He brought me up…out of an horrible pit, out of the miry clay, and set my feet upon a rock, and established my goings. *And he hath put a new song in my mouth…* (Ps. 40:2,3).

Here we find a man crying to God out of "a horrible pit." A pit of horrors, indeed, for the original implies a place of "chaos, confusion, conflict, noise, tumult, dimness, darkness, disorder, despair, death, and destruction." Rotherham translates it "the destroying pit," so all in it are doomed by the mere fact that they are there.

How did this man, who is typical of every man who has ever lived from Adam down, get there? Did God, who made him, put him there? Never. The Lord God planted a garden eastward in Eden; and there he put the man whom he had formed. And out of the ground made the Lord God to grow every tree that is pleasant to the sight, and good for food… (Gen. 2:8,9).

I have gazed enraptured at gardens made by human hands, which were so beautiful that they took my breath away; but what must have been the exquisite loveliness of this garden planted by the divine hand that put the shine into the stars, the majesty into the mountains, the sacred beauty into the dawn, the glory into the sunset, and tinted the petal of the rose!

Man had only to dwell there amidst noble trees, emerald green turf, gorgeous blossoms, flashing fountains, singing birds, beautiful, sleek animals, who fawned on him as their God-given head and enjoy uninterrupted communion and fellowship with the author of all this beauty, the Creator of the universe and the bestower of every good and perfect gift.

Whence, then, the pit? It was Satan, that malign and mysterious being, once the "anointed cherub...upon the holy mountain of God" in the mineral Eden of Ezekiel 28, with every precious stone for his covering, whose heart was lifted up because of his beauty and who corrupted his wisdom by reason of his brightness, who dug the pit of sin—rebellion against divine authority—and lured our first parents into his trap.

The bait was the knowledge of good and evil. The prize was won but at what a cost! For Adam and Eve fell into the pit; and all their progeny, from that day to this, were born there. And from the pit there is no human way of escape.

Men have sought out many inventions, embellished their pit dwellings with magnificent works of art, perfected systems of philosophy, even erected retaining walls, and laid down paving stones of ethical culture to prevent people from sinking deeper in the mire; but no man has ever been able to find a way out. In other words, with all the genius manifested by pit dwellers, there is no power in the pit to extricate anyone from its depths.

And when all is said and done, in spite of scientific discoveries, rapid transportation on earth and sea and in the sky, radio, and other wonders, the pit is the pit still; and it is a horrible pit; the Bible says so. Some are deeper in the mire than others; but all alike have sinned, and the wages of sin is death. (Rom. 6:23.)

As there is no power in the pit to deliver, it is evident that if anyone is to escape eternal doom, aid must come from above, and that is precisely what happened. One day, while heaven resounded with anthems of praise, Jesus Christ, the effulgence of the Father's glory and the expression of His substance, rose–"and the light in heaven grew dimmer as He left His father's side"—and came, down, *down,* DOWN, from the rainbow-circled throne on the sapphire pavement, down from the adoration of the living creatures who cease not day nor night crying, "Holy, holy, holy!" Down from the glory, which He had with the Father before all worlds. Down past whirling planets, burning suns, and rotating systems, to this dark world, to the very verge of the noisome pit, crying: ...Lo, I come: in the volume of the book it is written of me...to do thy will, O my God... (Ps. 40:7,8).

Plunged into the deepest depths of that awful abyss of darkness, a voice was heard from heaven proclaiming: ...Deliver him from going down to the pit: I have found a ransom (Job 33:24).

But none of the ransomed ever knew how deep was the water crossed; nor how dark was the night that the Lord passed through e'er He found His sheep that was lost. Away in the desert He heard its cry, sick and helpless and ready to die.

For He went down to the very "roots of the mountains," below your sins and mine, and from the awful profundities ascended a cry to the Father: ...Thou wilt not leave my soul in hell, neither wilt thou suffer thine Holy One to see corruption (Acts 2:27).

And God inclined unto Him and heard His cry and brought Him up, and set His feet upon a rock, and established His goings and put a new song into His mouth, a song of resurrection. And, thank God, He did not come up alone but brought with Him, out of the pit, all who through all the ages should believe on Him.

By faith we make His death ours. By faith we make His resurrection ours—ours the security, stability, safety, strength, and steadfastness of the rock, for "I hold not the Rock but the Rock holds me." Ours the song on the Rock, the song of resurrection.

Oh! There's a song I fain would sing,
A song of praise to my Saviour King;

It is high as the height where He intercedes,
    It is sweet as the tone in which He pleads,
It is low as the reach of His mighty arm,
    It is strong as His power over sin and harm;
To sing this song have you been set free?
    He can sing it through you,
He can sing it through me.

This song of praise shall yet be sung,
    In every tribe, by every tongue;
The angels desire its notes to swell,
    But redemptive love they cannot tell.
Creation groaneth this song to hear,
    All shackles melt as it strikes the ear;
Then the sons of God this world will see.
    Shall He sing it through you?
Shall He sing it through me?

Many years ago, in New York City, they brought a poor, degraded girl into an institution. The love of Christ in a Christian sister had won her from the life of the streets. I said to myself, "A familiar type enough!"

But was she such a familiar type after all? Poor, despised, desolate, and alone, with ragged garments and shoes out of which the water was squeezing with each step. That was familiar enough, only too familiar. But there was a light in her eye, a purpose in her being, and above all, a song continually on her lips that caught and riveted my attention in spite of myself, cultured heathen that I was at that time.

She seemed to have everything of the hardest—the business end of the broom and scrubbing brush. But the sweeping and scrubbing were just an obbligato to the solo that she sang continually:

"On Christ, the solid Rock I stand,
All other ground is sinking sand."

Christ had raised her from the death of sin, and she was singing the song of resurrection.

"Sarah," I inquired, "why do you sing all the time?"

"Because I'm happy."

"I suppose you think you're saved?" (I had seen cases before and thought I recognized the symptoms.)

"No, ma'am."

"You don't think you're saved?" I inquired, filled with wonderment.

"No, Ma'am; *I know it.*" And off she went with her scrub pail, singing, "On Christ the solid Rock I stand."

Well, might she sing? She was on the Rock, and she knew it. On the Rock she was delivered from everything that belongs to the pit—the guilt, condemnation, power, and penalty of sin, and its outworkings in the body, *sickness and debility.* Praise God!

If the pit is not the rock, neither is the rock the pit. Satan will try to pursue you with phantoms of darkness, sin, and sickness, but refuse them in the power of His resurrection.

Where are you? There are but two places for mortals. The horrible pit and the Rock of Ages. If you are in the horrible pit, cry unto God; and He will deliver you, For whosoever shall call upon the name of the Lord shall be saved (Rom. 10:13). If you are on the Rock, sing the new song that God has put in your mouth, the "song of resurrection."

Chapter 10
SPRING MEDICINE

It is about the time of the year that Grandmother used to give the children all around a dose of what she called "spring medicine."

"What is it good for, Grandmother?"

"Good for everything. Cleanses your whole system; strengthens you; increases your resistance to disease; prevents sickness from getting hold of you. It's a tonic that vitalizes you and makes it a joy to live and work and play."

"What is in it, Grandmother?"

"Everything good: sulphur, cleansing and purging; chamomile, clearing your blood and skin; sassafras to stir up your system; a little salts and senna, burdock, dandelion, and other herbs, and good old black New Orleans molasses."

Dear old Grandmother's "spring medicine"! How bitter it was and yet how sweet! "Bittersweet," we called it.

That is just like our "spring medicine."

You remember the little book that the angel gave to John, the Beloved, when for the Word of God and the testimony of Jesus Christ, he was in exile on that lonely rock, six miles by twelve miles, in the Aegean Sea, called the Isle of Patmos; where when every earthly door was closed, he saw one opened in heaven. The angel told him to take the book and eat it up, and it should be in his mouth sweet as honey, though it would make his belly bitter.

God believes in bitters and prescribes them when we need them. When Esther was being prepared to go in to the king she was six months in sweet odors and six months with oil of myrrh. Bitter, bitter myrrh! And they tell us, ancient cosmeticians—oh yes, they had beauty parlors then, too—that it was the oil of myrrh that had the marvelous property of removing every blemish from the skin and making it like living alabaster.

So don't let us be afraid of the bitter in the prescription, but take God's spring medicine, for we need it in the spring and in the summer, autumn, and winter as well. Grandmother's "spring medicine" may have been one huge blunder, or big mistake, like some other prescriptions, but there is no mistake about God's remedies. They are unfailing, and we surely need them.

Let us pick up the crystal vial and drink from Psalm 103:1-5: Bless the Lord, O my soul: and all that is within me, bless his holy Name.

Now notice the label on the bottle, the instructions for taking the medicine (v. 2): ...forget not *all* His benefits. Don't leave out any part of the medicine.

It reminds you of a loving mother packing her boy's trunk, putting everything he can possibly need into it, on the eve of his departure for college, and then writing a note and placing it on the very top of all, where it must catch his eye, saying:

"My darling son: Don't forget that your heavy underwear is at the bottom of the trunk in case the weather should turn cold. Be sure to wear it if you need it. And your best suit is on top. Put it on if you are invited out. Don't forget your good ties are in a box and your socks to match in another box. Mother loves you and wants you to be well and happy every moment. If you put your hand way down in the right-hand corner near the front you will find a big jar of those nut cookies you are so fond of, and beside it is a little tin box of Mother's chocolate fudge."

God has packed everything we need into this treasure casket we call the Bible, and He loves us so much that He even condescends to remind us of "His benefits"—all of them.

"Benefits" are available to members of lodges bestowing them—at least so I am informed—who have their dues all paid up and are in good standing. Thank God those conditions need not affright us for, as the old hymn says,

Jesus paid it all.
All to Him I owe,
Sin had left a crimson stain,
He washed it white as snow.

And as to our standing, He took our place and gave us His. He hung on the cross, where we belonged, and made us to be "accepted in the Beloved." So let us drink freely of the medicine He has provided for us. Who forgiveth all thine iniquities... (v. 3). Yes, it's there.

...who healeth all thy diseases. Praise God for that! Don't forget that great and glorious "benefit." Claim it, receive it, rejoice in it.

But you are only half healed when you do that.

There remains still in our mortal bodies the tendency to depreciation, disintegration, destruction. You might be well today and break all your bones tomorrow, or suffer some awful injury, or have a stroke of paralysis, if it were not for the keeping power of God. So quickly gulp down the next dose provided. "Forget not *all* His benefits."

Who redeemeth thy life from destruction (v. 4). You are walking through death all the time. As David said, ...There is but a step between me and death (1 Sam. 20:3). But God redeemed David's life from destruction, and He has promised to redeem yours.

And here is another dose, and oh, it is so sweet! ...Who crowneth thee with loving kindness and tender mercies (v. 4). It seems to me that people who have never experienced the healing power of Jesus in their own bodies cannot fully appreciate Him.

But the very best part of this wonderful medicine is yet to come. Tilt the crystal vial up and don't lose a single drop. "Forget not *all* His benefits."

Who satisfieth thy mouth with good things; so that thy youth is renewed like the eagle's (v. 5).

That is divine life after divine healing. How few people will drain the crystal vial!

But you need it all. You need continuous healing when you are well, as well as when you are sick. You need to be lifted above the plane where Satan can inoculate you with his germs. You need the overflowing life of God in your body as well as in your soul and spirit. God is holding the precious elixir of life to your lips this moment. "Drink, yea drink abundantly, beloved," He cries to you and me.

Chapter 11

HE GIVETH HIS BELOVED SLEEP

There is nothing more essential to our well-being—physical, mental, and perhaps even spiritual—than an adequate amount of refreshing, natural sleep.

Gene Tunney once stated in the course of an interview that, in his opinion, plenty of healthy sleep is of more importance than anything else in the training of an athlete. He rated it as of higher value than proper diet, suitable exercise, "work outs," or any other part of the training.

"If he sleeps, he shall do well," but how to make him sleep is sometimes a problem. It has proved insoluble by medical authorities until the present hour.

God, and God alone, can give sleep. You may place yourself in the most favorable surroundings, pillow your head on down, let the balmy breezes play gently over your couch, secure stillness, and count whole flocks of sheep, but unless the finger of Omnipotence touches your closed eyelids and distills through your frame that blessed blissful, delicious something that we call "sleep," there is no slumber for you. Not even a king can command it: On that night could not the king (Ahasuerus) sleep... (Est. 6:1).

In speaking on this subject I am on familiar ground, for I suffered from insomnia for years and could only lose consciousness by putting myself under the influence of the most powerful narcotics, regular "knockout drops," and I can testify that during that time *I never slept.*

Though I used to turn as purple as grapes and make such awful strangling sounds with respiration that my friends many times never expected me to awaken again, I *never slept* till God, for Christ's sake, delivered me from that awful incubus of morphine addiction that was crushing me. Then God gave me sleep, and *I slept.*

The difference between that blessed natural slumber from the hand of God, that heavenly dew gently distilling on my closed eyelids and the awful torture of the condition brought about by brain-twisting drugs, was as great as that between heaven and hell.

Does someone ask, "How am I to get this refreshing sleep from God?" Notice the words of Scripture: "He *giveth* his beloved sleep." (Ps. 127:2.) It is a gift and you have only to receive it.

John reposed on Jesus' breast. There is room there for you and me, too. He was called "Beloved" because he took the place. You can take it, too.

Dr. A. B. Simpson says somewhere in his God-given writings, "You have not gone far if you cannot lay your head on Jesus' breast and sleep by faith." What are the essentials for this?

First, a clear conscience made pure by the precious blood of Jesus.

We read in Acts 12:6 of the apostle Peter, doomed to execution by Herod, guarded by sixteen Roman soldiers, bound with chains, keepers before the door of his dungeon, sweetly sleeping! What a fulfillment of the promise, When thou liest down, thou shalt not be afraid...and thy sleep shall be sweet (Prov. 3:24). Sleep has healed more sickness, relieved more pain, and removed more symptoms than any medicine known to man.

Take up your Bible and read how God put Adam (Gen. 2:21), Abraham (Gen. 15:12), and Jacob to sleep, though the latter had only stones for his pillow (Gen. 28:11). The hardness of his couch did not prevent his having dreams of heaven and angel visitants.

"But, doctor, are you correct in saying that there are no drugs that will induce sleep? I thought that there were many that would put one to sleep: hypnotics, narcotics, sedatives, etc. Do you mean to say that there are no agents that will produce sleep?"

Emphatically yes. I mean to say just that. It is true that there are drugs that will produce drowsiness, torpor, partial or complete unconsciousness for shorter or longer periods—they will sometimes make you sleep the sleep of death—but these are for the most part virulent poisons, many of them habit-forming, and not one of them can impart natural sleep.

Peace, perfect peace,
In this dark world of sin,
The blood of Jesus
Whispers "peace" within.

If you cannot sleep, ask God if all is well with your soul. "Though your sins be as scarlet they shall be made as white as snow," (Isa. 1:18.) Then simply take sweet sleep just as you take salvation. Praise God for it before you feel it, and before you know it you will be fast asleep.

There are times when God wants to talk to us as He did to little Samuel. A sister told me that one night she could not sleep so she asked God why this was, and He answered her that He wanted to talk to her for a while. So she listened to the whispers of Jesus; and when the message was finished, praised Him for it. Then He said very tenderly: "Now go to sleep My child," and she slept. "He giveth His beloved sleep."

AS THEY WENT

And as he entered into a certain village, there met him ten men that were lepers, which stood afar off: And they lifted up their voices, and said, Jesus, Master, have mercy on us. And when he saw them, he said unto them, Go show yourselves unto the priests. And it came to pass, that, as they went, they were cleansed. And one of them, when he saw that he was healed, turned back, and with a loud voice glorified God, and fell down on his face at his feet, giving him thanks: and he was a Samaritan. And Jesus answering said, Were there not ten cleansed? but where are the nine? There are not found that returned to give glory to God, save this stranger. And he said unto him, Arise, go thy way: thy faith hath made thee whole

Luke 17:12-19

The healing of the ten lepers is worthy of especially careful study, presenting as it does features not found in connection with other miracles of healing performed by our Lord Jesus Christ during His earthly ministry.

First, it is *a group* healing. We have here ten men, a number that is often associated in the Scriptures with tests or trials. For instance, for ten days the children of Judah at the court of Babylon, including Daniel, were tested, or tried, on a diet of pulse, after which they were found ten times better than all the magicians and astrologers in the realm, and fairer and fatter in flesh than all the children which did eat the king's meat. (Dan. 1:3-15.) Likewise, the church at

Smyrna was promised ten days of tribulation to try them so that the faithful unto death might be awarded a crown of life. (Rev. 2:10.)

In the case of the healing of the ten lepers it would seem to be God's remedy for disease, His Word; He sent his word and healed them... (Ps. 107:20), which is tested or tried.

In establishing the therapeutic value of any remedy in a certain disease it is quite usual to try it out on a group of sufferers from that particular malady and that is precisely what was done in the case of the ten lepers. These men differed no doubt in other respects, mentally, morally, and socially, but they had one thing in common, their hopeless misery, for they were—all ten of them—lepers.

Even in their leprosy they differed no doubt, for among ten cases some would necessarily be more aggravated than others. There would be those still in the incipience of the disease, others further advanced with more marked symptoms, and others still presenting the appalling changes, such as sloughing of large portions of the flesh producing hideous deformity, which characterize the last stages, in which almost all resemblance to humanity is sometimes obliterated.

Lepers usually hid themselves from the public gaze in their lairs, for they were not permitted to mingle with their kind for fear of contagion. How then can we account for this public gathering of sufferers from the loathsome disease? Whence did they derive the courage to take such a daring step?

Some way there had been borne to them by the "wind that bloweth where it listeth" a name, a mighty name, a name above every name, Jesus of Nazareth, who healed even the leper; and faith came by hearing, and they determined to reach Him if they had to imperil their lives to accomplish it. Hence, this pitiful assemblage.

Rabbis, doctors of the Law, scribes, and Pharisees would have recoiled from them as from poisonous reptiles. Priests and Levites would have drawn their robes tight about them to avoid pollution.

But Jesus, the spotless Lamb of God, invites sinners and sick folks, no matter how awful their depravity or loathsome their disease, to come to Him and find rest.

And when He saw them, standing afar off, as the Law bade them (Thank God, we under grace are brought nigh by the blood of Christ), but lifting up their voices determinedly, concertedly, in the piteous chorus, ...Jesus, Master, have mercy on us! (Luke 17:13). He replied immediately. He always does. There is not a soul in existence who dares to assert that Jesus ever failed to answer when he cried to Him for mercy. He "saw" them through and through and recognized that it was a *heart* cry, and He answered it.

But what an answer? How startling His reply! How unexpected His command! "Go show yourselves unto the priests." (v. 14.) "Go *show!*" Why, they had been industriously hiding themselves, concealing, covering, cloaking, for they well knew that they were vile beyond expression, rotten, putrid, decaying, dying on their feet.

"Go show yourselves *unto the priests?*" The officials charged with the responsibility of making the minutest inspection and declaring the leper an outcast from human society if symptoms of the dread disease were discovered, also were empowered to issue a clean bill of health to the cleansed leper, which restored him to his privileges as one of God's people.

The word Jesus spoke to them healed and commanded them, because they were healed, to present themselves to the priests for official certification of the fact. Please note that they, not one, two or three, four, five or six of them, but all ten went. And as *they went,* not as they talked about it, sang about it, or even shouted about it; but *as they did it,* they were, all ten of them, the man in the last stages quite as much as the one who had but recently become infected with the deadly virus, cleansed, and had something to show that they were not afraid or ashamed to display before a whole conference of ecclesiastics, namely, perfect soundness through faith in the name of Jesus of Nazareth.

I am altogether devoid of theatrical aspirations, but I am free to confess that ever since the Lord healed me of hopeless conditions, resulting from morphine addiction, I have been in the "show business" (it is thirty-five years now) and never expect to retire. I long to tell with every breath what the Lord Jesus Christ is ready to do for the most hopeless cases of sin and sickness, and to point to myself as a monument of saving grace, to "go and show."

This Scripture verse was once brought home to me with great force during a time of fierce testing. I was working in a government office and also holding a number of meetings a week, and my eyes failed under the continuous strain. I felt sure that I could secure a prolonged leave of absence with salary, six months or even longer, by making application in the proper quarter, but I prayed earnestly before doing so.

To my surprise the healing of the ten lepers was brought vividly to my consciousness, and on reading the passage the words "*as they went*" stood out from the page as though they were for me personally. So certain was I of this that I abandoned all idea of applying for leave and was almost instantaneously relieved of all trouble in using my eyes. But it happened "*as I went.*" I had to do some "wenting" before deliverance was manifested.

Do not fail to note that ten went and ten were cleansed. God's remedy for all disease met the test as it always does. No matter what the ailment, whether incipient or advanced, how young or old the sufferer, Jesus never fails.

Leprosy is a type of sin, and there is no remedy for it but a cry of Jesus. Have you called upon the name of the Lord? If not, come in your sin and sickness, call upon Him, step out on His Word in the direction which He indicates and you will have something to show, for you can say, ...Behold the Lamb of God, which taketh away the sin of the world (John 1:29).

But now comes a sharper test. Ten were leprous; ten called on the name of the Lord; ten were cleansed. But only one, and he a stranger of whom nothing was expected, returned to give thanks; only one cast himself at the feet of Jesus; only one glorified God; and he was a Samaritan.

And Jesus answering said, Were there not ten cleansed? but where are the nine? (Luke 17:17).

During the last thirty-five years I have known directly and indirectly of the healing of thousands by the power of God through the grace of the Lord Jesus Christ. Where are they today?

If they were all like the Samaritan, at the feet of Jesus, I believe that many of the problems that constantly confront us in Christian work would be solved.

Shall we not like David who, when men went in jeopardy of their lives to fetch him water from the well of Bethlehem, refused to drink it but poured it out unto the Lord (2 Sam. 23:15,16), say of our lives, redeemed from destruction by His death:

"Love so amazing, so divine,
Shall have my life,
My love, my all."

Chapter 13
THRUST OUT FROM THE LAND

And it came to pass, that, as the people pressed upon him to hear the word of God, he stood by the lake of Gennesaret, and saw two ships standing by the lake: but the fishermen were gone out of them, and were washing their nets. And He entered into one of the ships, which was Simon's, and prayed him that he would thrust out a little from the land. And he sat down, and taught the people out of the ship, Now when he had left speaking, he said unto Simon, Launch out into the deep, and let down your nets for a draught. And Simon answering said unto him, Master, we have toiled all the night, and have taken nothing: nevertheless at thy word I will let down the net. And when they had this done, they inclosed a great multitude of fishes: and their net brake...And Jesus said unto Simon, Fear not; from henceforth thou shalt catch men

Luke 5:1-6,10

Behold this picture painted by the master artist, the Holy Spirit! The scene is laid beside the lake of Gennesaret, the time is the early morning and the rays of the sun are making "Blue Galilee" glint like a pavement of sapphire. On its shores is a press of eager men, women, and children. Hungry? Yes, but for more than the bread that perisheth. Thirsty? Famishing, with a thirst that no earthly fountain can slake.

There, beside that sea, stands One who is Himself the living bread that came down from heaven, the dispenser of the water of life of which when any drink they thirst no more. Mystery of mysteries!

He *stands,* inactive, while masses of people press upon Him, not only that their sicknesses may be healed and their empty stomachs filled with loaves and fishes, but that they may hear the Word.

Theirs is a profound hunger, an all-consuming thirst. ...man doth not live by bread only, but by every word that proceedeth out of the mouth of the Lord doth man live (Deut 8:3). They are dimly, dumbly conscious of their need of life. Like Bunyan's pilgrim who ran from the City of Destruction crying:

> "Life! life! eternal life!
> "Tis life of which our nerves are scant,
> "Tis life, not death, for which we pant."

And yet Jesus, who came that we might have life, stands apparently unmoved. He is not even looking at the starving, struggling mass of humanity that presses upon Him. Why? Because God is not only going to do exactly what He says, but He is going to do it exactly as He says. He has tied Himself irrevocably to human cooperation in the work of redemption. He has made man's faith a determining factor in the execution of divine purposes.

We then, as workers together with him (Gk. fellow workmen), beseech you also that ye receive not the grace of God in vain (2 Cor. 6:1). He who has constituted us His fellow workmen is He who hath said, ...My counsel shall stand, and I will do all my pleasure...I have spoken it, I will also bring it to pass; I have purposed it, I will also do it (Isa. 46:10,11).

God cannot fail, so man's cooperation in the work of redemption cannot fail. Individuals may fail; let us be passionately determined that, by God's grace, we shall not be among the number. But God's purposes will still be carried out according to His plan, in every detail, if He has to raise up from the stones under our feet "children to Abraham," in other words, "stagger-nots" who will, like Paul, believe God, that it shall be *even as it was told them.*

What is the Lord Jesus looking at? Study the picture limned by the brush of divine inspiration. He is gazing at two poor little ships standing idle on the shore, and a small group of bedraggled, discouraged fishermen, who have abandoned them and are washing their nets, preparatory to hanging them up to dry.

> I have toiled all night and for many a day,
> They say there are fish in the sea,
> But I've caught nothing, my labor is vain;
> There cometh no increase to me.
> I will wash out my net and hang it away,
> And my fishing boat draw to the shore;
> They are useless to me; I will cast out my net
> In these barren sea waters no more.

Did you ever feel like that? Did you ever look like that? Do you feel like that now? If so, it shows in your face, and you look like it.

I was rather dismayed on one occasion by something that happened. I was walking up a very steep hill from the ocean when a lady and gentleman in a car stopped and asked me if they might give me a lift. (I was laden with parcels.) They were strangers to me but I got into the car most thankfully. We exchanged a sentence or two—I don't remember just what I said—but the gentleman replied, "You must be a Christian." I felt like saying, "Don't I look like one?" For I felt they should have known it the minute they saw me. Evidently I didn't have on what a well-dressed Christian should wear, the outshining of the inner glory. Let your light shine; don't pull the blinds down.

Well, even if we are conscious that we have not been feeling and looking just as we ought, perhaps we don't look any worse than Peter and James and John did that day; yet, Jesus headed straight for their ships and took possession. Let us give Him a royal welcome, for I am sure He is coming to each of us this very hour!

And as He enters, He gives the word of command, which must be uttered *and obeyed,* before those poor, hungry souls on the shore can get so much as a crumb, for we are working together with God and cannot be dispensed with. Listen to the words: He entered into one of the ships, which was Simon's, and *prayed* him that he would thrust out a *little* from the land... (Luke 5:3).

The Lord Jesus Christ, the God-man, who threw the stars into their orbits and spheres into space; who swung the earth a trinket at His wrist; whom the winds and waves obeyed, pleading pitifully with His creatures to thrust out a little from land. "Oh, believe Me a little at least. Thrust out from land. Don't hug the shore so tight. Oh, thrust out from the shore of sensation, sight, sound, feelings, symptoms, human experiences, and intellectual deductions. Thrust out from it all."

Oh, it's heaven below to thrust out from land! Then Jesus can teach from your ship and the poor, starving folks on the shore get something to eat. Thrust out! How far? Just as far as you like. You can have just as much of the supernatural, the miraculous, the divine as you will take. The "age of miracles" is now for the one who will dare to thrust out.

After "Thrust out," comes the command, "Launch out." We may just as well do it. We are confronted with the supernatural these days. Hell is moved from beneath, and it takes the divine to cope with it. As we launch out, heaven comes to the rescue. The stars in their courses fight for us. Faith achieves the impossible and a draught of fishes is caught after a fruitless night of weary toil.

Chapter 14

SINGING SICKNESS AWAY

I speak from personal experience of the healing power that flows from some of our hymns. And why should I not do so? He sent his word, and healed them... (Ps. 107:20), and they are simply the Word of God in a musical setting.

When at the last gasp from mortal illness, which but for God's miraculous intervention would have terminated my life many years ago, I went to a meeting in church located four blocks from the place where I lay dying, walking every step of the way, and it was raining.

Like Paul, I can solemnly say, "I went up by revelation" (Gal. 2:2), and I should never have arrived at my destination if this had not been the case. An impossibility was achieved through me, *not by me,* but by God "who quickeneth the dead." (Rom. 4:17.)

When I reached the church, I sat on the cushions on a seat near the entrance and was not particularly alive to my surroundings until the strains of an old, a very old hymn, which has been called the crowning hymn of Methodism, "Jesus, Lover of My Soul," floated to my consciousness.

An old preacher said, "A song may reach us where a sermon fails," and the healing message of that old hymn flowed over my sinking soul and shattered body like "ointment poured forth."

All my trust on Thee is stayed;
All my help from *Thee* I bring...
Thou, O Christ art *all* I want; More than *all* in Thee I find;
Raise the fallen, cheer the faint,
Heal the sick, and lead the blind...

Plenteous grace with Thee is found,
Grace to cover all my sin;
Let the healing streams abound.
Make and keep me pure within.

Thou of life the fountain art,
Freely let me take of Thee;
Spring Thou up within my heart,
Rise to all eternity.

My recovery dated from that hour, and the experience led me to search hymns, ancient and modern, for more of the blessed elixir of life. Here I wish to share with others the rich treasures I unearthed.

We find divine healing in the "Song of Moses," which the children of Israel were commanded to sing and to teach to their children, as it should "not be forgotten out of the mouths of their seed." (Deut. 31:21.) How inspiring to their faith to join in with a mighty chorus singing the majestic words, "I, even I, am he, and there is no god with me: I kill, and I *make alive;* I wound, and I *heal.*" (Deut. 32:39.)

The Holy Spirit-inspired praise book, the Psalms, is filled with the precious truth that God provides for our physical as well as our spiritual well-being.

As the Psalms have been used in public worship all down the centuries, and are still so used throughout Christendom, including the Roman and Greek churches, it follows that even in ages of darkness and apostasy men have *sung* healing through trust in Christ, though they have not always had the faith and courage to preach and practice it.

Psalm 107:8 is largely used in public worship; the refrain, "Oh that men would praise the Lord for his goodness, and for his wonderful works to the children of men!" being sometimes sung by thousands of voices.

How clearly the relationship between sin and sickness and the unfailing remedy to be found in God alone is brought out in verses 17-20. I quote from Dr. Alexander Maclaren's version, *The Expositor's Bible,* Volume III:

> "Foolish men, because of their transgression, and because of their iniquities, brought on themselves affliction. All feel their soul loathed, and they drew near to the gates of death. And they cried to Jehovah in their distress. From their troubles He saved them. He sent His Word and healed them, and rescued them from their graves."

From a hymn by Ambrose, Bishop of Milan (340-397 A.D.), it would seem that the dauntless old saint who rebuked the emperor, Theodosius the Great, and refused to permit him to enter the church until he publicly confessed his terrible sin in massacring some of the inhabitants of Thessalonia, also withstood Satan's power in his own body and claimed a death like that of Moses, whose eyes were not dimmed, nor his natural force abated, when he was lifted out of mortality by the kiss of divinity. Here is the verse in question:

Grant to life's day a calm unclouded ending;
An eye *untouched by shadows of decay;*
The brightness of a holy deathbed blending
With dawning glories of eternal day.

Thank God that modern hymns on healing abound! We cannot have too many of them, providing they are inspired by the Holy Spirit, for in that case they are, like Paul's gospel, "*according to the*

Scriptures." Praise God for appointing singers to go before us in this conflict!

But let us never forget that it is not enough to listen appreciatively to these songs of victory over Satan's power to attack our bodies; not even enough to join in the chorus, no matter how lustily. We must not only confess with our mouths the Lord Jesus, but *we must also believe in our hearts that God hath raised Him from the dead,* which means that we, as we abide in Him, are lifted clean off the plane where sickness can have dominion over us.

The law of the Spirit of life in Christ Jesus hath made me free from the law of sin and death (Rom. 8:2). Disease is the death process, death working in our physical beings. Thank God for healing in hymnology! Thank God that we can "sing sickness away," if we will only believe unreservedly on the One who bore it away in His own body on the cross of Calvary! Thank God that "Christ is all"!

Let me give one instance of this from my personal experience. A certain sister found herself in the midst of a physical ordeal that ordinarily would have meant the attendance of physicians, nurses, etc., and medical, and possibly surgical, measures of a grave nature. But, led of God, she appointed singers ("praisers," Hebrew), and led the choir in the chorus of the familiar hymn:

Christ is all, all in all,
Christ is all in all.
Christ is all, all in all,
Yes, *Christ is all in all!*

They sang and sang and *sang!* And still they sang till God did what no human power could have accomplished, and heaven came down on their souls to meet as "glory crowned the mercy seat."

Balm
OF
Gilead

CONTENTS

FOREWORD

Long ago, a lonely hill,
    Crosses three, I see them still!
Long ago the Saviour said,
    As He bowed His dying head,
        "It is finished."

Balm of Gilead, heal my wound,
    Make me whole and strong and sound,
Thou the medicine I take,
    Forth with speed my health doth break,
        "It is finished."

Is there no balm in Gilead: is there no physician there? (Jer. 8:22). That there is balm in Gilead and a physician there is clearly implied, for the prophet goes on to inquire, Why then is not the health of the daughter of my people recovered? In the 46th chapter, verse 11, of the same prophecy, the daughter of Egypt is exhorted to go up to Gilead and take balm and is assured that it is vain for her to take "many medicines," as she will not be cured in that way.

In Ezekiel 27:17, we find that Judah traded in wheat, honey, oil, and balm. There we have the gospel: wheat—life; honey—the sweetness of the Bridegroom's love of the coming One; oil—the fullness of the Holy Spirit; and balm—healing. Balm of Gilead!

What does Gilead mean? Perpetual fountain. "...the water that I shall give him shall be in him a well of water springing up into everlasting life (John 4:14). There is no limit to the Balm of Gilead, the healing of the perpetual fountain, for we are told in Revelation 22:17, ...whosoever will, let him take the water of life *freely.*

Why then is not the health of the daughter of God's people recovered? Because ...they have forsaken me the fountain of living waters, and hewed them out cisterns, broken cisterns, that can hold no water (Jer. 2:13).

But if we have forgotten or ignored the physician of Gilead, He has not forsaken us and His sweet voice "like bells at evening pealing" still calls over land and sea, Come unto me all ye...heavy laden, and I will give you rest (Matt. 11:28).

This little book is a faint echo of His gracious invitation.

—Lilian B. Yeomans, M.D.

INTRODUCTION

What are our rights as to physical healing and health? All that was purchased for us by the sacrifice of Calvary, sealed to us by the glorious resurrection of the Lord Jesus Christ, is ours by right divine.

How can we ascertain exactly what was secured for us? In one way only and that is a constant, careful, diligent, reverent, prayerful study of God's Word. How lacking we all are on this line!

It seems to me that God had to allow me to go down to the very gates of death and the brink of a dishonored grave to *make* me study the Word on healing.

Sometimes when I see people, ostensibly studying their Bibles on the Lord for the body, turning the leaves carelessly, looking perhaps to the right or left as someone or something attracts their attention, I cannot restrain my righteous indignation.

In mental vision I see the sick and afflicted ones writhing in physical agony and mental despair on their beds of suffering waiting for messengers of healing.

As the book of Job says, they are exceedingly scarce, "One among a thousand." (Job 33:23.) Alas! How often these poor sufferers wait in vain for an "interpreter," or one who can bring them into vital contact with the Christ who died that they might have life and have it more abundantly. (John 10:10.)

If it is our inalienable right to enjoy health through the work accomplished on Calvary, it is our solemn responsibility to make this "saving health [known] among all nations." (Ps. 67:2.) To qualify for this ministry a study of the Word of God on this subject, that makes it an integral part of our beings, is absolutely essential.

When I practiced medicine, it was customary for physicians to carry certain drugs on their persons. If you were a doctor, you had at hand powerful stimulants to revive the dying, anodynes to relieve intolerable physical anguish, and other emergency remedies.

When we, as messengers, enter sickrooms, we should radiate from every part of our beings the power of the living Word. To this end it is necessary to study in accordance with instructions in Proverbs 4:20-22. My son, attend to my words; incline thine ear unto my sayings. Let them not depart from thine eyes; keep them in the midst of thine heart. For they are life unto those that find them, and health to *all their flesh*.

What does God demand here? First, undivided attention. When God says "attend," He means *attend*. Put every other thing out of your mind. Concentrate all your faculties on the Word of God. Second, drink it in through the ear gate. Open your ears to God's sayings. Close them to all else. He demands the exclusive use of the ear gate. He says "incline" your ear to His sayings. You don't understand? You don't have to. But you have to bow before Him and say, "Thy word is truth." (John 17:17.) Third, you are to look as well as listen. Let them not depart from thine eyes... (Prov. 4:22). Keep your vision fixed on Jesus. There is life, physical as well as spiritual, for a look to the Lamb of God. Fourth, "Keep them." (v. 21.) Where? In the very core of your being. David said, Thy word have I hid in my heart, that I might not sin against thee (Ps. 119:11). What did he hide? God's Word. Where did he hide it? In his heart. For what purpose? That he might not sin against God. When sin goes, sickness has to go, too. They came in together, and they have to go out together. Ye shall serve the Lord your God, and He shall bless thy bread, and thy water; and I will take sickness away from the midst of thee (Ex. 23:25). Fifth, the result of this—"Life...and health to all your flesh." (Prov. 4:22.) All is all: brain, eyes, ears, arteries, nerves, veins, heart, lungs, glands, stomach, spleen, liver, intestines, kidneys, muscles, and bones; in short, every part of you.

If you meet God's conditions, "There shall no plague come nigh thy dwelling" (Ps. 91:10); "Though a thousand fall at your side and ten thousand at your right hand, it shall not come nigh thee." (v. 7.) "Thy dwelling" means the tabernacle of clay in which you sojourn as well as the certain house on a certain street in a certain town where you receive your mail.

God can and will preserve us physically, as well as spiritually, under all conditions. Let us look at some of His gracious dealings with His ancient people, the Israelites.

The Egyptians, who comprised the greatest empire on earth at the time, sought to destroy the Israelites by hard bondage, But the more they afflicted them, the more they multiplied and grew... (Ex. 1:12). When Pharaoh ordered the destruction of the Hebrew male children at birth, the women doctors who were the obstetricians of the day, reported that the order could not be carried out as the Hebrew women were so "lively," i.e., full of vitality and vigor that they needed no assistance and could take care of themselves and their babies, too. (Ex. 1:19.)

When the Israelites went out of Egypt, there was not one feeble person among the tribes though Egypt was decimated with disease (Ps. 105:37).

God put a "difference" between the Egyptians and Israel (Ex. 11:7). ...I will put none of these diseases upon thee, which I have brought upon the Egyptians: for I am the Lord that healeth thee (Ex. 15:26).

Why the difference? Because the blood of the Passover Lamb was shed, and God said, ...when I see the blood, I will pass over you, and the plague shall not be upon you to destroy you, when I smite the land of Egypt (Ex. 12:13). Thank God that the blood is still ours, our sure defense! For we read, They overcame him [Satan] by the blood of the Lamb, and by the word of their testimony... to its power (Rev. 12:11). So let us extol it and put to flight all the armies of the aliens!

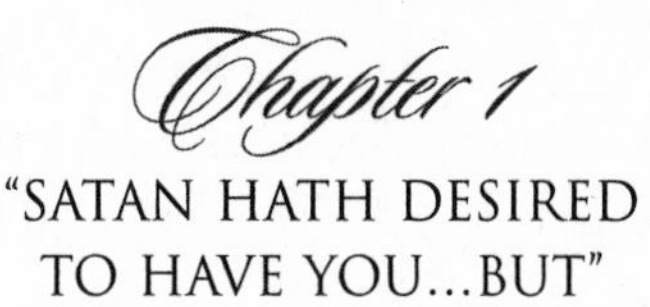

Chapter 1

"SATAN HATH DESIRED TO HAVE YOU...BUT"

Some time ago the Lord drew my attention to Luke 22:31-32, and said, "There is your life story. Satan hath desired to have you, but I have prayed for you that your faith should not fail. Now strengthen the brethren."

And as I meditated on these words, I realized that Satan was one of the first personages with whom I became acquainted. I was but a little child when it happened.

Perhaps you inquire anxiously, "Were you brought up among heathen or godless and vicious people?" By no means. My people were members of a fashionable church with stained glass windows, a wonderful tower, and a choir of artists. They stood high in the esteem of the community. Perhaps they were too refined to mention Satan and warn me of his devices. And our clergy, with the low, deep tones and the exquisite manners, were so lovely that one would never dream they had ever heard of Satan. How did I, a child, become acquainted with such an undesirable individual? He introduced himself to me, and he always said, "You are a naughty girl, and I am going to get you." That was partly true and partly a lie. And a lie that is partly true is the hardest kind of lie to fight.

It was true that I was a naughty girl. The Holy Spirit convicted me of sin when I was very small. But it was not true that Satan was going to get me. He tried hard, as he did for Peter; but thank God, the One who prayed for Peter prayed for me, too; and His prayer prevailed.

When the Civil War broke out, my father was a surgeon, practicing in Canada. He was a good surgeon and responded to the appeal for aid, which he received. Surgeons are always in great demand in wartime. He remained a surgeon in the U.S. Army till his death, and my mother received a pension from the government.

One of my first remembrances is of entering a great hotel in Washington, D.C., with my father and mother and two tiny sisters. I was able to walk alone and headed the little procession. Mother held the baby in her arms, and Father led the older baby by the hand.

As I walked in, fresh from a Canadian town where there were no black people, a figure almost gigantic in stature, gorgeously attired, and with a face as black as ebony, advanced to meet me. I was dumb with horror and amazement. No doubt I was sure that it was Satan himself. I realize now that he must have been a magnificently proportioned Negro, exceedingly handsome. But to me he looked like the devil himself coming after me. Petrified into a small marble image with terror, I saw him advance and pick me up in his arms to bear me away. Then the floodgates opened wide. I yelled as perhaps no child the ebony gentleman had ever seen or heard had yelled. He hastily dropped me. He was more frightened than I was, and I was nearly in convulsions. Employed at the hotel, he was accustomed to carrying the tiny tots in, but he had not reckoned with a little green Canuck.

I escaped that time from the one I thought to be Satan, but the real Satan is not always so easily dismissed.

I grew older and went to Sunday school where I learned my "duty to my neighbor"—to love him as myself; to do unto all men as I would they should do unto me; to love, honor, and succor my father and mother; to honor and obey the civil authority; to submit myself to all my governors, teachers, spiritual pastor, and masters; to order myself lowly and reverently to all my betters; to hurt nobody by word or deed; to bear no malice nor hatred in my heart; to keep my hands from picking and stealing and my tongue from evil speaking, lying, and slandering; not to covet or desire other men's goods but to learn and labor truly to get my own living; and to do my duty in that state of life unto which it shall please God to call me.

Perhaps you might think that all that good counsel would have helped me; but it worked the other way, for Satan said, "That's all right, but you haven't done it. I'm going to get you." So things grew worse than ever.

One day when my dear mother was dressing me for Sunday school in a white dress, with all its frills and tucks and fluffy ruffles—I had to hold my hands out horizontally for fear of mussing it—the awful thought of my black heart inside of my white dress and of Satan who was going to get me so overwhelmed me that I burst into a storm of weeping and cried, "I am lost! I am lost!" My mother was terrified at first—she was not saved then—but when she realized that it was my soul and not my body I was wailing about, she said, "I only wish you hadn't found it out when you had your best dress on."

With no one to guide me, I drifted along trying to banish the thought of Satan and to have as good of a time as possible under the circumstances.

Schools, college, and universities succeeded one another in rapid succession. By the time I graduated in medicine, I was practically an agnostic. I became so hardened that I absolutely hated the missionaries who were at college with me. Ye are the salt of the earth... (Matt. 5:13) and their Christ-likeness convicted me, for I was a sinner and knew it.

Satan did not worry me so much now. He almost made me believe there was no devil. He was sure he had me.

But the Lord Jesus Christ hadn't forgotten to pray for me. Blessed Lord Jesus, who ever liveth to make intercession for us! (Heb. 7:25.) He proved, in my case, able to save to the uttermost.

I finished my work in college and hospitals and went to Canada to practice in partnership with my mother, Dr. Amelia Le Sueur Yeomans. She was a very brilliant woman who was vice-president of the Canadian W.C.T.U. and president of the Suffrage Club. (I can always get a hearing in Canada, for people think I am my own mother and come to my meetings.)

I worked very hard in my profession, both in private practice and hospital work. The burden of responsibility was crushing and the strain terrible. Sometimes, when it seemed more than I could stand, I resorted to narcotics. One awful day I awoke to the fact that I was an absolute slave to morphine. How I struggled for deliverance!

But Satan, my ancient enemy, taunted me and said, "There's no hope. No one ever gets delivered in the last stages, and that's where you are. You are my slave forever. I've got you! *I've got you!* I'VE GOT YOU!"

Thank God that I come from a long line of Puritan ancestors on my father's side! They were people who unhesitatingly believed every word in the Bible. They knew that there is a real live devil. I saw the old family Bible with the names of my forebears—one of them was "O Be Joyful Yeomans." I have always envied him (or her, I don't know which it was) the name. I had a Grandfather Yeomans who was a preacher and lived more in heaven than on earth. No doubt he claimed me among all his descendants.

Let me assure you that *God answers prayer!* Now in a moment of absolute despair there came to me the thought, "Unless there's hope for me in the Bible, there's no hope anywhere." So I shut myself up with the Book, "the only Book," as Sir Walter Scott called it. And there I found *the living Christ,* who had been praying for me all along, though I had not known it.

I was so sick, so weak, so almost demented, that I *couldn't* pray, but then I would breathe a sigh to Him, "Lord Jesus, I am past praying now. You must pray for me." And He did.

He made me know that I was accepted in Him, and He prayed a prayer in me that I would never have dared to utter, so fully did He identify Himself with me in all my awful failure. It was, "Thou wilt not leave my soul in hell, nor suffer thy Holy One to see corruption." (Acts 2:27.)

Thank God for such a Saviour, who went down to the profoundest depths of the horrible pit in which I lay weltering and brought me up by the power of His resurrection!

Chapter 2

FEELING AND HEALING

Before I was saved God graciously sent me many of His faithful messengers who told me of my awful condition and inevitable doom if I remained in it.

Once a most venerable old man, a stranger, addressed me on the streets of New York and told me, without any ceremony, that he did it because he could discern my need of salvation. And I was holding my head as high as anybody on the avenue! But the old man was right for all that. Oh, how hungry my heart was for God, the living God!

Then there was the old Salvation Army soldier who did my laundry and always gave me a good stiff warning and exhortation, even stiffer than the collars she did up for me. And there was Sarah! I shall never forget her. I met her in an institution; and she always sang, "On Christ, the Solid Rock I Stand," as she worked. Whether it was sweeping, washing, potato peeling, or scrubbing, it made no matter. She never left the solid Rock.

I was impressed and interested. I realized that these good people possessed something that I lacked and greatly needed. I noticed, however, that some of them did not always seem to be certain about their salvation; and I used to think, "That would never satisfy me. I must have something that doesn't depend on my feelings, for I know that they are apt to vary with circumstances."

One day I came across some writing by the late F. B. Meyer, of England, in which he gave his testimony to salvation. He said, "I am saved; and if the whole world stood against me, I would say, 'Stand thou on that side, for on this am I. *I am saved.*' Nothing can make me doubt God's Word."

And I said to myself, "That's the kind of salvation I want." And I began to seek for it, and I found it in the Bible. I saw there that I was saved because of *Calvary.* I'm not saved because I feel good but because the Lord Jesus Christ bore my sins in His own body on the cross. ...thou shalt call his name Jesus: for he shall save his people from their sins (Matt. 1:21). "When he had *by himself* purged our sins." (Heb. 1:3.) And the One who did the work "by *himself*" cried, "It is finished!" (John 19:30). Believe the Word, and your feelings will fall in line with it.

Healing is part of salvation. The blood that was shed on the cross fully atoned for the whole race and provided perfect cleansing for every guilty soul. He tasted death for every man. (Heb. 2:9.) The breaking of His sacred body by the atrocities that deprived Him of the semblance of humanity guaranteed "perfect soundness" to our bodies (Acts 3:16). "By his stripes ye were healed." (1 Peter 2:24.)

Because He bore those stripes for your healing, there is no power on earth or in hell that can place disease on you or hold it there. You are free! But you have to believe God's Word. He sent his word, and healed them... (Ps. 107:20). The only way to take the medicine is to believe it, no matter how you feel. "Thy word is truth" (John 17:17).

When you let symptoms and feelings make you doubt that you were healed (*past tense*) by those stripes that the Lord Jesus Christ bore for you, you simply turn off the healing power, the heavenly electricity.

How do you think Job *felt* during his awful affliction? (He evidently had leprosy, at least I would judge so from his symptoms.)

We know how he felt, for we have in the third chapter of the book the most eloquent expression of despair ever uttered in human language. We know that his flesh was rotting off, his breath like a graveyard, his fitful sleep tormented with awful visions; but what did he believe, nay *know*? "I know that my redeemer liveth." (Job 19:25.) My Redeemer, the One who redeems me—liveth. Three diamonds strung on a chain that cannot break—I know. *Know*—what's feeling compared to knowing? Give me knowledge every time. Away with "I feel." I don't care what I feel when I know! I know that He is my Redeemer and that He liveth; and because He lives, I live and shall live forever. I live this moment. My Redeemer liveth and is doing His work. What is His work? Redeeming me. From what does He redeem me? From the curse of the broken law, which includes every disease that flesh is heir to. Christ hath redeemed us from the curse of the law, being made a curse for us... (Gal. 3:13).

What remains for us but praise?

WALKING ON WATER

And...Jesus constrained his disciples to get into a ship, and to go before him unto the other side, while he sent the multitudes away. And when he had sent the multitudes away, he went up into a mountain apart to pray: and when the evening was come, he was there alone. But the ship was now in the midst of the sea, tossed with waves: for the wind was contrary. And in the fourth watch of the night Jesus went unto them, walking on the sea. And when the disciples saw him walking on the sea, they were troubled, saying, It is a spirit; and they cried out for fear. But straightway Jesus spake unto them, saying, Be of good cheer; it is I; be not afraid. And Peter answered him and said, Lord, if it be thou, bid me come unto thee on the water. And he said, Come. And when Peter was come down out of the ship, he walked on the water, to go to Jesus. But when he saw the wind boisterous, he was afraid; and beginning to sink, he cried, saying, Lord, save me. And immediately Jesus stretched forth his hand, and caught him, and said unto him, O thou of little faith, wherefore didst thou doubt? And when they were come into the ship, the wind ceased. Then they that were in the ship came and worshiped him, saying, Of a truth thou art the Son of God.

Matthew 14:22-33

Every four years the eyes of the world are turned to the Olympics where the best athletes of all nations compete for perishable crowns and fleeting honors. Paul says, "They do it to obtain a corruptible crown; but we an incorruptible." (1 Cor. 9:25.) And he urges us in connection with the heavenly race, "So run, that ye may obtain." (v. 24.)

As we are specially told that we are a "spectacle to angels" (1 Cor. 4:9), I think we have a right to believe that those in that heavenly city are intensely interested in our prowess.

Part of Peter's race ran through water where there was no foothold for the natural man. Peter succeeded in walking on the water, but Peter also failed in walking on the water.

What a valuable lesson this incident has for us, for from it we can learn how to succeed in walking on the water and how not to fail in walking on the water.

First, note that this opportunity for "water walking" was God-given. Many things contributed toward making the test a very hard one: the darkness of the night, the violence of the tempest, the frailty of the ship, the weirdness of the hour (between 3 and 6 A.M. when all vital forces are at their lowest ebb) and above all, the absence of Jesus. And when the Lord at last came to them, it was in an unfamiliar guise, a gleam through the gloom. But He spoke and they knew His voice! There is no voice like His.

It is said that the great tenor Caruso once called for a registered letter in a village where he was unknown. The clerk refused to deliver it without identification. The tenor hesitated a moment, then stepped back a little and opening his mouth poured forth a Niagara of glorious, golden melody that almost lifted the clerk out of his skin and set the people running to the post office from every direction. They knew his voice.

And Jesus said, ...Be of good cheer; it is I; be not afraid (Matt. 14:27). No wonder Peter wanted to go to Him, water or no water. But he was not fanatical, for he said to the Lord, ...*bid* me come unto thee on the water (v. 28). There's a difference between faith and fanaticism. Faith refuses to take one step unless she has the Word of God under her feet, whereas fanaticism is ready to be guided by feelings and impressions alone. George Mueller said, "I must have the Word before I move."

The Lord Jesus said to Peter, "Come." (v. 29.) Blessed Jesus! He always says "Come," never "Go." But there is a day coming when He will say "Depart." (Matt. 7:23.) God grant that no reader of this may hear that awful word from His lips!

And Peter stepped out of the boat, left all human aid, and *walked* on the water to go to Jesus. He walked on the water; and if he walked one foot, he could have walked ten miles just as well.

Then he failed to walk and began to sink. Why? The Bible tells us exactly why. Let us study it so we will not fail to walk on water when it comes in our race.

"He saw the wind boisterous" (Matt. 14:30)—he had no business to see it for he should have been looking at One only, His objective—the Lord Jesus. And when he saw, he was afraid.

Many times this remarkable verse has helped me in crises. When I was addicted to morphine and at my last gasp, I had a lovely friend, a beautiful woman, cultured, wealthy, and most important, deeply spiritual. She lived in her Bible and lived it out in her daily life. I never knew a woman of her refinement who had such tender compassion for outcast girls as she possessed. She took them into her beautiful home and gave them of her best.

She and I had a strange experience that drew us *very* close together. We were dying at the same time; she of a malignant growth, I of morphine addiction, hopeless cases both of them.

We used to sit together "beside the silent sea," waiting the sound of "the muffled oar" with our Bibles open in front of us. As we turned the pages, we found the "leaves of healing" (Rev. 22:2) for there was divine healing on every page. But we could not seem to grasp it, for there was a stretch of water to be walked upon.

How to take the leap? Yet it must be done if we were to survive. We were not afraid to go, and yet we felt as though we *ought* to be healed in view of God's promises.

At last I somehow got out of the boat and walked on the water. I think God had to make it nearly capsize to get me out. When I saw the waves boisterous and I sank, He caught me. By this time my lovely friend had been taken by her devoted husband to some sanitarium where, though I tried my best, I could not reach her. I never saw her again.

Very recently, I had a deliverance through this passage. For some time, possibly as the result of doing a great deal of manual work to which I was not accustomed, I suffered from pain, at times excruciating. I became so stiff that it was all but impossible for me to move. My spine was particularly affected.

Satan, who is an expert diagnostician, gave my trouble a name, but I shall not flatter him by according him any publicity. He also gave me a prognosis painted in the most lurid colors. I prayed and got relief but failed to obtain complete victory. One morning in the very early hours, I said, "Well, I hardly feel able to get up at all. I suppose the Lord won't talk to me if I don't."

Then I heard that voice. He said, "Walk on the water. You have been looking for improvements in symptoms, a change in the natural order of things. Stop it. That isn't it at all. My Word is absolutely true. My healing is supernatural. It doesn't matter how you feel. *Step out.*" And I did.

A spiritual song the Lord gave my sister, Amy, has been singing in the air and in my spirit ever since.

> Drear was the hour, tossed with the bark,
> A spirit seemed coming to them through the dark,
> Walking the waters, whoever heard?
> Someone cried joyful, "See 'tis the Lord."

Refrain
Step out like Peter, walk upon the water,
Step out like Peter, walk upon the sea! Come!
Step out like Peter, walk upon the water,
Step out like Peter. Thy Lord will walk with thee.

"Lord, if it be Thou, bid me to come,
Walking beside Thee the waves are my home.
Off with my fisher's coat, now for the sea.
Seeing Thee only I walk with Thee.

Boisterous the billows, Peter looked round;
"Lord, in this tempest I'll surely be drowned."
Sinking I perish, "Lord, pull me out!"
Kind was the answer, "Why didst thou doubt?"

Some walk quite boldly with Christ on the land,
Joyful and eager to fill His command;
But should He call them to Him on the sea,
Fainting and fearful their poor hearts would be.

Chapter 4

HAPPINESS AND HEALTH

We are *commanded* to be joyful. "Be glad and rejoice." (Joel 2:21.) Joy, even poor human joy, is the greatest stimulant, the most powerful restorative, the most effective tonic I know anything about in this world.

What is the greatest joy, the most blissful experience in the natural order that a human being can have? I am going to give you my opinion about it. You will find this joy spoken of in the Bible—everything is there. It is the joy of the mother when her firstborn comes into the world. The Bible tells us that this joy is so great that it swallows up all remembrance of anguish. (John 16:21.)

When I practiced medicine, my favorite tonic for my little mothers was letting them see their tiny babies, hold them in their arms, and gloat over them as often as possible. And, oh, the dose was such a sweet one! Sarah said that God had made her laugh so that all that heard her had to laugh with her when He gave her Isaac. (Gen. 21:6.)

But there is a much more poignant joy than any that earth can give, and God wants us to have it constantly. It is also the most effective tonic in existence, for God says, ...the joy of the Lord is your strength (Neh. 8:10).

We are *commanded* to be joyful, and part of the punishment for failure to obey this command is being laid open to the inroads of every kind of disease.

Could anything be plainer than the following scripture? Because thou servedst not the Lord thy God with joyfulness, and with gladness of heart...therefore shalt thou serve thine enemies which the Lord shall send against thee...Moreover He will bring upon thee all the diseases of Egypt, which thou wast afraid of; and they shall cleave unto thee. Also every sickness, and every plague, which is not written in the book of this law, them will the Lord bring upon thee, until thou be destroyed (Deut. 28:47,48,60,61).

This joyfulness does not have its rise in any earthly things or circumstances. It is as far as heaven is from earth from hysterical, senseless mirth. In olden times they used to say to young folks who were giggling in the morning, "Be careful or you will cry before night," and alas, there was only too much truth in the homely proverb.

Whence, then, is this joy, which God demands of us, to be derived? The answer to this question is written so plainly in the Word that the wayfaring man need not err therein. David tells us in Psalm 43:4, "God, my exceeding joy!" Just God, in all His glorious attributes and our eternal union with Him in Christ Jesus. Surely this is enough to fill any reasonable being with joy unspeakable and full of glory. "In whom believing ye rejoice with joy unspeakable and full of glory." (1 Peter 1:8.) *Believe* and you will rejoice; doubt and you will despair.

And this supernatural joy, *the joy of the Lord,* is our strength, spiritual, mental, and physical. We are forbidden in Nehemiah 8:10 to be sorrowful. If we are not joyful and happy, we cannot be physically sound and healthy.

Some people may say, "Oh, that is all for Old Testament saints." I do not agree with them; but let us turn to the New Testament, and we shall find that it opens with a proclamation of "good tidings of great joy." (Luke 2:10.) The very word "gospel" means "good news," and people are happy when they receive glad tidings.

When Mary, the mother of our Lord, entered the presence of Elizabeth, John the Baptist, *yet* unborn, leaped within her for joy! That was scriptural, for the Lord told His disciples, These things have I spoken unto you...that your joy might be full (John 15:11).

The kingdom of God is not meat nor drink; but righteousness, and peace and joy in the Holy Ghost (Rom. 14:17). That this joy is absolutely independent of circumstances, the letter to the Philippians called "The Joyful Letter," abundantly proves. It is a "cup running over with joy."

What were Paul's circumstances? He was a prisoner in a filthy cellar under Rome, the Mamertine Prison, a damp, dirty hole. He was Nero's prisoner, and Nero is esteemed the most repulsive monster that ever wore mortal flesh. He murdered his own mother.

Over and over again in this epistle we find words as these: "I rejoice and will rejoice," "joy of faith," "fulfill ye my joy," "I joy and rejoice," "joy and rejoice with me." He winds up with "Finally, my brethren, rejoice in the Lord..." (Phil. 3:1). And then he can't refrain from saying it again, *Rejoice in the Lord always: and again I say, Rejoice* (Phil. 4:4). Paul knew how to take the *joy tonic.* Let us imitate his example.

Chapter 5

THE LIFE...WHICH IS IN THE BLOOD

"The life is in the blood." This is scientifically accurate and would be accepted as such by any physiologist. Do not fear that I am going to try to teach you physiology. Nothing is further from my thoughts. Is it not important? Immensely. And interesting? Fascinatingly so. But we are concerned just now with weightier matters, even the God-breathed oracles of Scripture. In the light of that Word we can find divine messages in rocks and trees and in the bodies of men and animals, for the God of the Bible is the God of nature. I am studying human blood in this chapter, viewing it as a feeble shadow and representation of the blood of Jesus Christ, the Lamb of God, by which He washed us and made us kings and priests unto God.

The subject is a vast one. I cannot do more than touch upon some outstanding matters in connection with it.

A distinguished physiologist, Trevor Heaton, M.D., Oxford University, said, speaking of the human body: "At present we can only explore the outer fringes of this extraordinary organization, and as in all scientific discovery, this is all we can hope to do." This is true of the body as a whole and also of each of its component parts, including the blood.

First, what is the blood? As it flows from a wound, it looks like a uniformly red liquid; but turn the microscope on it, and you find a fluid—the plasma—with solid particles floating in it, some red, some white. These are the corpuscles. The bright scarlet color is due to hemoglobin, the coloring pigment of the red corpuscles.

Second, what is its function? What does it do for the body? *Literally everything.* Everything comes to the body through the agency of the blood. There is a passage in Hebrews 9:7, just three words, "not without blood," referring to the precious blood of Jesus Christ. Sometimes I feel like saying, "Nothing without blood."

God has given us all things richly, but above the entrance to redemptive fullness we read, "Not without blood."

To be more specific about human blood, the following may be mentioned among its functions:

(a) The removal of waste and carbon dioxide, conveying the various excrementitious materials to the proper channels of elimination. What a fitting illustration of the cleansing power of the blood of Christ! "How much more shall the Blood of Christ...purge?" (Heb. 9:14.) ...the blood of Jesus Christ His Son, cleanseth us from all sin (1 John 1:7).

So important is this function in the natural order that it has been said that nine tenths of disease is caused by failure in elimination. Well may the apostle exhort us, Having therefore these promises, dearly beloved, let us cleanse ourselves from *all* filthiness of the flesh and spirit... (2 Cor. 7:1).

(b) The blood carries to each cell in the body (there are millions of them) its necessary food, making a complete circuit of the body in 45 to 50 seconds. Of the blood of Christ, the Word says, "Except ye eat the flesh of the Son of man, and *drink his blood,* ye have no life in you....my blood is drink indeed." (John 6:53,55.) It is summed up in the words in Luke 22:20, "This cup is *the new testament* in my blood." Everything God has promised us comes to us through the blood of Jesus Christ.

(c) The blood aids in keeping the temperature of our bodies normal. God wants our spiritual temperature kept normal. Because iniquity shall abound, the love of many shall wax cold (Matt. 24:12). "Because thou art lukewarm...I will spue thee out of my mouth." (Rev. 3:16.) When Peter followed afar off he had to warm himself. We are brought ...nigh by the blood of Christ (Eph. 2:13).

(d) It brings each cell of the body into contact with the atmosphere and its life-giving oxygen by means of the hemoglobin of the red blood corpuscles. The oxygen brought to the cells sets fire to the waste matter, and the ashes are carried off by the blood. In cases of hemorrhage that cannot be arrested, the patient endures unspeakable agony as every cell in the body suffers from air hunger. Never shall I forget some cases of the kind that I have witnessed, nor some cases of God-hunger I have seen. What is the remedy in hemorrhage from the blood vessels? Transfusion of blood. When we are hungry for God and cannot find Him, what do we need? The blood of Jesus, which gives us access to His presence (Heb. 10:19).

(e) The blood also conveys emergency supplies (hormones—substances manufactured by certain organs for crises) from the place of manufacture to the organs that have to meet the emergency. For instance adrenalin, made in the little cocked-hat shaped glands (suprarenal capsules) situated on top of the kidneys, a most powerful stimulant, which is said to put the pounce into the lion; and pituitrin, the strongest restorative known, which is made by the pituitary body, a hazelnut shaped gland on the floor of the skull under the brain, are conveyed by the blood in this way. Adrenalin sometimes seems, if we can believe reports, to conquer death, for the time being. Of the blood of the Lord Jesus Christ we read that by His death on the cross He destroyed him that had the power of death, that is, the devil (Heb. 2:14), so that saints of God can now overcome Satan by the blood of the Lamb. (Rev. 12:11.)

(f) Human blood defends the body by actually conquering deadly microbes when they get into the circulation. The soldiers of the blood, tiny white corpuscles, called leukocytes, stand up and fight them to the death. So the blood of the Lamb overcomes all Satan's power of sin, sickness, and death if we will but believe and use it. We are made "priests unto God." (Rev. 1:6.) As priests, it is our prerogative to use the *blood*. It will bring victory every time if we do it in faith, for faith will never let go till Satan is beaten down under our feet.

(g) By its marvelous power of coagulation the blood stops bleeding, seals up the wound, and starts repair work at the point of injury. So the blood of Jesus heals our wounds, makes us "whole, and strong and sound" with "perfect soundness." (Acts 3:16.)

(h) The blood continually bathes every cell in the body in tissue lymph. This is their proper atmosphere without which they could not live. The blood of Jesus Christ brings us into communion and fellowship with God, the Father and His Son, Jesus Christ. (1 John 1:3.) God said, "I will appear in the cloud upon the mercy seat" (the place where the blood was sprinkled) (Lev. 16:2). "I will commune with thee from above the mercy seat" (Ex. 25:22).

As we study human blood, we realize the truth of the words in Romans 1:19-20, That which may be known of God is manifest in them; for God hath shewed it unto them. For the invisible things of him from the creation of the world are clearly seen, being understood by the things that are made, even his eternal power and Godhead....

The things that human blood does for us are faint pictures, shadowy representations of what the blood of the God-man, Christ Jesus, does for those who have believed on Him and have life through His Name.

SALT

The Lord Jesus Christ compares His people to salt. How apt the comparison! How true the similitude! Ye are the salt of the earth... (Matt. 5:13).

What is salt? How is it brought into existence? By the union of two substances: one, something from above, a gas or vapor, chlorine (ancient chemists called gasses "spirits"); and second, something from below, of the earth, a dark, dull, grayish black metal called sodium. From this union a totally new substance, sodium chloride, or salt, is born.

Of course, salt is found in nature widely distributed, but all the salt so found in mines, the ocean, vegetables, etc., is formed by the union of something from above with something from beneath and is properly called, in chemical parlance, sodium chloride.

Please note that the new substance is utterly different from the dull, dark metal of the earth, sodium. It is white, pure, beautiful (in its crystalline form), healing, health-preserving, decay-preventing, and characteristically different from everything else in the universe. It is salt! Nothing else will take its place.

The dark, dull, unlovely metal of the earth represents man in his natural state—The first man is of the earth, earthy... (1 Cor. 15:47). In John 3:3 it says, ...Except a man be born again [marginal reading 'from above'], he cannot see the kingdom of God.

Something spiritual, something from above, even the Spirit of God unites with this being of earth; and a mighty *re-creation* is affected. He is born of the Spirit, born again, born from above and becomes a new substance, or creation, in Christ Jesus. As it is utterly impossible to obtain natural salt except by the union of something from above with something from beneath, so is spiritual salt unobtainable except by the moving of the Spirit of God on the human heart.

It does not come by effort, good resolutions, or reformation; but by the Spirit of God coming upon us, the power of the Highest overshadowing us. We are born of God, made partakers of the divine nature, heirs of God, joint heirs with Christ. Beloved, now are we the sons of God... (1 John 3:2). "Now." When? After we have believed on the Lord Jesus Christ—Ye are the children of God by faith in Jesus Christ (Gal. 3:26). And as salt is not sodium, so you are not the old Adam but a new creation in Christ Jesus. "Not I but Christ." White? Yes, *white* through the blood of the Lamb.

A poor girl who had been saved from awful vileness by faith in the sacrifice of Calvary was ordered by the surgeons in the hospital where she had been placed to have an operation. She was told that ether would have to be administered. She turned pale and asked the nurse to come to her bed.

"What is the matter, dear?" inquired the nurse. "Are you afraid of the operation?"

"No, nurse, I am not afraid of that. If I should die, I have a home waiting for me in heaven. But, oh, I am so afraid that when I am intoxicated by the ether, I may say something to dishonor my Lord. You don't know what awful things I have heard and said, too. Will you promise me to tell me truly what I say when I come out of the anesthetic?"

When she regained consciousness she asked the nurse if she had been quiet under the ether.

"No," said the nurse, "you were not quiet all the time."

"Oh, what did I say?"

"You did not speak but you sang."

"What did I sing?"

"Just one hymn, 'Safe in the Arms of Jesus.'"

A little girl who was dug out of a foul den and saved at a Sunday school in the slums got sick and lay dying. She sent her only penny to the Sunday school and said, "Grandmother, see that Jesus gets it all."

"Pure?" Yes; "though your sins be as scarlet they shall be as white as snow." (Isa. 1:18.)

I was much touched at the inscription on a monument erected in a New York cemetery by a number of girls of the streets who were saved in connection with a work in which I was interested. They desired to lie around it rather than anywhere else. Alas! Their lives were curtailed by their awful experiences, and they themselves prepared this resting-place for their bodies and chose the inscription, "These are they which came out of great tribulation, and have washed their robes, and made them white in the blood of the Lamb. Therefore are they before the throne of God." (Rev. 7:14,15.)

Beautiful? Yes, and like salt, the beauty, which is of the Lord, our God, is more apparent the closer you look at it. Viewed through a microscope salt assumes beautiful crystalline forms.

Healing, health preserving, antiseptic, causing unsound places to heal up? Yes, it is all of these, and sometimes it makes people who have these unsound places on them smart in the process of healing them.

Arresting decay, destruction, and putrefactive processes? Yes, God's salt does all of these things, for we are told to have no fellowship with the unfruitful works of darkness, but rather reprove them (Eph. 5:11).

The Lord Jesus says He sends us out as the Father sent Him, and the works that He did we are to do also and greater works. (John 14:12.) God's plan for His salt is that it should be distributed as widely as its type is in the mineral world. How widely salt is distributed in the great oceans touching every shore, in the earth in combination with various minerals, in caves hung with innumerable stalactites, in vegetables and animals; in short, everywhere. So God's salt is found everywhere from hovel to palace, and He commands us to scatter it to every land till all have heard the message of salvation.

God alone knows the power that dwells in the presence of His people! For the sake of ten righteous men God was willing to avert the awful doom that fell on Sodom and Gomorrah. (Gen. 18:32.) On Paul's eventful journey to Rome God gave him the lives of all who sailed with him, some 275 souls. (Acts 27.)

But if the salt has lost its savor, what is it good for? Nothing. A young university student who had been trained by a fine Christian mother said to me once: "You know we have a theological faculty at the university, but I find that the students in theology don't believe the Bible. I can't help believing it; and when they don't, I can't imagine why they are studying theology. What good can they be to God or man?"

The Lord answers that question—"If the salt have lost his savour...it is...good for nothing...but to be cast out" (Matt. 5:13).

HIMSELF

...Himself took our infirmities, and bare our sicknesses (Matt. 8:17). I wish that all who read this chapter would precede it by reading Matthew 8:1-17 at least three times. Indeed, it would be well to commit the verses to memory. They seem to cast a flood of divine illumination on the whole subject of divine healing.

We must never forget that it is the Word that heals. He sent His *word,* and healed them... (Ps. 107:20). Perhaps you ask, "Does not the *word* mean the Lord Jesus Christ?" Certainly, but as we read the written Word in faith, the Lord Jesus Himself meets us in its pages.

In order to experience the full power of the Bible in healing our bodies, it is essential to have it hidden in our hearts (Ps. 119:11; Prov. 4:20-22). Then we can "meditate on it" day and night, let it flow through our beings, ...a pure river of water of *life,* clear as crystal, proceeding out of the throne of God and of the Lamb (Rev. 22:1).

I sometimes suggest lists of scripture verses bearing particularly on the truth of the Lord for the body, but experience has taught me that it is much more effective for each person to make his or her own list, as they are lighted up to them by the Holy Spirit. Jot down the references and commit them to memory so that they become a part of your consciousness. In that way they are easily accessible at all times, day or night, on the street, traveling, and even when you are unwillingly compelled to listen to unprofitable conversation or radio broadcasting. By means of the memorized verses you can mount up on wings like an eagle. (Isa. 40:31.)

Glancing at the verses in the eighth chapter of Matthew which precede our text, "Himself" (Matt. 8:17), we have the case of the leper, who doubted the willingness of the Lord to heal while he was fully convinced of His ability to do so. (vv. 2,3.) Possibly the wretched creature was so conscious of his repulsiveness and the vile nature of his malady that he could not believe anyone would have mercy on such an outcast from human society. But the Lord Jesus settled that misgiving forever, for *all lepers,* no matter how loathsome, by His "*I will.*" Praise God for that!

Next a very different figure appears upon the stage. A Roman centurion (Matt. 8:5-13) enters, with dignified bearing and martial mien. The Romans were masters of the world, and they let the world know it. But how is this? His proud head is bowed before the gentle Nazarene, whom he addresses as "Lord" (Gk.. *kurios*). He says, in effect, "I know what power is. Caesar has power over me, power of life and death; I have power over my subordinates, but in Thee I acknowledge power *over all power.* Speak but the word. 'Tis all I ask. I crave it as a bounty, for I am not worthy."

And then the Lord Jesus declared that He had not found such faith in Israel, and gives him admission to the heavenly feast where he is told his place card will be beside Abraham, Isaac, and Jacob. "And his servant was healed in the selfsame hour." (v. 13.)

In verses 14 and 15, we have a picture of the Lord Jesus as the family physician. I always felt the relationship of a truly good and devoted physician to the families of which he was in charge was a very sacred one. My ideal family physician, I may as well own, was my own mother. I knew how she loved her charges and truly bore them on her heart day and night. She had families, every junior member of which she had brought into the world. How they reciprocated her affection!

On one occasion she left town on a speaking tour and placed her practice in the hands of a very able doctor whose only fault was that he was a man.

One morning the children were told that the doctor was coming. This was always the cause of great rejoicing. Glad expectancy reigned among the youngsters. At last the door opened and the nurse came in and introduced a very fine looking gentleman with a bright smile on his face. But it didn't help him with the children. They had never had any doctor but Mother, and the youngest cried indignantly, "Go away! I won't have you. You aren't a doctor at all. You are *a man!*"

But how beautiful is the ministry of the Lord Jesus as the family physician! How the children love Him! How readily the little things trust Him! They put us to shame with their simple faith. The dear old hymn, "God Will Take Care of You" was inspired by a tiny child whose mother was ill and whose father (a minister of the gospel) hesitated to leave her to fulfill his engagements. The little fellow crept up close to his mother and whispered in her ear, "Mother, God will take care of you." This so rebuked their unbelief that the father made full proof of his ministry and returned to find the mother healed and rejoicing in the beautiful song the Lord had given her. He then sat down and played the words to a tune God gave him, and so we have it:

> God will take care of you,
> Through every day, o'er all the way.
> God will take care of you.

In the 16th and 17th verses of Matthew 8 we have a mass meeting for healing, though the doctors of divinity, or at least some of them, say we have no Bible authority for holding them. When the even was come, they brought unto him many that were possessed with devils: and he cast out the spirits with his word, and healed all that were sick: that it might be fulfilled which was spoken by Esaias the prophet, saying, Himself took our infirmities, and bare our sicknesses.

This mass meeting is linked by the Holy Spirit to the prophecy of Isaiah in the Atonement chapter (Isa. 53), announcing the Messiah as the bearer of sickness and infirmity. It was not some exceptional manifestation of His power with which to convince people of His deity, but it was to fulfill His Messiahship. He had to heal all who came to Him for healing, otherwise He would not have been true to the picture painted of Him by the Holy Spirit 700 years before. We can find no warrant for accepting a Christ who does not heal the sick. There is no such Christ in the Bible. We read of our Lord in 1 Corinthians 15:3 that He ...died for our sins *according to the scriptures*. The Scriptures tell us that He bore our sicknesses, as well as our sins, on that cross of shame where He died His sacrificial death. Surely he hath borne our griefs, and carried our sorrows... (Isa. 53:4).

"The words in Isaiah 53:4, for 'griefs,' choliy (*kholee*), and 'sorrows,' *makob,* literally mean 'sicknesses' and 'pains.'" — *Bodily Healing and the Atonement,* Dr. T. J. McCrossan.

And now the climax. It was He *Himself* who took our infirmities and bore our sicknesses. Not Himself and physicians; not Himself and surgeons. When it tells us in Hebrews 1:3 that "He...by himself purged our sins," we should not dare to add one iota of human effort or merit to that supreme sacrifice. There is nothing that can be added. When the Bible tells us that He Himself forever consummated and finished our healing, can any addition be made thereto?

Dr. A. B. Simpson relates that on one occasion he had to speak on divine healing before a large audience, presumably including a large number of unsympathetic persons. He had no opportunity to make any preparation, and so asked God to mightily illuminate him by the Holy Spirit, giving him Scripture verse, subject, and sermon. One word, "Himself," was flashed into his spirit; and it was all sufficient, for Himself is our medicine, and He never fails. He is the healing and the health. The healing cannot be had apart from Him. He is the life of our mortal bodies as well as of our spirits. It is all wrapped up in Him, and we have to receive Him in all His fullness to get the healing in its perfection. He abides in us by the Holy Spirit, and one thought of discouragement will shut out the fullness of His abiding.

He Himself took and bore, not once but for always. He is always lifting us and bearing us.

Chapter 8

"HOW SHALL I CURSE WHOM GOD HATH NOT CURSED?"

The startling question of this chapter is asked by one of the most awful and mysterious personages in holy writ, Balaam, the son of Beor, brought from Aram, out of the mountains of the East, by Balak, king of Moab, to curse Jacob and defy Israel. (Num. 23:7.)

That Balaam was possessed of extraordinary powers is evident from the absolute confidence placed in him by his fellow men as represented by Balak, who said to him: ...I wot that he whom thou blessest is blessed, and he whom thou cursest is cursed (Num. 22:6).

The wonderful testimony to God's faithfulness which he uttered, God is not a man, that He should lie; neither the son of man, that He should repent... (Num. 23:19), and the sublime prophecy of the Messiah as the Star and Scepter that issued from his lips when for the third time Satan vainly tried to use his tool to the destruction of Israel, mark him as one singularly gifted of God.

What a tragedy that such splendid powers should have been prostituted to earn the "wages of unrighteousness"! But it is with his confession of absolute inability to accomplish that for which, with great care and effort, he was brought from the mountains of the East to do, that we are concerned.

Three times he tried; no expense was spared; money was poured out like water. No effort was too great. To the high places of Baal, seats of Satan, they betook themselves. Seven altars smoked with sacrifices of bullocks and rams. Balak and the princes of Moab with him stood by the burnt offering. Expectantly the king and his train waited for the awful word that should curse the people of God. At last the seer, prostrated by the prophetic impulse, with wide-open eyes, staring yet blind to things of earth, speaks in solemn accents:

...Hath he [God] said, and shall he not do it? or hath he spoken, and shall he not make it good? Behold I have received commandment to bless: and he hath blessed; and I cannot reverse it. He hath not beheld iniquity in Jacob, neither hath he seen perverseness in Israel; the Lord his God is with him, and the shout of a king is among them. Surely there is no enchantment against Jacob, neither is there any divination against Israel... (Num. 23:19-21,23).

In despair Balak implores—...Neither curse them at all, nor bless them at all (v. 25). But his plea is in vain. Balaam says, If Balak would give me his house full of silver and gold, I cannot go beyond the commandment of the Lord, to do either good or bad of mine own mind; but what the Lord saith, that will I speak (Num. 24:13).

Then from his controlled lips pour sublimely glorious prophecies of the coming Messianic kingdom: "There shall come a Star out of Jacob, and a Sceptre shall rise out of Israel...Out of Jacob shall come He that shall have dominion" (Num. 24:17,19).

Note that in every instance increased effort to curse only results in augmented blessing. Had there been iniquity in Israel? Alas the Bible makes it clear that they had repeatedly failed God. Did God condone it? Never. He condemned and punished them, but when Satan rose against them to curse them by means of his tool Balaam, He stood like a lion and defended His people. For the Rock had been smitten and abundant life-giving water (type of salvation by grace) had reached the need of the people.

The brazen serpent, type of the cross of Christ, had been lifted up in their midst; and they had received life for a look. Who shall lay anything to the charge of God's elect? It is God that justifieth (Rom. 8:33).

We read that these things ...happened unto them for examples: and they are written for our admonition, upon whom the ends of the world are come (1 Cor. 10:11). The curse for disobedience to God's commands includes every disease to which humanity is liable. This is explicitly stated in Deuteronomy 28:58-62. Satan comes with all his power and exhausts his resources to curse us with some blighting, blasting, devouring disease; but if we will look in simple faith to the One who was made a curse in our stead, the enemy is inevitably defeated.

He *cannot* curse whom God has not cursed; nay more, his very efforts to do this only result in increased blessing for us. On his own confession we learn this, Behold, I have received commandment to bless: and he hath blessed; and I cannot reverse it (Num. 23:20).

If you are threatened with alarming symptoms in your body, *have no fear!* The children of Israel were abiding in their tents, "according to their tribes," when God wrought this mighty deliverance for them. See to it that you are in the circle of His arms, in the center of His will. If the Holy Spirit shows you that you have strayed, come home to *your tent* by the appointed path of repentance toward God and faith in the Lord Jesus Christ. Then rest securely in the knowledge that Satan *cannot* put disease (part of the curse) upon you.

Does someone ask, "But Dr. Yeomans, what about Sister "So and So," or Brother "This or That," who is suffering at this moment from an awful ailment; and how can you explain the case of a saint who died of a deadly disease?"

There is an answer to every legitimate question in the Bible, a solution to every problem; and I find it in this case in Deuteronomy 29:29: The secret things belong unto the Lord our God: but those things which are revealed belong unto us and to our children forever, that we may do all the words of this law.

It is clearly *revealed* that Christ hath redeemed us from the curse of the law (Gal. 3:13), including every sickness to which humanity is liable. This truth belongs to us and our children, and we are responsible before God for the use that we make of it. Things that God has not seen fit to reveal to us at this time *are not our property,* and we do well to remember this and refrain from touching them even in thought.

The fact that the prophet Elisha, who raised the dead in his ministry, fell sick "of his sickness whereof he died" (2 Kings 13:14) does not exonerate us from our responsibility in regard to God's provision for our healing and health; neither does it justify us in judging the prophet. If we feel any inclination to do this, it would be well for us to note that when a dead man was put into Elisha's tomb, he was revived and rose to his feet the moment he touched Elisha's bones. (2 Kings 13:21.) Just so, we are healed the moment our faith *really touches* the sacrificial death of our Lord Jesus Christ on Calvary.

When I was on the very brink of the grave, the holiest person I ever met nearly rolled me in by the fact that she was so ailing and frail. The enemy would ask, "How can *you* hope to be healed when Mrs. "So and So" always has one foot in the grave and the other on the brink? You know you are not holy like she is and have no hope of ever being her equal spiritually. Explain her condition before you expect restoration to health."

How much precious time I wasted trying to explain Mrs. "So and So's" case. But one day I got desperate and said, "I don't care if every saint on earth dies of disease, the Word of God promises me healing; and I take it, and I have it." I have had it ever since.

I may say that years after I met this lovely saint (I had not seen her for years and did not know if she was on earth or in the glory) in a great department store purchasing a new dress. That didn't look as though she contemplated casting off these earthly cerements. I took courage and approached her, and a fresh surprise waited me. Her terrible illness had caused her to lose all her hair but now her beautiful, abundant silvery locks were a halo of glory around her face.

I stared at them until she said sweetly, "Were you looking at my hair, Lilian?"

"Is it real?" I stammered, forgetting my manners in my astonishment.

"Quite real. God gave it to me in answer to prayer. Do you like it?"

"Like is a feeble word; I love it, I never saw anything more heavenly in the way of hair."

The Bible says, The hoary head is a crown of glory, if it be found in the way of righteousness (Prov. 16:31), so perhaps I was not far wrong in calling her hair "heavenly." And while that dear woman was going on from faith to faith until she was able to pray the hair back on her head even in old age, I, at the enemy's behest, was beholding lying vanities and forsaking my own mercy until it nearly cost me my life.

A word to the wise is sufficient.

Chapter 9

"LET US GO OVER UNTO THE OTHER SIDE"

"Let us go over unto the other side." (Luke 8:22.) These words were addressed by the Lord Jesus Christ to His disciples who were safely on board a ship captained by the Creator of "all things visible and invisible."

It was evening and Jesus was exceedingly weary as the result of His labors with a multitude of people who had just dispersed to their various homes. As He lay asleep on a pillow in the rear of the boat, the disciples obediently went about their various duties.

Possibly Peter's thoughts may have been something like this: "If the Master had not commanded it—His very words were 'Let us go over unto the other side'—I would never have ventured on the sea this night. But no matter how the storm clouds lower, we must be safe, for He is in the ship."

So they labored on in spite of rising wind, lashing waves, and threatening skies. And "other little ships" took courage to follow in the wake of the boat that contained the Lord. But the tempest increased in fury; the waves towered mountains high, beating against the frail bark till its destruction seemed inevitable.

From their knowledge of seamanship, the disciples were well aware that, barring a miracle, they were no better than dead men. Surely the Master will arise and come to their aid! Why this mysterious delay?

They venture to creep to His side and look upon the sublime spectacle of God incarnate, sleeping like a tired babe upon its mother's breast, while demons of hell shriek round the boat that cradles Omnipotence in a vain effort to founder it.

How profound is the peace that envelops the divine sleeper! Somehow they dare not disturb Him. His repose is so holy!

Meantime the ship is filling fast. Now it is full, and the sea is actually engulfing them. They are sinking into a watery grave.

As the pangs of death seize them, they cry in anguish, ...Master, carest thou not that we perish? And he arose, and rebuked the wind, and said unto the sea, Peace, be still. And the wind ceased, and there was a great calm (Mark 4:38,39). The Lord can talk to the sea, rebuke the winds, speak to fish and birds—the fish released Jonah at His command, and the ravens obeyed Him.

If you have known what it is to have the tempest of sin, sickness, anxiety, or sorrow stilled by that voice, you know how great is the calm, how exquisite the relief, how unutterably glorious the deliverance that comes with His word of power.

With the disciples you cry, "What manner of man is this?" And you answer, "The God-man, the Word made flesh, Immanuel, God with us."

This narrative is full of invaluable lessons to us. Let us take heed how we hear! Note that, though He delivered them, the Lord was far from satisfied with the conduct of the disciples during the awful ordeal. He had a rebuke for them—and a scathing one—as well as for the elements warring under the command of the prince of the power of the air. For Satan had not only stirred up an awful storm on the Sea of Galilee but had succeeded in creating a tempest of unbelief in the hearts of the disciples.

The Lord Jesus told them that they were fearful for one reason alone, namely, because they had no faith. He had said, "Let us go *over,*" and they should have known that they could not go *under.*

Then again He said, "Let us go over," assuring them of His presence with them, so no evil could befall them.

Under similar circumstances Abraham would have known that he would land high and dry, safe and sound on the other side of the lake, even if the boat turned upside down. Of him it is said, "Under utterly hopeless circumstances he hopefully believed" (Rom. 4:18 WEYMOUTH).

Paul dared to stand forth when ...all hope that we should be saved was then taken away and say, ...be of good cheer: for there shall be no loss of any man's life among you... (Acts 27:20,22). Why was he so fearless? He tells us in the 25th verse of the same chapter, ...I believe God, that it shall be even as it was told me.

If a storm, whether of temptation, physical suffering and weakness, or financial disaster imperils your frail bark, ask yourself one question: "Is the Lord Jesus Christ on board?" Then follow it up with a second one if the answer to the first is in the affirmative, "Is He the Captain?" If you can answer these inquiries satisfactorily to your own conscience, enlightened by the Word and the Holy Spirit, you are absolutely safe from every ill. God will take care of you. I say it most reverently, He *must* in order to be true to His Word, which He has magnified above His Name.

Let me relate a recent happening in my own immediate environment. A young minister, a very consecrated man, an invaluable worker in the responsible position he holds, was suddenly smitten with the most direful symptoms, including excruciating abdominal pains. He summoned God's servants, according to the Scriptures, and earnest prayer was made for his relief. The physical anguish subsided but later returned.

This was truly a tempest of satanic origin. As his wife and children clustered about him and believers stood fast holding on to God, an ambulance arrived, and surgeons came to his bedside. They examined him but said that they could not arrive at a diagnosis without taking him to the sanitarium and added that as the case appeared to be a very serious one, there should be no delay about doing this.

Truly the waves were dashing high, the lightnings were flashing and the thunders were rolling.

But, thank God, as he lifted his heart to heaven for guidance, he was reminded that he was called by his Captain, the Lord Jesus, to "go over" from sickness to health, by the prayer of faith (James 5:14), nothing being said about "going under" an operation. So commending himself to God he said, "I will trust and not be afraid." And the word of power was spoken, the wind ceased, and there was a great calm.

That was several months ago, and there has been no return of the symptoms; and like the disciples after they had crossed over at the Lord's command, he has witnessed marvelous manifestations of God's healing power. His mother was healed of cancer (diagnosis made by one of the very best men in the large city in which she lives), and his little girl was snatched from the very jaws of death.

Another verified case came to my notice lately. A woman was told that she must have her foot amputated. General septic poisoning was feared, I presume. She consulted the Lord and was given Proverbs 3:26, For the Lord shall be thy confidence, and shall keep thy foot from being taken. On that ship, with the Lord in command, she safely weathered the storm and came out on the other side high and dry, with two perfectly good feet. Praise God for His faithfulness!

Chapter 10

"AENEAS, JESUS CHRIST CURES YOU"

Now Peter, as he went to town after town, came down also to the saints at Lydda. There he found a man of the name of Aeneas, who for eight years had kept his bed, being paralyzed. Peter said to him, 'Aeneas, Jesus Christ cures you. Rise and make your own bed.' He at once rose to his feet. And all the people of Lydda and Sharon saw him; and they turned to the Lord.

Acts 9:32-35 Weymouth

Here is a case of healing of hopeless chronic disease, which took place after Christ's ascension, in the present dispensation of the Holy Spirit.

If the eye of some sufferer from chronic disease is scanning this page, let me lovingly entreat him to pray, before reading further, in the words of the psalmist, Open thou mine eyes, that I may behold wondrous things out of thy law. Make me to understand the way of thy precepts: so shall I talk of thy wondrous works (Ps. 119:18,27). For in these brief verses *opened* eyes behold the truth, "and the truth shall make you free." (John 8:32.)

To such, "talking of His wondrous works" becomes the one purpose in life, and there is no power on earth or in hell that can shut their mouths once their eyes have been opened to see the risen Christ as their life, physical as well as spiritual.

Can you not see in this Scripture passage busy Peter hurrying from town to town, ministering everywhere in the "power of His resurrection," reaching Lydda and being lovingly greeted by the brethren there?

It is probably not long before some brother says to the apostle, "We have a very sad case here. A man by the name of Aeneas has been bedfast for eight long years. Could you visit him? He is a great sufferer."

And as the apostle stands by that bed of pain, Aeneas' sad eyes that have looked so long for deliverance in vain are fixed upon his face. What does Peter do? Nothing. He knows better than to try to do anything but fade out of the picture and let the One who has already done it all shine forth in all His power and glory—the One by whose stripes Aeneas was healed already if he would only believe it.

"Aeneas, *Jesus Christ* cures you." (Acts 9:34.) The messenger delivers his message; the "interpreter, one among a thousand" brings the sufferer face-to-face with Jesus, anointed with the Holy Spirit and with power "who went about doing good and healing all." (Acts 10:38.)

One look of faith to the risen One and Aeneas' eyes, sad no longer, flash with superabundant vitality. He rises immediately. We can't blame him for being in something of a hurry to get up after eight years of helpless recumbence.

He makes his own bed, as Peter told him to do. What a luxury after being hauled and mauled round by well-meaning but oftentimes awkward people who ministered to his helplessness! Only those who know by sad experience what it means to lie an inert mass of flesh at the mercy of others, can appreciate Aeneas' feelings on this joyful occasion. How he enjoyed walking! And by merely walking about and letting people see him do it, he is used to bring about a revival that sweeps all the people of Lydda and Sharon into the fountain of cleansing. All that dwelt at Lydda and Saron saw him, and turned to the Lord (Acts 9:35). Worthwhile, wasn't it?

As I meditate over this account, a question continually rises in my mind: If the Word of God says of Aeneas, "Jesus maketh thee *whole,*" have we any right to be one half or even three quarters whole? If Peter told Aeneas, "Jesus Christ cures you," are we justified in remaining sick? Or was this wonderful gift only for Aeneas and some other special favorites?

I think we can find the answer to this query in Luke 4:16-30. Jesus had returned to His hometown after going about all Galilee, teaching, preaching, and healing. His fame had gone forth, and He well knew that His fellow townsmen felt that they had a special claim upon Him. ...Ye will surely say...Physician, heal thyself: whatsoever we have heard done in Capernaum, do also here in thy country (v. 23).

Knowing their attitude He reads, when the roll is given Him, from Isaiah 61, where it is written, The Spirit of the Lord is upon me, because he hath anointed me to preach the gospel to the poor; he hath sent me to heal the broken hearted, to preach deliverance to the captives, and recovering of sight to the blind, to set at liberty them that are bruised, to preach the acceptable year of the Lord (vv. 18,19).

Then closing the book and sitting down, when all eyes are fastened upon Him, He said unto them, ...This day is this scripture fulfilled in your ears (v. 21). In other words, He proclaimed salvation, healing, deliverance, the opening of blind eyes, physical and spiritual, for all who would accept it, then and there. Nobody in Nazareth need to let the sun set that night upon his or her sin, sickness, affliction, or captivity. What a jubilee they might have celebrated! What a revival would inevitably have resulted!

What hindered? One thing only—their failure to acknowledge, accept, believe upon, and submit to the Word of God made flesh, who stood among them offering Himself freely to all. "He sent His Word and healed them." (Ps. 107:20.) But what if they will not take the medicine? "I would...but ye would not." Naaman humbled himself, believed the message in the mouth of a serving maid, obeyed God, and was healed. (2 Kings 5.) The widow of Sarepta believed so thoroughly that she took the bread from the mouth of her son, who was threatened with death from famine, at God's command; and both she and her son and her house were saved from death. (1 Kings 17:7-16.) If you really believe the promise, you will obey the precept that accompanies it.

"Aeneas, Jesus Christ cures you." Put your name, whether James, John, Jacob, Joy, or whatever it may be, in place of Aeneas in this verse and *believe* it. Your disease will vanish—I say it on the authority of the Word of God— ...I am the Lord that healeth thee (Ex. 15:26); I am the Lord, I change not... (Mal. 3:6). It matters not whether your ailment is acute or chronic, "He healeth all thy diseases." (Ps. 103:3.) And when you step forth, you will find that your "Lydda and Sharon" will turn to the Lord.

Chapter 11

GOD CALLED ABRAHAM ALONE

Among the most vivid recollections of my early childhood is the story of my mother's wedding dress. I never saw the garment, as it was unfortunately stolen before I was born. Perhaps that made it all the more interesting. At any rate I shall never forget the description of its beauty and costliness, which always ended with, "It was real silk brocade from London and would *stand alone.*" (The last two words always *very* emphatic.)

I never quite understood what "standing alone" as applied to a dress meant, nor why it was deemed an essential quality for a perfect wedding gown, but I listened with almost reverential awe nevertheless.

There is another wedding dress I want us to consider, the wedding garment of the bride of the Lamb. This dress is of "fine linen, clean and white; for the fine linen is the righteousness of saints." (Rev. 19:8.) In other words, it is "the righteousness of God which is by faith of Jesus Christ unto all and upon all them that believe." (Rom. 3:22.) Here is a wedding dress that will "stand alone."

Real faith will stand alone anywhere for any length of time in the face of all contradictions and in the teeth of any opposition, for it rests on the "forever settled" Word of God.

There's a walk for every soul in God alone,
    There's a stand in God for every soul to take.
There's a walk none else can take but only you,
    For this path is trod by you and God alone.
He calls, He apprehends your soul to stand in Him,
And as you praise and stand the work is done.
    God called Abraham alone!

Yes, God called Abraham alone and blessed him and increased him. (Isa. 51:2.)

As I read the story of the healing of blind Bartimaeus, the Holy Spirit impressed me of this man's aloneness with God throughout the entire transaction (Mark 10:46-52). There he sat, alone in a crowd—the loneliest kind of loneliness—hopeless and helpless. No one volunteered a hand to assist him to get within range of the Great Physician.

But he could *hear,* and he used what he *had* to secure what he *lacked.* The moment his ears told him that it was Jesus of *Nazareth* who was passing by (many were called Jesus in that day), he filled his lungs and emitted a cry so piercing that it brought down stern rebukes on his head. For Jesus of *Nazareth* was He who said, The Spirit of the Lord is upon me, because he hath anointed me to preach the gospel to the poor; he hath sent me to heal the broken-hearted, to preach deliverance to the captives, and *recovering of sight to the blind,* to set at liberty them that are bruised, to preach the acceptable year of the Lord (Luke 4:18,19).

Poor blind beggar! How easily the crowd could have silenced him forcibly. But Bartimaeus had lost all consciousness of the crowd. By faith he wrenched himself clean out of his surroundings and stood alone with God incarnate in the person of His Son, Jesus Christ the Lord. There were to him just two people present, Jesus of Nazareth and the blind beggar, Bartimaeus.

Alone and unaided by any favoring circumstance, he undertook by his voice, the only thing he had, to bring the two into vital contact. Opposition only made him cry the "more a great deal." (Mark 10:48.) That is its invariable effect on real faith, for real faith will stand alone. "And Jesus stood still!" (v. 49.) Amazing words! His every step controlled and directed by the Spirit of God, Jesus was on an errand to some definite objective, yet at the cry of Bartimaeus—no, at the cry of *faith*—He stood still.

Marvel of marvels, God incarnate, creator and sustainer of the universe, arrested in His course, brought to a full stop by a blind beggar's cry. Yes, for ...all things are possible to him that believeth (Mark 9:23).

Bartimaeus received his sight and followed Jesus in the way.

Chapter 12
OUR DAILY BREAD

And he said unto them, When ye pray, say, Our Father which art in heaven...give us day by day our daily bread (Luke 11:2,3).

The Lord Jesus Christ asked His Father, with utter simplicity and child-like confidence, for His bread, a day's supply at a time.

The Father of our Lord Jesus Christ is our Father, too, by virtue of the new birth; and we should ask Him for our bread just as confidently as our elder brother did, realizing that our Father heareth us always, and we have only to ask in order to receive. What problems would be solved, what anxieties stilled, what cares banished if we always did this!

> If our love were but more simple,
> We should take Him at His Word.
> And our lives would be all sunshine
> In the sweetness of our Lord.

The Lord Jesus knew, as we never can know, what intricate adjustments and complex arrangements have to be effected by divine wisdom and omnipotence in order to answer that simple little petition that any tiny child can breathe, "Give us our daily bread."

When have we our daily bread? When we have a bank account or a meal ticket reposes safely in our pocket, or we have a standing invitation to the hospitable board of some kind friend?

No indeed, in any and all of these situations we may still be far from our daily bread.

Driving through thousands of acres of golden grain in the Canadian Northwest, I said to myself, "There's our daily bread from our Father's hand." Then, as I watched the men working like tigers to gather the precious grain before the frost or storm could blight it, I said, "And our Father knows that it is good for us to eat our bread in the sweat of our faces, and so He lets us work hard for it and do much toward answering our own prayers."

But as in thought, I turned from the external and apparent to the internal and invisible and remembered the elaborate process and complex changes every atom of food has to undergo before it can be utilized by the system; I changed my tune and said, "Oh, the work those men are doing is just child's play; they are like little ones running errands for Mother who is doing all the real work. God alone can give us our daily bread."

When have we our daily bread? When we take it into our mouths, taste, masticate, and swallow it? By no means. Do you realize that you are inconceivably complex, made up of millions of units, microscopic cells, each of which is eagerly waiting for its daily bread, and a goodly number of which require a special diet to enable them to perform peculiar functions upon which the continuance of life depends?

When you say, "Give us this day our daily bread," you are praying for the necessary food supplies for a whole community, so to speak. And the raw materials which you take into your mouth have to be acted upon by a number of secretions of various organs, beginning with the salivary glands in the mouth, passing on to the gastric juice of the stomach, pancreatic juice from the pancreas, and so on through the intestines, being modified during the whole progress by glandular secretions of the most complex chemical nature poured in from the various organs.

Not until this work is fully accomplished and the digested food is carried into the circulation and duly distributed do the cells hear the dinner bell and get their daily bread. So essential is every detail to the answer to the prayer, "Give us our daily bread," that failure at one point may be fatal even to life itself.

For example, sugar is necessary to life, and normal blood contains it in the proportion of 1-1000. But before the sugar taken with the food can be utilized by the body cells, which cannot exist without it, it has to be acted upon by a glandular secretion produced in the so-called "islets" of the pancreas, from which fact it takes its name "insulin" (Latin *insula,* an island).

In the absence of insulin the sugar taken into the system is thrown into the blood as refuse, and upon the kidneys devolves the task of excreting it. Meantime the cells are starving for sugar, and ultimately the individual dies of sugar starvation with his blood loaded with it—just as a man may die for lack of water in an open boat in the middle of the ocean.

Surely we are "fearfully and wonderfully made"! Well might the Lord Jesus say, "Take no thought...what ye shall eat, or what ye shall drink...Is not the *life* more than meat?" (Matt. 6:25.)

What is the corollary from all this? God and God alone can give us our daily bread. We may have it in the bank, in our hands, in our mouths, in our stomachs, in our blood even; but only God can *give* it to us. This He does by making His Word health to all our flesh, including every gland and cell.

So this beautiful prayer, Give us this day our daily bread (Matt. 6:11), is a petition not for food only but for *life,* which is more than meat. In other words, it is a prayer for *perfect health* put in our mouths by the Lord Jesus Himself.

Chapter 13

A MIRACLE THAT SPEAKS TO OUR OWN TIMES

Jesus came again into Cana of Galilee, where he made the water wine. And there was a certain nobleman, whose son was sick at Capernaum. When he heard that Jesus was come out of Judea into Galilee, he went unto him, and besought him that he would come down, and heal his son: for he was at the point of death. Then said Jesus unto him, Except ye see signs and wonders, ye will not believe. The nobleman saith unto him, Sir, come down ere my child die. Jesus saith unto him, Go thy way; thy son liveth. And the man believed the word that Jesus had spoken unto him, and he went his way. And as he was now going down, his servants met him, and told him, saying, Thy son liveth. Then enquired he of them the hour when he began to amend. And they said unto him, Yesterday at the seventh hour the fever left him. So the father knew that it was at the same hour, in which Jesus said unto him, Thy son liveth: and himself believed, and his whole house"

John 4:46-53

The Bible states that Jesus came into Cana of Galilee, where He had made the water wine. Close at hand was Capernaum, where dwelt many Roman officials in their beautiful mansions. From the Greek it is evident that the man of this story was a ruler, or courtier, a resident of Capernaum.

It is possible, probable, perhaps almost certain, that he had heard of the first miracle, for we read in John 2:11, This beginning of miracles did Jesus in Cana of Galilee, and *manifested forth his glory;* and his disciples believed on him. It is within the bounds of possibility that he was present at the wedding ceremony. He may have been an eyewitness of the marvel and tasted of the water that was made wine. From the perturbation manifested when the supply of wine proved insufficient, the family may well have been prominent persons in the society of the district. What better lesson in faith could he have had than the miracle at the wedding? God expected him to profit by it, and He expects us to profit by similar experiences.

There was a need, a real need, a great one. No wine? Forever and forever in the conservative East this would be quoted against the honor of the family, "The wine gave out at the wedding!" The mother of the Lord Jesus revealed to Him the awful situation. "*They* have no wine!" And then, confident that He would do something though His words sounded discouraging, she said to the servants. ...Whatsoever he saith unto you, do it (John 2:5). He will speak, only believe and obey, no matter what He tells you to do.

That is *faith. "Whatsoever he saith unto you, do it."*

If He tells you to walk when you have no legs, step out; or to speak when you have no voice, open your mouth wide immediately; or to believe when you are not conscious of an atom of faith, do it; or to sing His praises when you feel like chanting a dirge, shout, "I will extol Thee, my God. I will bless Thy name forever and ever." That is *faith.*

When He spoke, He told them to fill up the water pots. A hard task; their combined capacity was about 162 gallons. "*Whatsoever.*" No doubt the water had to be carried some distance, and what use would it be when they brought it? It was wine, not water, that was needed. "*Whatsoever.*" And they filled them to the brim.

Then came a much harder test. (They always get harder as you go from faith to greater faith.)

"Draw out now, and bear unto the governor of the feast." (v. 8.)

"But it *is water!*"

"*Whatsoever!*" And they obeyed. And when the governor had tasted it—I don't believe there was any change till then—he said, "Well, this is good wine for sure!" (v. 10.)

This Roman nobleman who approached Jesus concerning his son presumably had this happening to go upon, and he asked the Lord Jesus to "come down" and heal his son, lying at the point of death. (John 4:47.) He wanted the personal, physical, visible presence of the Lord. That's what we want and what we lack. So this miracle is specially suited to our own time and condition.

Once my sister and I were having a great test of faith. We had the promise, but our eyes failed to report anything, our ears gave no testimony to its fulfillment, though the Word said, "It is finished." We wanted the Lord Jesus to "come down" and show us "signs and wonders." But that was not to be. Instead the Holy Spirit sang a song through my sister, one verse of which was:

> Let Me *close* the eyes of your *senses*
>   And *open* your *heavenly sight;*
> For only thus shalt thou see Me
>   In that world of which I am the Light;
> And thus thou mayest now behold Me,
>   Fully trust My power divine,
> And sing the song of the ages long,
>   "I am Thine, and Thou art mine."

Let us note three points:

1. Distance was no obstacle to the Lord Jesus then, and it is no obstacle to Him now. He healed this child by His Word, in spite of intervening distance. He will do the same for you or me if we trust Him. In view of the fact that man has largely annihilated distance by his inventions, such as rapid transportation, radio, telephone, wireless, telegraph, television,

etc., and executives of great corporations daily contact London, New York, Tokyo, Bombay, Melbourne, or any other part of the earth and make their power felt wherever they desire; surely it is not hard to believe that distance is no barrier to the working of the divine will in the fulfillment of His Word.

2. This miracle of healing was performed in answer to simple faith in the Word of God. The Lord Jesus Christ led the seeker away from everything but His Word. ...Except ye see signs and wonders, ye will not believe (John 4:48). Then He tested him with a word. The word of the Lord *tries* you. It tried Joseph when he was in prison. (Ps. 105:19.) Never say that you "tried divine healing." The Word of God is tried ...as silver tried in a furnace of earth, purified seven times (Ps. 12:6). Divine healing, which is the Word of God, tries you and me. God grant that we may not be found wanting!

The Lord Jesus gave the father the word, "Go thy way; thy son liveth." (John 4:50.) The man met the test, and believed the naked word. He ceased all clamor for the Lord to come to his home and went quietly about his business.

3. This case was definitely gradual in its manifestation. The healing "began" at a certain moment. Temperature went down to normal at the "seventh hour." (John 4:52.) The boy became convalescent. In other words, it was not a case of instantaneous healing, like most of those in the ministry of the Lord. In the eighth chapter of Matthew, for instance, we have three cases of instantaneous healing in the first fifteen verses: the leper who was cleansed "immediately" (Matt. 8:3), the centurion's servant "healed in the self same hour" (v. 13), and Peter's mother-in-law, who rose and ministered to them when Jesus touched her. (v. 15.) On the other hand, we see many gradual healings in our own day; though, praise God,

> dazzling miracles are still seen, sometimes lightning-like in their manifestation.

Is there such a thing as having *gradual* faith? Is it possible that the father in this true story possessed it? Notice that he asked when his son "*began to amend.*" (John 4:52.) We might modernize that into "When did he show the first symptoms of improvement?"

Let us never forget that the unchanging law is ...as thou hast believed, so be it done unto thee... (Matt. 8:13).

Chapter 14

A SPIRIT OF INFIRMITY

And he was teaching in one of the synagogues on the sabbath. And, behold, there was a woman which had a spirit of infirmity eighteen years, and was bowed together, and could in no wise lift up herself. And when Jesus saw her, he called her to him, and said unto her, Woman, thou art loosed from thine infirmity. And he laid his hands on her: and immediately she was made straight, and glorified God. And the ruler of the synagogue answered with indignation, because that Jesus had healed on the sabbath day, and said unto the people, There are six days in which men ought to work: in them therefore come and be healed, and not on the sabbath day. The Lord then answered him, and said, Thou hypocrite, doth not each one of you on the sabbath loose his ox or his ass from the stall, and lead him away to watering? And ought not this woman, being a daughter of Abraham, whom Satan hath bound, lo, these eighteen years, be loosed from this bond on the sabbath day? And when he had said these things, all his adversaries were ashamed: and all the people rejoiced for all the glorious things that were done by him.

Luke 13:10-17

Time—the Sabbath day, a sacred time.

Place—a synagogue, a sacred place.

Act—healing, a sacred thing, part of redemption. (Isa. 53:4.)

Case—paralysis, accompanied by hideous, repulsive deformity. (Luke 13:11.)

Character—chronic, of eighteen years' standing. Hopeless.

Call—The Lord Jesus Christ summoned the sufferer to Him. We beg and plead and pray while all the time Jesus is calling us to leave all else and come to Him. He sees us in our sickness. He saw that sufferer because He was looking for that sort of thing. He said, ...They that are whole need not a physician; but they that are sick (Luke 5:31). If you are sick, He is calling you—"Come unto me, all ye that...are heavy laden." (Matt. 11:28.)

Cause—(as given by the Great Physician) Satan. (Luke 13:16.) What a flood of illumination is here thrown on many cases of suffering! Jesus did not ascribe this case to natural causes. He distinctly declared that it had a supernatural origin and was inflicted by Satan himself, through the agency of an evil spirit. A "spirit of infirmity" saps the power out of muscles, nerves, and tendons so that they cannot support the body in its normal posture. I have seen cases of this character; and, thank God, I have witnessed their deliverance through the power of the Name of the Lord Jesus Christ. Note that our Lord does not recognize this disease as a providential dispensation but speaks of it as the direct result of Satan's devices.

Fault-finders—certainly. They are always present when God is working. Satan takes care of that. Jesus answered them and made them ashamed. (vv. 14-16.) He will answer them for you, too, by mighty manifestations of His power if you contend earnestly for the faith once delivered to the saints. The signs will follow the Word faithfully preached. (Mark 16:20.) Fault-finders will be confounded by your *lips and life*.

Condition of Healing—faith. (v. 16.) A faith like Abraham's believes without seeing in the face of seeming impossibilities and acts on God's Word alone. Noah began building an ark on dry ground by faith in God's word, which proclaimed the coming of the deluge. Dr. Simpson began to build a life work for God on an existence that physicians pronounced at an end. No, it was on God's Word that said, ...I am the Lord that healeth thee (Ex. 15:26).

Cable—binding God and man. "Ought." The most powerful word in human language for it implies moral obligation. God says that the sick *ought* to be healed, and He was so determined to heal them that He allowed His Son to bear such awful atrocities that His mangled body lost almost the semblance of humanity. (Isa. 52:14.) By His shed blood He made provision for the cleansing of all sin from every human soul, and by His broken body He provided perfect soundness for every human body born into this world. God acknowledges the force of this "ought" and has fully met His responsibility. Now it remains for us to discharge ours by entering into our heritage by faith.

Chapter 15

JESUS IN HIS HOMETOWN

And he came to Nazareth, where he had been brought up: and, as his custom was, he went into the synagogue on the sabbath day and stood up for to read. And there was delivered unto him the book of the prophet Esaias. And when he had opened the book, he found the place where it was written, The Spirit of the Lord is upon me, because he hath anointed me to preach the gospel to the poor; he hath sent me to heal the broken-hearted, to preach deliverance to the captives, and recovering of sight to the blind, to set at liberty them that are bruised. To preach the acceptable year of the Lord [to proclaim the year of acceptance with the Lord WEYMOUTH]. And he closed the book, and he gave it again to the minister, and sat down. And the eyes of all them that were in the synagogue were fastened on him. And he began to say unto them, This day is this scripture fulfilled in your ears [in your hearing WEYMOUTH]

Luke 4:16-21

This is a most striking incident, which reminds me of one that occurred in my own ministry. I was holding meetings, which were being very well attended, in a prosperous rural district. On one occasion I was clearly guided to ask a young farmer, son of a very godly family, to give the message at an evening meeting. He did not want to say yes, dreading to face his old friends in the capacity of a preacher, and he dared not say no, for he was not sure that God did not demand it of him. So he went away and waited on the Lord with the result that it was revealed to him that he was to preach that evening and tell his friends and neighbors that the call of God was upon him to devote every moment to the service of the Lord in the ministry. Never shall I forget his simplicity and humility.

He said, "I was asked to preach this evening; and when I asked the Lord if He wanted me to do it, He said to me, 'I don't want you to do anything else as long as you live.' Well, boys, whatever you think of my preaching, I am sure there's one thing you will never say and that is that I went to preaching because I didn't love farming." I think it possible that there wasn't a dry eye in the church when his message was finished.

And the inhabitants of Nazareth were touched by the presence of the gentle Nazarene who had grown up in their midst. No doubt He had done little carpenter jobs for them when He was helping Joseph. Some of the mothers in Israel had handed Him some little "goodies" when He was still a child and had seen the heavenly light in His eyes as He lifted His eyes and thanked them.

Then, too, there hung about Him the halo of notoriety, for ...there went out a fame of Him through all the region round about. And He taught in their synagogues, being glorified of all (Luke 4:14,15). No wonder that the eyes of all were fastened upon Him as He began to speak. And what a message it was—no, is! For He is the same today and says the same word of power. (Heb. 13:8.) He cannot change. He proclaimed unto them the fulfillment of the words of the prophet, uttered seven hundred years before. He proclaims to us their fulfillment today, for He says, I am the Lord, I change not... (Mal. 3:6).

Then He answered their thoughts, for they were saying in their hearts, "If all these wonders we hear He has performed elsewhere really took place, let us see some of the same sort here. There is plenty of sickness and suffering, poverty, and blindness in Nazareth.

Physician, heal thyself. Minister to your own townsmen who have the first claim upon you."

And He did not withdraw His gracious offer, did not modify His claims in the smallest degree. He said, in effect, "The only hindrance to My doing the same works I have performed elsewhere lies in you. You do not accept Me for what I am. '...No prophet is accepted in his own country' (Luke 4:24). God is the same; He is unchanging. He is the same to you that He was to Naaman. But your attitude toward God is not that of Naaman. He received God's messenger and obeyed his command. He humbled himself to the very dust before God as He was represented in the message of His messenger. When the prophet did not come out and speak to him, he did as he was commanded and dove seven times into Jordan. Thus Naaman received healing, and so will anyone else who will follow his example. It cannot be otherwise, for God is the same God to you that He was to Naaman."

And the audience immediately proved the truth of His words concerning them. For they were so proud, not humble like Naaman, that His words turned their kindness toward Him to absolute hatred; and they tried to murder Him then and there by casting Him headlong over the hill on which Nazareth was built.

They desired to be healed no doubt. They could have been healed had they met the conditions, for God is unchanging. They could not be healed without meeting the conditions, for God is unchanging.

Now if you desire to be healed and are not healed, there has to be a change. And that change must be in you, for God never changes. He is the Lord that healeth "all thy diseases." If you will humble yourself before Him and pray believingly, He will reveal to you exactly what the needed change is. More than that, He will enable you to make it. For it is God which worketh in you both to will and to do of His good pleasure (Phil. 2:13).

Chapter 16

THE VOICE OF ELIJAH

And the Lord heard the voice of Elijah; and the soul of the child came into him again, and he revived (1 Kings 17:22).

This is a lesson on the power of prayer, spoken prayer, in the ministry of divine healing.

You remember the story; Elijah, that mighty man of God, had come by divine command from his refuge at Cherith to Zarephath to be sustained by a widow.

What a test it was for his faith to be obliged to leave Cherith! The word means "promise," and God had said, "…hide thyself by the brook Cherith, that is before Jordan. And it shall be, that thou shalt drink of the brook; and I have commanded the ravens to feed thee *there*" (1 Kings 17:3,4).

And as he sat by the brook that flowed through the rocky gorge, it seemed to sing as it rippled, "God is faithful, God is faithful. He will always keep His Word, to the uttermost fulfilling every promise I have heard." How sweet, so pure and sparkling the waters were to his lips!

And the punctuality of the ravens, never failing to bring bread and flesh in the morning and bread and flesh in the evening (v. 6), solemn and stately in their black plumage as so many servitors in some palace!

...And he drank of the brook (v. 6). Oh, Cherith is a delightful place in which to dwell! Never shall I forget a sojourn there! The Lord told us to name our home Cherith and put it on an electric light on the front door. He gave my sister a song, which began:

Oh, the earth was very dry,
    Parched beneath a brazen sky;
Humbly see the prophet stand,
    Listening to his God's command:
"Go to Cherith, I will feed thee there;
    Go to Cherith, drink its waters fair.
Lo, I speak to fish and bird,
    My commands the ravens heard,
Go to Cherith, I will feed thee there."

But the brook dried up! (v. 7.) Explain that if you can; I can't, and I know better than to try. What is to be done in a case like that? What did Elijah do? Listened for the next command. ...Whatsoever He saith unto you, do it (John 2:5). That is all we need.

And the word of the Lord *came*... (1 Kings 17:8). It always does when we listen for it with a fixed determination to obey. Arise... Take higher ground. Get thee to Zarephath...I have commanded a widow woman there to sustain thee (v. 9).

Zarephath means "fiery furnace, crucible." Yes, the gold must be further refined, for there is stern work to be done, and Zarephath is the place for the refining process.

When Elijah arrived at Zarephath, the widow was on the spot as promptly as were the ravens. But what a change in the menu! And what unutterable humiliation for the prophet to order a cake made from meal snatched from the mouth of a child ready to die of starvation and watered with the mother's tears! And yet what glorious things God was bestowing on that widow! He is the husband of the widow and the father of the fatherless. (Ps. 68:5.)

I remember a widow of my acquaintance and a little incident in her life that may seem an interpolation, but I believe it belongs here. She was living by faith and that encouraged her to take in boys and young men who were not always able to pay their board promptly. She felt she could trust God for them and help them spiritually. God never failed her, but one Saturday she had a hard test. She had prepared a big baking, bread, buns, pies, and cakes for Sunday, so as to be able to be free for worship on the Lord's day. Going to the coal bin she found, to her dismay, that she could not possibly bake the things she had made because of the shortage of coal. Some of the boys who were at home followed her footsteps and laughed loudly when they realized her predicament.

"Now, Mother, what are you going to do? Look at that bread rising fast; and your coal has given out."

"Well, God hasn't given out," she answered. "I am going to have a little talk with Jesus." And she vanished to the attic, which was her sanctuary. But before she could get on her knees there was a loud call from the boys downstairs:

"Mother, come down. Here is a load of coal."

Sure enough there was a man at the door with a truckload of coal.

"I didn't order any coal."

"Well, it is for this number," the man replied.

"Take it away. I never order coal unless I have money on hand to pay for it. There's some mistake."

And she retraced her steps to the attic, leaving the boys, who were much interested in the baking of the pies, disappointed. Closing her eyes she began to pray; but before she could frame a petition, the Lord said, "Open your eyes, the answer is before you." And she opened her eyes and saw something she had been unconscious of before: rows and rows of old, worn-out boots and shoes. They had been given her for her boys. Instantly she understood and filled her apron with them and sent the boys up for more, till everything was baked. Just as the last pie was coming out, the truck returned with the coal and a message that it was paid for by a friend.

The widow of Zarephath stood the test. She literally took the last morsel from her son to feed the prophet. That was real faith. Of course, there was no famine in that home after that. There could not be. But there was a crucible for her as well as for Elijah. The presence of the man of God brought awful conviction to her heart. We are not told what her concealed sin was, but she herself acknowledged that it merited no less punishment than the death of her son. As the child lay there dying, she confessed and found mercy. (Prov. 28:13.)

If you have on your conscience unconfessed sin, my advice to you is to go at once to God and pour out your heart to Him. It is no use to seek for physical healing unless you are prepared to do this.

"Doesn't God ever heal unsaved people?" That is not the question. It is not for us to set limits to the grace of God. But as sin is the first cause of sickness, we cannot expect to be delivered from the latter while we are hugging to our bosoms the serpent who produces the deadly virus. When I struck an epidemic of typhoid, my first step was to shut off the source of the disease.

Elijah, as the servant of God, now takes the case into his own hands. He says, "Give me thy son" (1 Kings 17:19). That means leave the case in God's hands. Take your hands and *eyes off*. How the distracted mother would cling to the little form, watching for some sign of returning animation! It might not be. Watching to see if God is healing is unbelief, pure and simple. "And he took him out of her bosom." (v. 19.) And she let him do it! If you have never had an experience like that, you will not understand the depth of meaning covered by the simple words. Perhaps you will recall them and understand them better some day.

Elijah took the lad up to the loft, where he abode and laid him upon his own bed. And he cried unto the Lord. *"And the Lord heard the voice of Elijah."* (v. 22.) Oh, the power of the human voice! It can speak life or death. The judge says, "I sentence you to die," and the prisoner at the bar is legally dead from the moment the words are uttered. The power of the human voice, *speaking to God in believing prayer, is limitless.*

God heard the voice of Elijah and the child revived! Do you desire something from God? Let Him hear your voice, in confession of sin if necessary, like the widow of Zarephath, and in believing prayer, like Elijah, and *God will answer you.*

Health AND *Healing*

CONTENTS

Chapter 1

THE HUMAN BODY

Not long ago I was staying with a friend who is a fine cook. She would go into her kitchen and after a very short time, come out with a beautiful fluffy cake, a chiffon pie, or a pan of lovely rolls. I followed her into the kitchen one day to find out how she did it, and what do you suppose I saw? Beautiful appliances, all white enamel and glittering chromium. They were puzzles to me. I would not have known what to do with them or how to take care of them. But the riddle was solved when I found that with each appliance the maker had provided a book of instructions that had to be carefully studied and faithfully followed if you were to have rolls light as feathers and pies and cakes that made people's mouths water just to look at them. The books with the appliances told what they were made to do and warned the owner against misusing them. Also, they gave the names and addresses of the makers so that they could be sent for to make repairs or put in new parts when needed.

You have of your very own a machine so wonderful that the most costly ones made by men are just tinsel toys from the dime store in comparison with it. That machine is your body. Man-made machines may look all right at a distance, but when you get close to them, you always find flaws and defects. But this machine I am telling you about now is more beautiful the nearer you get to it; and if you magnify it four or five hundred times, it is found to be made of rich tissues arranged in lovely patterns. The tissues in their turn are made of tiny cells of different shapes (some are star-shaped) all of them beautiful. The cells are different because they have different tasks to perform, and they all work together for the good of the whole. For in this machine, the most wonderful of God's works in the material universe, His law is, "No schism in the body." (1 Cor. 12:25.)

Your body was made expressly for you by God Himself. It was not turned out with thousands of others like buttons from a factory. God tells us that all our members were written in His book ...when as yet there was none of them (Ps. 139:16). The wisest men confess that they never expect to be able to find out all the secrets of this wonderful living machine. (As you use it, don't forget that it is a love gift from God. Say to yourself, "God thought of me and loved me, so I am here.") Over this machine, worth more than all the millions in the world, God has given you control.

NOTE: You will notice that I give chapter and verse for everything I tell you. I hope you will look up these references in your Bible. Then this little book will be a great blessing to you, for it will teach you how to use the Bible when you need to be healed or when you have to pray for sick people. The only medicine God gives us is His Word. He says, He sent His Word, and healed them.... (Ps. 107:20.)

Count some of the treasures you own and see how rich you are. There is the most marvelous engine pump ever known—the heart. It never goes on strike but forces pure blood through pipes to every cell in the body, feeding muscles, bones, and nerves; working day and night, even when you are fast asleep, as long as you live. The blood gathers up worn out matter as it goes and takes it to the right side of the heart from which it is pumped into the lungs to be made pure again by the air we breathe. Then it is sent back to the left side of the heart from which it is pumped again to the millions of cells that are always waiting for the dinner bell to ring.

I wonder if you know that you have a pair of self-adjusting telescopes in your body. Some of the telescopes men make have to be moved and changed by heavy machinery to focus on objects at different distances, but you can look up from darning socks to watch a silver cloud sailing across the blue sky with *your* telescopes. Even a child can do this. Your wonderful telescopes adjust themselves!

We live in an age when it seems everybody has a camera. Some camera enthusiasts have extensive outfits that amaze most of us. They have a close-up lens, a telephoto lens, all types of light filters, films for different situations, light meters, and many other accessories, all designed to improve the quality of pictures. But God has placed in your body the smallest cameras in the world, your two eyes. Did you know they are taking pictures all the time? The images these cameras make on the rear wall of your eyes are carried to your brain and *you see.* Only God, who made you, knows exactly how this is done. But wonders do not stop there. You have in your brain an art gallery called memory in which some of these pictures are hung, never to be removed while you live. You will agree with me that all the wealth in the world would not buy some of them; for instance, your mother's tender face and the baby sweetness of your children. With them you are rich.

In order to make no mistakes about the use to which you should put your wonderful body, you must study your book of instructions, the Bible, every day.

As I said, God has placed your body under your control. But He has taught you very plainly what He made it for and that is His own glory.

He tells us that the things we cannot see are shown to us by the things we *can* see. (Rom. 1:19,20.) We cannot see God, yet as we look at the mountains, oceans, stars, and flowers, as well as many other things God made, His strength, power, majesty, and beauty are seen in them. But when it comes to man, God can unveil Himself much more fully than through rocks, stars, oceans, and flowers. Man is made in God's image and so formed that God can dwell in his body and shine His glory through it. He can speak with man's tongue, think through his mind, and love in his heart. In that way we can glorify God with our "bodies which are His." (1 Cor. 6:20.)

To glorify means to make glorious. We cannot add to God's glory, but we can let those who look at us see it shining through our bodies. Doesn't it make you glad that you have a body that can be used to make men see the glory of God?

Let me tell you some things you will find in the Bible about man's body. (1 Cor. 6:13-20.)

1. It is the Lord's. He claims it for Himself.
2. He loves it so much that He is going to raise it from the dead.
3. It is a member of Christ.
4. It is the temple of the Holy Spirit.
5. It was bought with a price.
6. When the Lord Jesus Christ comes to take those who are in Jesus to be forever with Him, their bodies are to be changed and made like unto His glorious body. (1 John 3:2; 1 Cor. 15:52,53.)

I have always admired the beautiful body God made for man. Perhaps because when I was still very young, I studied it so closely. Preparing to be a doctor, I had to know every bone, muscle, nerve, and blood vessel. The more I studied it, the more wonderful it seemed. I was not saved then, and the first time I saw a human brain it made God so real to me that I was afraid. When I thought of what the brain of man had done, I could not help thinking how mighty the One who made it must be. And I was afraid! But when I came to Jesus, I learned to love Him so that I was no longer afraid, for I knew my sins were washed away in the precious blood that He shed for me on Calvary. Have you that knowledge? If not, repent and believe the gospel (John 3:16), for only in the strength that God supplies through His eternal Son can you glorify God in your body and your Spirit, which are His.

My friend, the good cook I told you about, is able to do such good work because she knows how to use her appliances as the makers intended them to be used. She carefully studies the books of instruction to find out what to do and what not to do and obeys every rule. That is why she can feed her friends such good things. If we will do that with our book of instructions, the Bible, the Word of God, we shall be able to use our bodies to glorify God and help every one with whom we come in contact. We shall feed the hungry with the living bread that came down from heaven so that they will hunger no more.

In the first book in the Bible, Genesis, we are told how God made our bodies (Gen. 1:26). He who is three in one, Father, Son, and Holy Spirit, made us in His own image and likeness. Likewise, man is in three parts, spirit, soul, and body. (1 Thess. 5:23.)

Before this, God had created many wonderful and beautiful things: trees, plants, flowers, great whales, fish, animals, and birds. The air was filled with the scent of blossoms, the whir of swift wings, and the music of bird songs.

But when He made man, He did not form him like any of these. He made him like Himself, godlike, *like God.* And God gave man dominion over His works. He was the ruler of them all. After all was done, God looked at His work and said it was "very good." (Gen. 1:31.)

How fine the body of the first man was! God called it "very good." That means every part of it was perfect. No trace of sickness or weakness. Not the slightest blemish upon it. Our first father, Adam, walked this earth in a body fit for the king that he was. God gave him work to do that no man living today could do. He was told to name all the animals; and as they passed meekly before him, he gave to each bird and beast the right name. (Gen. 2:19,20.) What a brain he had to be able to do that! How strong he was to stand such a strain on mind and body!

Now I know the question that you want to ask. It is, "Why are we not like that today? Almost everybody I know has something wrong with him or her. It is nothing but sickness, sickness everywhere. Can you explain it?"

Yes. The book of instructions, the Bible, tells us all about it. Sickness came because the first man failed to obey the rules God had given him about his body, the wonderful living machine.

In the garden in which God placed Adam (the most beautiful garden that ever was because the Lord planted it), there were all sorts of trees bearing luscious fruits. Man could enjoy the most delicious meals, for God told him that there was no limit. Of every tree, excepting one, he might freely eat. But if he dared to disobey and eat of the fruit of the forbidden tree, God told him he would surely die. (Gen. 2:16,17.)

Man disobeyed and dared to take into the wonderful living machine what God had forbidden him to eat; and through his sin, disease and death came to him and all of his children down to this day. That is the cause of every case of sickness you see. There was no disease till man sinned. It was not known on earth till then.

From that sad day tiny babies come into the world with bodies that are apt to get sick. Sometimes they are even born with some awful disease in their blood.

People sometimes bring sickness upon themselves by their own sins; for, as with Adam, sin and sickness go together. There were two men who were called Mr. Chang and Mr. Eng. If you asked one to dinner, the other came whether you wanted him or not. They were the famous Siamese Twins who were joined by a band of flesh that could not be cut without killing them. Sin and sickness are like that. If you invite sin, sickness comes along.

Chapter 2

A PROMISE AND A COVERING

If Satan, who tempted Eve to eat the forbidden fruit and share it with Adam, tempts you to do wrong, you need not yield. We are warned that he goes about like a roaring lion seeking whom he may devour. One way he devours those who yield to him is by eating up their flesh with terrible sicknesses so that they are just skin and bone. The Bible tells us to "resist" him and he will flee from us. (James 4:7.)

Obey your book of instructions, and you will be kept, body, soul, and spirit by the power of God.

A little old hymn—I wonder if you ever sang it when you were a tiny tot in Sunday school—tells how this may be done.

> Yield not to temptation
>   For yielding is sin,
> Each victory will help you
>   Some other to win.
> Fight manfully onward,
>   Dark passions subdue,
> Look ever to Jesus,
>   He will carry you through.

Now we find God in the cool of the day going to the beautiful garden He had made for man's first home to visit Adam and Eve.

But alas, they were nowhere to be found. Instead of running to the One who had so loved them and given them such precious things, they ran away from Him and hid among the trees of the garden. As He called Adam by name, they came trembling and afraid, for they had sinned and told the saddest story earth has ever heard—the story of the Fall. They stood ashamed and helpless before God. They had listened to Satan and disobeyed their maker.

The awful sentence was pronounced, the death sentence. ...The soul that sinneth, it shall die (Ezek. 18:4). God always keeps His Word; and He had warned them that if they ate of the forbidden fruit, they would surely die. (Gen. 2:16,17; Rom. 6:23.) So He said to them, "Unto dust shalt thou return." (Gen. 3:19.)

Right then and there death began to work in those wonderful living machines, their bodies. From that time sickness, which is just slow dying, began to be seen and felt by the children of men.

But even then God did not forsake them. He gave them two wonderful things: a promise and a covering.

The promise was that there was to come one glad day a virgin-born Son, the "seed of the woman," who was to destroy the old serpent who had deceived Eve, by bruising his head. (Gen. 3:15.) When a serpent's head is mashed, that is the end of the serpent.

This was partly fulfilled when the Lord Jesus Christ was born in Bethlehem of Judaea of the Virgin Mary. Then when the Lord Jesus was crucified on Calvary, Satan was brought to naught; and his power over all who trust in the precious blood of Jesus was broken (Heb. 2:14).

The second precious gift was a covering (coats) that God Himself made and put on them because without them they could never dwell in His presence. What were these coats made of?

For the first time, suffering and death entered that beautiful Garden of Eden. Innocent animals cried in anguish as their lives were sacrificed and their blood shed. Of their beautiful skins God fashioned coats for Adam and Eve. Those coats covered them, spirit, soul, and body. They are a picture of Christ made unto us righteousness (rightness) when He died on the cross to redeem us. (1 Cor. 1:30.) He made us right in spirit, soul, and body. And a right body is a healthy body.

When disease began to show itself in the bodies of men (because the Fall had made them apt to get sick), God told them to pray to Him in faith in the Christ who was to come and die for them, and He would heal them.

In the book of beginnings, Genesis, we have the story of a king, Abimelech by name, who was stricken with a sore sickness in his own body, as well as among the members of his family, because he had taken another man's wife, intending to make her his wife. (Gen. 20.) He did not know that she was Abraham's wife or he would not have done it; but he had done wrong to take her, and God told him that if he did not make the wrong right he would surely die and all his family with him. God promised him healing if he obeyed and told him exactly how to obtain it.

(You will remember that I told you that this book of instructions tells us how to have the wonderful living machines repaired by their Maker; so listen carefully for God says, "I am the Lord, I change not.") (Mal. 3:6.)

God told Abimelech that he must first make restitution by taking Sarah back to her own husband and then have her husband, Abraham, pray for him that he might be healed. (Gen. 20:7,17.)

Abraham trusted in the Lord Jesus Christ. He spoke of Him as the Lamb of God and saw Him *by faith* though He had not come yet. The Lord Jesus said Himself, ...Abraham rejoiced to see my day: and he saw it, and was glad (John 8:56).

So it was by faith in the name of the Lord Jesus Christ that Abimelech was healed all those thousands of years ago, and it is by faith in that same name that the sick are made well today. We who believe are told to lay our hands on sick people in the name of the Lord Jesus, and they will recover. (Mark 16:15-18; James 5:14-16.) Just after the Lord Jesus gave this command in Mark, He was caught up into heaven and sat on the right hand of God. (Mark 16:19.)

God never changes and never will change. We are just as sure of healing as Abimelech was if we go about it as he did, according to our book of instructions, the Bible.

I was on the platform of a church where I had been asked to pray for the sick; and as I was talking to them and telling them from the Bible that God would heal them if they came His way, I happened to look at the ministers on the platform with me. There were three besides myself, one woman and two men. I had known all of them for many years and positively knew that all four of us would have been under the ground for many years if God didn't heal just the same as He did thousands of years ago.

One of them had diabetes mellitus. Doctors had pronounced the death sentence. He was told that he could pass into a stupor and die any moment and must never be left alone. He became blind from the disease. He was prayed for just as Abimelech was, not by Abraham but by a daughter of Abraham who by faith saw the Lamb of God dying for our sins and sicknesses. He was made well and has been working for the Lord ever since—about six years.

The other brother had stone in the kidney. He suffered absolute agony and his friends sent an ambulance and surgeons who said he must be removed to the hospital at once. He said he could and would trust God. His wife stood with him in faith and believers were sent for to pray for his healing. That was about four years ago, and he has been perfectly well and active for his Master ever since.

The sister who was with us had had seven serious operations by some of the greatest surgeons in the United States. At last she heard of Jesus of Nazareth and was prayed for and healed, though the doctors (on whom a small fortune had been spent) said there was no hope.

I was dying the morphine death 40 years ago and had nothing to look forward to but a funeral, and not much of one at that. No one could help me but God, and at last I found the way to Him. It was just the same old path that Abimelech trod, repentance and faith in the Lamb of God; and it brought the same results. *It never fails.*

Chapter 3

HEALING PICTURES IN THE BIBLE

Books of instructions sent with machines are well illustrated. People, especially children, learn more easily from pictures than in any other way. They will turn over the leaves of a picture book for hours, and teachers find that the time is well spent if the book is a good one.

God has placed many beautiful pictures in the Bible, our book of instructions. From some of these we learn how to be free from sickness. Let us look at the picture of the Passover Lamb in Exodus 12.

The great-grandchildren of Abraham came down to Egypt to live because there was no food in Canaan. They had a very hard time there for the Egyptians were cruel to them. Worse still, they failed to do some things the God of their fathers had told them to do. But when they cried to God, He was merciful and took them out of Egypt to lead them to a new home. When the king of Egypt, who was very strong with his army and war chariots, would not let them go (though God told him to), God warned him that He would send an awful plague that would leave one dead in every house. (Ex. 11:4,5.)

But before God did this He told Moses, His servant, to tell the children of Israel (as they were called) what to do to keep the plague away from their homes.

The father of each house was told to take a pure, spotless lamb without any flaw in it for himself and his children. I can see the picture; can't you? The little ones gather round as the father brings in the lovely little creature, and cry, "Oh, isn't it snow white! May I have it, Father? Its coat is as soft as down. I want it for a pet."

But the father shakes his head sadly, "No, my child, you may not have the little lamb."

"What are you going to do with it, Father?"

"I am going to kill it and put its blood on the door so that when the death angel comes to our house he will pass over it. This night he is bringing death to every home on which there is no blood."

"O Father, must the lamb die?"

"Yes, it must die that you may live."

And that night there was a great cry in all the land of Egypt, for there was not a house where there was not one dead. (Ex. 12:30.) But in the blood-marked homes of the children of Israel, all was well. Not so much as one tiny child sick. And Paul the apostle tells us that in this scene we have a picture of what the Lamb of God does for those who trust Him, for he says, ...Christ our Passover is sacrificed for us (1 Cor. 5:7).

Beneath the blood-stained lintel
    I, and my children, stand.
A messenger of evil is flying through the land.
    There is no other refuge from the destroyer's face.
Beneath the blood-stained lintel
    Shall be our hiding place.

I knew a lady who had a very large and very sickly family. People used to joke because there seemed to be almost always a placard on the house with measles or scarlet fever or chicken pox (once it was small pox). But it was no joke to the lady, for she had so many children that it took a great deal of her time to nurse them through these awful sicknesses; and besides, she loved her boys and girls and feared she might lose them.

About that time God was pouring out His Holy Spirit on us in that town and some of us were praying and reading our Bibles day and night. This poor mother heard of our meetings and crept in one day. She told us her troubles, and we talked to her about the Lamb of God who bore all our sins and sickness. We said, "Put the blood on the door, and it will keep these plagues away. But you and the children must feed on the Lord Jesus in the Word, as the children of Israel ate the flesh of the Passover Lamb." She did what we said.

I knew her for years after that, and she never had another health department card on her house. She read and read the book of instructions and taught it to others so that sick people used to go to her house (the blood of the Lamb of God was on the door) to be made well through prayer, just as Abimelech went to Abraham. And many of them were healed.

When the awful influenza plague was killing its millions and almost every house bore a placard, my sister, Amy Yeomans, said to everybody she could reach, "There will never be a placard on our home. Not because we are any better than anyone else, but because the blood is on the door and the destroying angel must pass over. God said so." She made her boast *in the Lord,* and God honored His own Word. I visited some stricken ones that sent for me, but it never entered our home.

After the Passover, Pharaoh was in a hurry to get the children of Israel away. (Ex. 12:31-33.) The Egyptians were so frightened at what had happened in their homes that they gave them silver and gold, as well as clothing to help them on their journey. (v. 35.) They took food, but Moses, who was a doctor (Acts 7:22), did not take any drugs but trusted God to keep them from disease as He did during the terrible plague that killed the Egyptians. And the Bible says that there was not one feeble one among them. (Ps. 105:37.) All were ready for the day's march and set out with shining faces and shoulders squared.

When they came to the Red Sea, God rolled it away; and they walked over on dry land and sang a hymn of praise to God on the other side. When Pharaoh tried to follow them to take them back to Egypt (he was sorry he had let them get away) (Ex. 14:5-8), he and all his host and chariots were buried in the Red Sea, which came rolling back when God's people were safely over. (vv. 23-28.)

Now we shall look at another picture. Let us call it "The Wonderful Tree."

When the Israelites had gone some distance they met a great trial. The water was so bitter that though they were thirsty, they could not drink it. (Ex. 15:23,24.) Sometimes very bitter water makes you sick at the stomach.

I am sorry to say that they did a very wrong thing. They complained against Moses who had been sent by God to deliver them from the iron furnace of Egypt. Over and over again in the book of instructions we are warned that if we misuse our tongues, which God gave us to glorify Him, we shall be sick. (Prov. 13:3.)

But if they did the wrong thing, Moses did the right thing, for he cried to God. And God did the most wonderful thing for them. He showed Moses a tree! It was a wonderful tree, and it was there all the time; but even Moses did not see just how wonderful it was till God showed it to him. He told him to throw this tree into the waters, and they would become sweet. And sure enough, when the poor people with their tongues cleaving to the roofs of their mouths for dryness dared to take a drink, it was sweet to their taste. Oh, how they drank and drank of the sparkling water! And right there God gave them a promise which still stands and will stand forever, for God does not change. We call it the "Covenant of Healing." As you know, a covenant is a solemn pact or bargain.

It says, If thou wilt diligently hearken to the voice of the Lord thy God, and wilt do that which is right in his sight, and wilt give ear to his commandments, and keep all his statutes, I will put none of these diseases upon thee, which I have brought upon the Egyptians: for I am the Lord that healeth thee (Ex. 15:26).

Water is a type of life. Our bodies are largely made up of it. But the water of human life is bitter at its very source because of sin. Even a newborn baby may get sick and die. It may be born sickly. There is only one thing that can make life's water pure and sweet, free from sin, sickness, and other defilement, and that is *the* tree. Do you ask, "Oh, tell me where it grows! I want to find it and cast it into my life for the bitterness of sin and sickness is more than I can bear. What shall I do?" Exactly what Moses did. Cry unto the Lord; and He will show you the cross on Calvary's hill with One hanging on it, dying under the double burden of your sins and sickness. (John 1:29.) A great prophet saw it seven hundred years before Jesus Christ was born in Bethlehem and cried, "Surely He hath borne our diseases and carried our pains" (Isa. 53:4, literal translation).

When the Lord Jesus Christ came and lived on earth seven hundred years after this was written about Him, the evangelist Matthew tells us that when they brought sick people to Him, He healed them *all,* that this word of the prophet might be fulfilled. (Matt. 8:17.) It had to be fulfilled because it was the word God put into his mouth. It has to be fulfilled today, for God cannot lie.

Remember, you must cast the tree into the water of your life by looking at the cross of Calvary and believing God who says, ...I am the Lord that healeth thee (Ex. 15:26).

Chapter 4

SONGS OF INSPIRATION

I want to turn to the wonderful lessons about our bodies, which we learn from songs in the Bible. Yes, the most wonderful songs that have ever been sung are in our book of instructions. That may well be, for they are not of earth but of heaven. The Holy Spirit sang them through men's lips.

Does it seem strange to teach from songs? It is really a very old way of teaching and has never gone altogether out of fashion. Moses taught the children of Israel a song, which he commanded them to teach to their children for all time. They were to have it in their mouths and never to forget it. It tells of the faithfulness of God to His people and their unfaithfulness to Him.

But the "sweet singer of Israel" was David, who was also a prophet and king. He had some very hard attacks of sickness and learned how to pray and sing himself well again. Some of the songs he sang have been the means of making many other sick people well. That is because they are God's words, and He says, He sent his word, and healed them... (Ps. 107:20).

One lesson that David teaches us from his own experience is very important, and that is that we must humble ourselves and confess our sins when seeking to be made well. He says in one psalm that when he kept silent about his sins, "his bones rotted away," and he was "roaring all the day." (Ps. 32:3.) How he must have suffered!

There is an old proverb that says, "He who will not speak his sin to God has to groan." Another says, "A dumb conscience makes a loud voiced pain." But when he said, "I will confess...to Jehovah," we find him "compassed about with songs of deliverance." No more rotten bones and roaring but glad praises to God for healing. Fully recovered from his awful disease he turns round and calls upon us all to be glad in the Lord and rejoice...and shout for joy, all ye that are upright in heart (Ps. 32:11).

When I was a child, I was afraid to have my Mother line me up before the doctor for he always said, "Put out your tongue." And when I put it out it seemed to tell him all the naughty things I had done. For he would say, "This child has been eating trash," though I had not told him one thing about the candy I had had and the extra piece of pie I had begged from the old cook. But he knew the signs of a healthy tongue; and when mine wasn't healthy, he would make me go to bed early and worst of all, take a dose of castor oil before I went.

David gives us the signs of a healthy tongue for the Christian; and they are, first, confession of wrongdoing when our consciences tell us that we have sinned. Second, a testimony to Christ; and third, praise and more praise. Why he calls his tongue "glory"! (Ps. 30:12.) If the name of yours is "grouch," you had better have it changed to "glory."

One of the songs he sang is "The Lord Is My Shepherd." It is a portrait of Jesus Christ, the Good Shepherd, who laid down His life for the sheep that they might have life and have it more abundantly. Those who have abundant life, great vitality, are well because the healthy body fights off disease.

This song of the Good Shepherd has been sung in more places by more different kinds of people than any other song. When we read or sing it or listen to it being sung, we should remember that the health of the sheep is the Shepherd's care. He does not trust the sheep and lambs to keep themselves well but at their cry is always ready to heal them. The Good Shepherd is not only ready but able also to make you perfectly well if you will call on Him. David says, O Lord my God, I cried unto thee, and thou hast healed me (Ps. 30:2).

God is the only One who can heal every disease. The greatest doctors will tell you that there are cases of sickness for which they can do nothing. Sometimes people who are not very well off think if they had plenty of money they could get cured. But this is not always so. I have known those who spent fortunes trying to find health. Some of them went to the finest surgeons who told them that there was no hope. Others tried climates, took all kinds of cures, dieted till they were nearly starved, with no results.

But God says that He heals *all* our diseases just as He forgives all our sins. You will find this in one of the psalms of David, Who forgiveth all thine iniquities; who healeth all thy diseases (Ps. 103:3).

Some who have tried everything else in vain have called upon Him and proved that He says what He means and does what He says.

In some psalms David teaches us of the tender watchful care of God over His own. Psalm 121 has been called by some who have proved its truth "The Sleepless Sentry." It says that the Lord "who neither slumbers nor sleeps" shall preserve us from all evil. That means sickness, as well as other things, for sickness is part of the curse upon those who break God's law. (Deut. 28:58-61.)

There is a beautiful psalm, which God's people dearly love. I have heard a congregation of those who had been healed by faith in the Lord Jesus Christ or who were seeking divine healing repeating it together. Every one of them knew it by heart. (It is a very good thing to commit verses about the Lord's healing to memory.) God tells us that if we attend to His words, listen to them, keep them before our eyes and hide them in the midst of our hearts, they are "health to all our flesh." (Prov. 4:20-22.)

The psalm the whole congregation was saying from memory is called by some, "The Hiding Place," because it tells of a place where we may hide so that no sickness can find us, not even the most contagious pestilence. (Ps. 91:10.) Do you long to know where that safe shelter is? I can tell you, for God gives it in the book of instructions. You will find it in Psalm 31:20: Thou shalt hide them in the secret of thy presence.... That is what our Lord Jesus Christ meant when He said "Abide in me." (John 15:4.) The great apostle Paul could say, "For me to live is Christ." (Phil. 1:21.) He tells us to follow his example so this was not for apostles only. (Phil. 3:17.)

If you lived in a poor little house in a dangerous place where evil persons might break in any moment to do you and your loved ones grievous harm, and were invited into the finest palace on earth where you and yours would be safely guarded night and day, wouldn't you move at once?

Of course you would. That is exactly what God offers you and yours, for this wonderful salvation, which includes the body, is for your "house," meaning your family as well as yourself personally.

The 91st Psalm says of those who live in the hiding place, which is Jesus Christ, There shall no evil befall thee, neither shall any plague come nigh thy dwelling (Ps. 91:10).

Let me tell you right here about how God made this word good to one who trusted Him to do so. A Christian businessman, who trusted God for his family as well as for himself, was away on a trip of inspection for his company. During his absence, which lasted some time, one of his children, a daughter who is now an ordained minister, was taken ill. In his absence a very fine physician was called who at once pronounced the case as diphtheria and ordered all the usual precautions, including a rigid quarantine.

Just as this was about to be carried out, the father returned. As soon as he heard the sad news he took to prayer. (I did not see him do it but am as certain as if I had for he *always prayed over everything.*)

After prayer he rose from his knees filled with courage and faith. Going straight to the doctor he said, "Doctor, I learn that you have ordered my house into quarantine for diphtheria." The doctor said, "I am sorry to say that is the case. Little Ruth has the disease."

"I beg your pardon, Doctor, but I have to tell you that there is no diphtheria in my house. It is impossible for it to be there." The doctor gazed at him as though he thought he had gone mad.

"I have a question to ask you, Doctor. Was a swab taken from the child's throat and sent to the Provincial Laboratory?"

"No. It was unnecessary. The case is a clear one of diphtheria."

The Bible says that if we constantly think about God's Word we have more understanding than our teachers, and so it proved with my friend for he asked, "As the child's father, have I not a legal right to insist upon the laboratory test before my house is quarantined?"

The doctor had to yield to this; and after carefully swabbing the throat, sent the specimen to the laboratory. The report came back "negative," and there was no serious illness. In answer to prayer the child was running round as well as ever in a day or two; and needless to say, there was no quarantine.

I am thinking as I remember this case of a beautiful psalm that shows us God's thought for the family. If you note it carefully you will see that it includes health for every one in the home.

I love to call it the "Home Sweet Home Psalm"—number 128. Read it with me and first of all see that it is for "*everyone* that feareth the Lord." (v. 1.) That means to fear Him as you feared your father; if you had a good one, too much to willingly disobey him. You feared him because you knew he was so good that he would have to punish you if you did wrong. But you loved him for that very goodness which made him so careful to train you in the right way.

Verse 2 promises the father health and strength to earn a living for himself and family and a good appetite to enjoy what he had earned.

Verse 3 tells of a healthy mother and "children like olive plants" round the table.

Verse 6 promises this man long life and his "children's children" playing round his feet.

If we only had more homes like that, how much better it would be for everybody!

There is a very joyful psalm that people who have been healed by faith in the Lord Jesus Christ love to use in praising God. It is Psalm 30. David has been very sick, has gone down to the grave; but God has in mercy brought him up in answer to his prayer. O Lord my God, I cried unto thee, and thou hast healed me (Ps. 30:2).

He is so happy about it that he asks all God's people to help him praise. (v. 4.) In the 11th verse he says that the Lord has girded him with gladness and turned his mourning into dancing.

Some people think it is very wrong to dance in worshiping God, but David got so full of glory sometimes that he had to praise God with every muscle in his body. Do you remember how he danced before the Lord "with all his might," when he brought up the Ark of God to the city of David? (2 Sam. 6:14.)

Chapter 5

WILL THE LORD HEAL ME?

In the last book of the Old Testament written by the prophet Malachi (his name means the messenger of Jehovah), we read of a glorious sunrise of which God gave him a vision. It was a very dark age, and perhaps the messenger was almost ready to give up hope. But God knew how to cheer his heart and the hearts of others who were longing for the coming of the Christ. He said, Unto you that fear my name shall the Sun of righteousness arise with healing in His wings; and ye shall go forth, and grow up as calves of the stall (Mal. 4:2).

It was four long, dark centuries before this Word came true in the coming of the Lord Jesus Christ, the Light of the world, who cried to men, ...He that followeth me shall not walk in darkness, but shall have the light of life (John 8:12).

That was the true light, which lighteth every man that cometh into the world (John 1:9). All we have to do is to get close enough to Him and we shall find healing in His wings.

To get the light and warmth of the sun you have to turn toward it like the sunflower, which always looks sunward. So we must look to the Lamb of God for healing. Let the blessed rays of divine light and life play all through your whole being.

One of the most wonderful healings I ever saw was given through this "sunrise" Scripture—Malachi 4:2. A Baptist minister, whose wife was a beloved sister in Christ, was very sick. He had a deep-seated abscess—or pocket full of pus—under his tongue. His throat, tongue, and all the parts nearby were swollen to many times their normal size. His tongue was so large that it would not stay in his mouth but hung out, a large purple mass. He could not swallow or say one word. He was in awful pain. They had a very good surgeon, but he would not operate because he said it was too dangerous. He said he would watch the case for a while but could not promise that the man would live. The minister and his wife had been believers in divine healing; and when they saw that all human hope was gone, they made up their minds to cast themselves on the Great Physician. So the wife asked the doctor for his bill.

He said, "I do not want to give you a bill; I have done nothing for you. I would rather wait and see if I can operate."

The minister's wife said, "But Doctor, we are sure you have done your best, and we want to pay you. You would be willing to say that everything had been done that could be done, would you not?"

"Yes," said the doctor, "but I would rather not take any money."

The wife insisted and said, "We are going to have another doctor."

"Well, let me call him in consultation."

"This doctor does not consult with other doctors."

"He has to," said the doctor. "The law demands it."

And then the wife said, "Our new doctor is the Lord Jesus."

So that night some believers were sent for to pray for the man. After prayer, I begged the sister to go to bed because she had not had any sleep for many nights. I told her to believe God for a real healing. Just then the Lord flashed this verse (Mal. 4:2) into my mind and said, "Give it to her and tell her to believe it." It seemed almost heartless to talk about "gambolling like a calf" when her husband was so far gone, but that was the reading in the margin of my Bible; and I gave it to her. She pillowed her head on this Word of God and went to sleep.

A brother took care of the groaning sick man. After a while the Lord said to the brother who was acting as nurse, "Sit on his bed and make him rest his head on your breast. I will give him sleep."

This was done and the brother dimmed the light. In a few moments the sick man was fast asleep. He had not slept for many nights. As the brother supported the sick man's head, he rested his own head on God's Word. In twenty minutes he smelled the most awful odor he had ever smelled. Turning up the light he found the whole bed, and all their clothing, simply soaked in vile smelling, poisonous pus. God had operated and removed the poison. The sick man wakened perfectly well, and together they had a bonfire and burned up everything, even the mattress. Then they scrubbed the place; and when the little wife wakened, she had a well husband who was hungry for breakfast. A year or so afterwards when they had moved out of town, the minister made a great big sled on which he used to draw his wife to church. It was a bright winter's day and he played that he was a skittish colt and kicked up his heels. Then the Lord said to the wife, "What is that?" And she remembered the Word of God, which promised that he should go forth and gambol, or play, like a calf.

That Word has never lost its power, as the Baptist minister proved for himself. But we have to be very careful when we are trusting God's Word to make sure that we are in the place where we can claim it for our own.

This promise is addressed to those who "fear my name," God's name, and that means that we ask in submission to His will. Indeed it is because we see in the book of instructions that it is His will that our bodies should be strong and healthy, that we feel it to be our duty to ask Him to heal us.

Then this promise is for those who have childlike confidence, like the apostle John who lay on Jesus' breast. To receive the healing we must draw near to His heart of love, get under His very wings.

The Lord Jesus said in His sad farewell to Jerusalem, ...How often would I have gathered thy children together, even as a hen gathereth her chickens under her wings, and ye would not (Matt. 23:37). Let us be as simple as little chickens and nestle under His great strong wings. No disease can enter there.

It is so much easier for us than it was for those in Malachi's time, for his vision has come to pass. The Lord Jesus Christ was made man and dwelt among us. We have beheld His glory. He was crucified for us and buried; but death could not hold Him, and He rose from the dead and ascended to the right hand of God where He is exalted, and He hath shed forth the Holy Spirit upon those who believe.

Through men like Matthew, Mark, Luke, John, Paul, and others, the Holy Spirit has given us the wondrous story of the life of the Lord Jesus Christ. We find Him going about "healing all that were oppressed of the devil." (Acts 10:38.)

One time He came into a synagogue on the Sabbath to teach and saw there a poor woman who was bent double and could not lift herself up.

And He called her to Him. That is the first step; get near to Him. It was very hard for her to come, deformed as she was and unable to lift up her head. It was very humiliating, too; and to make it harder for her, the ruler of the synagogue was angry and did not want her healed on the Sabbath day. But she came to Jesus. Don't let anything keep you from coming to Him.

And the Lord Jesus said, "Woman, thou art loosed from thine infirmity," and He laid His hands upon her and immediately she was made straight and glorified God. (Luke 13:10-17.)

When the ruler of the synagogue spoke angrily because the Lord Jesus Christ had made this woman well on the Sabbath day, the Lord said, ...Doth not each one of you on the Sabbath loose his ox or his ass from the stall, and lead him away to watering? And ought not this woman, being a daughter of Abraham, whom Satan hath bound, lo, these eighteen years, be loosed from this bond on the Sabbath day? (vv. 15,16). So Jesus said she ought to be healed, and He loves you just as much as He loved her and died to take your sins and sicknesses away just as much as hers. If you "ought to be healed," whose fault is it if you stay sick? Not the fault of the Lord Jesus. He bore your sickness and sin on the cross, and all you have to do is to take pardon and healing. I was called to pray for a neighbor lady who was suffering a great deal. She is saved and has the Baptism in the Holy Spirit, as in Acts 2:4, but she was in such pain and felt so weary of suffering that she hardly seemed to want to get well. But I told her this great truth from the lips of the Lord Himself that she *ought* to get well. It was her duty, I told her. And she saw that she owed it to her Lord to be well and go about her Father's business. So she took healing like a dear little obedient child and fell into a sweet healing sleep. The apostle Paul says that he could hardly know what to choose, to depart and be with Christ, or stay in this sad world to help people here. But much as he longed to see Jesus, he chose to stay and do all he could to save and help. (Phil. 1:21-25.)

In the last chapter I told you how blessed it is to learn by heart Scripture verses on healing so that when we are tempted we can use them to inspire our faith. You know the Bible says that "above all" we must take "the shield of faith, wherewith ye shall be able to quench all the fiery darts of the wicked." (Eph. 6:16.) (It is "wicked one" in the Greek and means Satan.) And ...faith cometh by hearing, and hearing by the word of God (Rom. 10:17).

I have asked a great many people to commit to memory the first 17 verses of the eighth chapter of Matthew, for I have found that almost every question about healing is answered there. Also, I have seen such wonderful healings where this Word is studied. In the Old Testament the animals that God called "clean" chewed the cud, as well as had divided hoofs. Doesn't that mean that we are to "chew" the Word of God? The first Psalm says that the "blessed" man "meditates" in God's Word day and night. (v. 2.)

It is not hard to do that when you know it by heart. When you waken in the small hours of the morning and thoughts of difficult things in your life trouble you, just open your heart to the Holy Spirit by praises to God; and He will faithfully bring the Word you have learned to your remembrance. It will flow like a river of living water through your thoughts, driving doubt and fear away. Many of God's people have learned that sweet secret, and I want to teach it to you if you do not know it.

I am supposing that you have learned these verses, Matthew 8:1-17, and I am giving you some of the light and comfort people have found in them.

Verses 1-3. A poor leper came and worshiped Him. He would have been afraid to come near anyone else because his place was among the tombs. But he could not fear the Lord Jesus Christ. He is the Lamb of God. No one is afraid of a lamb. Even a child will hug a snowy lamb. Come to Jesus no matter how unworthy you feel. But the leper has a doubt: he knows that the Lord Jesus can heal him; somehow he cannot look into His eyes and doubt it. But *will* He? Tremblingly he says, ...Lord, if thou wilt, thou canst make me clean. (v. 2.) Jesus snatches the "if" out of his mouth with His glad, "I will; be thou clean." (v. 3.) And immediately his leprosy was cleansed, and it was a joyful man who went to the priest to receive his bill of health.

Do you ask, "Will He heal me?" You have His answer, "I will." He tasted death for you as well as for the leper. He cannot say "Yes" to him, and "No" to you.

Then in verses 5 to 13, we have a very different case. The leper had "incomplete faith," which the Lord Jesus finished for He is the author and finisher of our faith (Heb. 12:2), but the Roman centurion had "great faith." Jesus said so. Why was it so great? Because in spite of his unworthiness (he said, "I am not worthy"), he believed that Jesus would heal because He was Jesus. And he was sure that the word of Jesus had power to drive sickness away. Just as sure of that as he was that his servant would obey his orders. He knew everything had to obey the Lord Jesus.

Jesus said this Roman officer would sit down with Abraham, Isaac, and Jacob in the kingdom. (v. 11.) Why? Because we sit down with our equals and all Abraham, Isaac, and Jacob did was to believe God's Word. It is so easy to please God; only believe Him and He will do the rest. But without faith it is impossible to please Him. (Heb. 11:6.) You can please Him if you will. Put away anything you know to be wrong ("They repented not that they might believe") and rest your heart on His promises. They cover your every need. (Matt. 21:32.)

In verses 14 and 15 the Lord enters Peter's humble home and finds the dear old grandmother very sick. Dr. Luke says she had a "high or great" fever. (Luke 4:38.) Peter's little house belongs to Jesus. Peter says he forsook all to follow the Lord. Everybody in the house is under the Master's special care. So Jesus touched the hand, hardened by much toil, and the fever left her; and she rose to minister to Him and those with Him. Have you given your home and all your loved ones to Jesus? As the old hymn asks...

Is your all on the altar of sacrifice laid,
Your heart does the Spirit control?

You can only be blest
And have peace and sweet rest,
As you yield Him your body and soul.

I once lived with some saints who had given their house and all who lived in it to the Lord. When three of their little children were very sick and it seemed sure that there would be death in the home, we prayed together. After we had done this, I went to my room and there the Lord told me to give them the words, I exhort you to be of good cheer: for there shall be no loss of any man's life among you, but of the ship (Acts 27:22). I had a fierce fight of faith before I was ready to give the message. From a medical viewpoint, death seemed certain for at least one of the little ones. The devil told me I would raise false hopes in their hearts and get into awful trouble myself. When I was ready to trust God, I said, "But Lord, why should I say the words 'but of the ship'?" He said, "Give My message as I give it to you." I called them and solemnly told them what the Lord said. They received it as from God and never had a shadow of a doubt. They did not seem to notice about the ship so I felt I must say, "But God told me I must say 'but of the ship.'"

They were so happy about the children that they didn't seem to mind about the ship. Soon after they lost their house, but of course, all the children got well and are living yet.

Now perhaps you will say, "I have not found a case like mine, yet, in this Scripture passage." Well, wait a moment and read verses 16 and 17: When the even was come, they brought unto him many that were possessed with devils: and he cast out the spirits with his word, and healed *all* that were sick: that it might be fulfilled which was spoken by Esaias the prophet, saying, Himself took our infirmities, and bare our sicknesses. (A quote from Isaiah 53:4.)

Here we see that He healed *all* that were sick; and you can't get outside of all, can you? And He did it because the Scripture cannot be broken; and it had been prophesied by Isaiah, seven hundred years before Christ came, that He would do just this. That Word still stands today.

Chapter 6

HEALING FOR CHILDREN

I know what mothers want to hear and that is how to trust the Lord to keep the little ones well and strong. Also any who may have children who are not as sturdy as they should be want to know how to bring the little ones to the Great Physician and get them healed. There are no stories in the Bible, our book of instructions, sweeter than those that tell of the Lord Jesus taking the little ones into His arms, laying His hands on them and blessing them. When I was working in a hospital in New York many years ago, I saw a beautiful oil painting—I think it was lifesize—which a very rich man gave. It almost filled the wall at one end of the ward. How the sick people loved to look at it, for it showed the Lord Jesus Christ bringing life and healing to the little daughter of Jairus, a ruler of the synagogue.

The story is told three times in the New Testament: Matthew 9:18-26, Mark 5:22-43, and Luke 8:40-56. I like to read about healings in Luke's Gospel, for he was himself a doctor and sometimes tells us things the others leave out.

In verse 41 we read that Jairus—who was a great man among the Jews, "a ruler of the synagogue"—came and fell down at the feet of Jesus and besought Him to come to his house. How simple his faith! How humble he was! While others were denying that Jesus was the Christ, this spiritual leader fell at His feet in public. It might cost him his job. Perhaps he would be put out of the synagogue of which he was a ruler. But he did not mind that. His only child, his darling daughter, a sweet damsel of twelve years lay dying. He knew in his soul that Jesus of Nazareth could save her life.

Perhaps it took that awful trial to bring the proud ruler to Jesus. I know a lovely young couple—educated, rich, but alas, without God—whose only child, a beautiful boy, lay dying. The family doctor held out no hope; but the baby's grandmother knew that Jesus is the same today, for she had been healed herself. And God gave her faith to go to her son and daughter and tell them that if they would fall at Jesus' feet and receive Him as their Saviour and Lord, the child would get well. She said, "The Lord told me to tell you this. If you do not surrender, the baby will die." They believed the Word and did just what Jairus did. And the child is a big boy now.

Jesus set out for Jairus' house, but a poor woman who had been sick many years and spent every cent on doctors, touched the hem of His garment and was made whole immediately. Then the Lord stopped the whole procession—there was a great crowd following Him—so that this woman could tell what had happened to her. How hard that was for the poor father!

Why was Jesus so anxious to let the woman speak? Perhaps so that her faith might be made strong and steadfast. Nothing helps you more than telling of His goodness and praising Him for His mercies. Then this wonderful healing of a hopeless case of twelve years' standing would help Jairus to believe that his daughter too would be healed. But someone came and said the little maid was dead. Even then the Lord Jesus told the father not to fear but believe. And when Jesus got to the beautiful home of Jairus—I am thinking of the picture I saw in the hospital—some people there wept and mourned, and others laughed Him to scorn. Jesus put them all out.

When I hear a person say, "Well, they talk of healing by faith in the Lord Jesus Christ, but I never saw one," I cannot help think of the people who were put out. The Word of God does not promise that you will see if you are weeping and mourning, for *that* is unbelief. Do you dare to scorn the truth that Jesus Christ is the same today? He tells us the ones who will see His wonderful works, and they are those who believe. ...Said I not unto thee, that, if thou wouldest believe, thou shouldest see the glory of God? (John 11:40). Peter, James, and John didn't weep and mourn. They knew too well the power of the Lord Jesus. The parents did not laugh Jesus to scorn. The father bowed himself at His feet. If you want to *see,* cease your mourning and fall at His feet in adoration. Oh, how sacred the hush that fell as the Lord stood beside the deathbed of the little maid and taking the cold, limp hand in His (which had all power in heaven and earth) said tenderly, "Maid, arise." (Luke 8:54.) And she arose with shining face. Jesus, ever thoughtful, said to them, "Give her meat." (v. 55.) Do you think that was strange? Not at all; I have seen people healed of sore sickness when their friends would ask half afraid, "Would it be right to give them something to eat?" It seemed too good to be true that they were really well and able to eat like other folks.

In the gospel of John we have the story of the healing of the son of a nobleman who lived in the city of Capernaum, where a great many rich Romans had fine homes (John 4:46-54).

This case is very helpful to us for Jesus did not go to the child as He did to Jairus' daughter! He just spoke a word and the work was done because the child's father believed the word. We do not see the Lord Jesus walk in at the door when we pray to Him for our loved ones. But He is with us. He says, "I will never leave you nor forsake you." (Heb. 13:5.) We don't have to *send* for our doctor. He says, If a man love me, he will keep my words: and my Father will love him, and we will come unto him, and make our abode with him (John 14:23).

The nobleman wanted Jesus to go to his house with all speed to heal his son who was at the point of death. But Jesus read his heart, and saw that he wanted to see something before he would believe. He had things turned the wrong way. We must believe that we may see. David says, "I had fainted, unless I had believed to see." (Ps. 27:13.) "Faith is the evidence of things not seen." (Heb. 11:1.) The nobleman still pleaded for a visit from the Lord. He said, ...Sir, come down ere my child die (John 4:49).

Then Jesus gave him a word, "Go thy way; thy son liveth. And the man believed the word that Jesus had spoken." (v. 50.) And because believing the word of God is seeing, his son was healed.

When the children for whose healing we are praying are too young to take hold of the promise for themselves, we must get the parents to unite in faith for them. I have a big feather pillow made out of carefully selected feathers, which always reminds me of a tiny child I prayed for years ago at a camp meeting in Canada. She was terribly deaf as the result of scarlet fever. The mother, who was very anxious to have the Lord heal her little darling, brought her to the altar at a meeting and asked for prayer. I asked, "Is her father saved?" The mother, who was saved, seemed a little doubtful about it. "Well, go and tell him that I would like to see him. You must bring the child between you to the feet of Jesus." When they came with the little thing toddling between them, and together we bowed at the altar in simple faith in the blood as our only plea, the child was instantly healed. I received the beautiful pillow and a home-made blanket as a thank offering. There was a note pinned to the pillow on which the child's name was written and a statement that she could hear a pin drop. I have always valued the pillow almost beyond anything I possess.

When children are old enough to believe for themselves, we must read the Word of God to them, especially stories about the healing Christ. ...Faith cometh by hearing, and hearing by the word of God (Rom. 10:17). They are often more ready to believe than adults. Sometimes their faith helps older people to get well.

There is a hymn that we all love called, "God Will Take Care of You." I happened to hear from someone who knew all about how it came to be written and composed. A minister had been called to preach one Sunday in a large city and had brought his wife and little boy with him for the trip. They were at a hotel. Sunday morning, near church time, the minister's wife was taken very sick. She was so sick that the minister made up his mind to break his promise to preach, a thing he had never done in all his life. As he was going out of the door to take a message to the office, the tiny child ran over to his mother's bed and whispered in her ear, "Mother, God will take care of you." The childish faith stirred the mother to believe God, and she called her husband back. "Don't break your promise, dear," she said. "I would not have you do it for all the world. God will take care of me."

The minister's faith rose to meet the test, and he went and did God's work. When he came back, his wife met him with a smiling face and said, "God gave me a little hymn," and she read him the beautiful words:

No matter what may be the test,
God will take care of you.
Lean weary one, upon His breast,
God will take care of you.

The husband, who was a musician, sat down and played the sweet melody to which we sing it.

Children can often lead people to Christ for salvation and healing when older persons fail.

We have a wonderful story in the Old Testament (2 Kings 5:1-27), which tells how a little maid, who had been taken captive by the Syrians, was the means of healing the great Naaman, commander in chief of the army of the king of Syria. She was a servant to Naaman's wife; and when she saw that the commander was a leper, she said to her mistress in simple faith in God, ...Would God my lord were with the prophet that is in Samaria! for he would recover him of his leprosy (v. 3). She was so sure that her faith moved the great General Naaman, and even the king of Syria who no doubt greatly longed to have his faithful general's life spared. If you read the story you will see that the king of Syria wrote a letter to the king of Israel asking *him* to make Naaman well. That was not what the little maid told them to do. She had said that the prophet who was in Israel, Elisha, would make Naaman well. Not because he had the power himself but because God worked through him. Naaman took a great fortune with him, and costly raiment, to buy his healing. That was not the little maid's fault. She had said nothing about taking anything but himself, dying of a fatal disease for which there was no human cure. When we come to Jesus for healing, we have to sing in our hearts:

> Just as I am without one plea,
> But that Thy blood was shed for me,
> And that Thou bidd'st me come to Thee
> O Lamb of God I come.

Never forget that, "Jesus paid it all."

Naaman had to learn that the king of Israel could not make him well; that all his money and rich gifts could not help him at all. But one thing would heal him and that was the Word of God. That word was spoken by Elisha, for he was God's mouthpiece. Naaman had to believe it. That was all. What did Elisha say?

...Go and wash in Jordan seven times, and thy flesh shall come again to thee, and thou shalt be clean (v. 10). He sent this word by a messenger. Naaman didn't have any chance to show what a great officer he was, how many servants he had, or to present his costly gifts.

He was angry. No doubt he said to himself, "The prophet turns me away like a beggar." That was all he was. Just a poor beggar, with his flesh falling off his bones from leprosy. Sometimes God has to bring us down very low before He can heal us. But thank God, Naaman believed the word enough to obey it to the letter. Down he went seven times and received such a wonderful healing! His flesh that had sloughed off came again as fresh as a little child's. (v. 14.)

The Lord Jesus Christ used Naaman's case to teach the people in His hometown, Nazareth, what real faith meant. (Luke 4:27.) And it all came about through the faith of a little captive girl. How happy she must have been when her master, the splendid Generalissimo Naaman, came marching home to his wife and children, as well as to his king and country.

I could tell you many stories out of my own life where children, even tiny ones, have been used in the Lord's healing. I think I shall tell you a funny one here and hope you will read it to your little ones if you are so happy as to have some.

We had a beautiful fox terrier puppy given to us, a fine dog and very bright—almost too bright for us. So we decided to give him to a sister who had a number of children who loved to play with him. She was glad to have him. One day she noticed that the puppy was sick. She told the children that they were not to play with him or even touch him. He had run under the big kitchen range after refusing to eat.

She noticed that the children—she had them of all ages down to three—went into a huddle and talked very earnestly. The one who was only three years old took a very active part in the discussion.

Then she saw them all go to a corner and kneel down. They stayed there some time.

Then they came out in a solemn little procession and said, "Mother, we have prayed for Puppy, and we are sure he is well. You said that when he was well he would come running when we called him, wagging his tail, and would eat his breakfast. And you said, too, that his nose would be cold. May we call him to his breakfast? We know he will come running and wagging his tail. And Mother, may we just touch the tip of his nose, just barely touch it. We are sure it is cold as ice." As she hesitated one of them offered the crowning argument by saying, "Mother, you said that God blessed His people's cattle and kept them well. He is our cattle, isn't he?"

Rather weakly she said, "Well, you may call him." This was done in a chorus and the dog ran out wagging his tail and rushed to his breakfast plate. Then one of the children cried, "O Mother, I just touched his nose the least teeny-weeny bit, and it is cold as an icicle."

I think this story shows that we are not to despise the faith of children, even tiny ones, but try to encourage it all we can.

Perhaps I might tell one more case of victory through the faith of a little child. The father of the child, who is a man of God, is my authority. The child's mother suffered for years from neuralgia in her face. The child, a little girl, loved her mother dearly; and when she had these awful attacks, she suffered with her. She was taught and believed that the Lord Jesus bore our pains on the cross. One day—I think she was five years old at the time—while her mother was in awful agony she jumped up and ran to her and laid her hands on her *in faith*. That was the last attack.

Faith is faith, whether in children or adults, and faith is the victory that overcomes. (1 John 5:4.)

Chapter 7

YOU HAVE AUTHORITY

Supposing we consider healings that happened after the Lord Jesus Christ led His apostles out to Mount Olivet, a short distance from Jerusalem, and was caught up to heaven, a cloud receiving Him out of their sight.

How hard it was for them to see Him vanish from their eyes! But God gave them one great comfort. What was it? He sent two messengers to say, ...This same Jesus, which is taken up from you into heaven, shall so come in like manner as ye have seen him go into heaven (Acts 1:11).

This is the blessed hope of all God's dear children. I am sure that it reminded the disciples that their Master, who was coming again, had left them some work to do for Him. Don't you think it ought to make us all pray, "Lord, what wilt thou have me to do?" (Acts 9:6.)

What had the Lord told them to do? You will find it in Luke 24:49: Behold, I send the promise of my Father upon you: but tarry ye in the city of Jerusalem, until ye be endured with power from on high.

They remembered His words (Acts 1:12), and we find them returning to Jerusalem to an upper room, where with other disciples—120 in all—they continued in prayer until the promise of the Father, the gift of the Holy Spirit, came upon them all and they began to speak in other tongues as the Spirit gave them utterance. (Acts 2:4.)

Have you obeyed that command of the Lord Jesus Christ yet? If not, lose no time about it for His coming draweth nigh! The promise is unto you, and to your children...even as many as the Lord our God shall call (Acts 2:39).

They needed the Holy Spirit in those days but not any more than we need Him in these days. They were His witnesses for that time, and we are His witnesses for this time.

Very soon after this we find the mighty power of the Holy Spirit shown in the healing of a most desperate case. (Acts 3:1-16.) For years and years a poor man had been laid each day at the Beautiful gate of the temple in Jerusalem. There good people, who might give him alms as they entered that holy place to pray, would be sure to see him lying helpless, for he had never walked. He had been born a cripple. He was forty years old at the time of which we are talking.

It seems almost certain that the Lord Jesus Christ had seen him, for we know that Jesus loved to go to the temple because it was His Father's house. Why did not the Lord Jesus heal him? We do not know the answer to that question, for the Bible does not tell us. Perhaps the poor cripple had not yet come to the place of repentance and faith. It may be that the crucifixion of the Lord on Calvary and His Resurrection from the dead brought faith to the heart of the poor sufferer. He would be sure to hear of these things, for they were noised abroad all over the holy city.

The Lord Jesus had made the healing of the cripple possible before He left for His heavenly home, for He had told His disciples that they were to lay hands on sick people in His name and that the sick people would get well. (Mark 16:15-18.)

And so that they would not be afraid to do this, He said to them, Verily, verily, I say unto you, He that believeth on me, the works that

I do shall he do also; and greater works than these shall he do; because I go unto my Father (John 14:12).

Did the Lord Jesus ever heal a lame man? Yes, many of them. We are told that the lame came to Him in the temple, at the gate of which the cripple lay, and He healed them there. And in many other places besides, He made the lame to walk. One man who had lain for thirty-eight years, helpless to move himself, got up and took up his bed and walked at the Word of the Lord. That story is in John 5:1-9.

So when the apostles, Peter and John, saw this lame man reaching out his empty hand—all he could move—and asking for an alms, they remembered the words of the Lord. And Peter fastened his eyes on him with John. Oh, how we need to work *together* in healing! And he commanded, "Look on us." (Acts 3:4.) Whether you get healed or not depends *entirely* on where you look. If that man had fixed his gaze on his legs (mere bags of skin and bone, for they had never been used, and the muscles had not grown), he would not have been healed no matter how earnestly the apostles had prayed for him. Jesus Himself, "did not many mighty works" in His own hometown. Why? Because of their unbelief. (Matt. 13:58.) It is "according to your faith," the Lord Himself said so. When the brazen serpent was lifted up on a pole in the wilderness by Moses at God's command to heal the stricken Israelites who were bitten by fiery serpents, we are told that if a serpent had bitten any man, when he beheld the serpent of brass, he lived. Not when he was looking at his sore wounds but when he fixed his eyes on God's cure for them—the brazen serpent. (Num. 21:8,9.)

The brazen serpent is a picture of the Lord Jesus made sin for us, that we might be made the righteousness (rightness) of God in Him. The Lord Himself says so in John 3:14-15: As Moses lifted up the serpent in the wilderness, even so must the Son of man be lifted up: that whosoever believeth in Him should not perish, but have eternal life.

Here we have the lame man looking at Peter and John, messengers of the Lord Jesus, and "expecting to receive something of them." (Acts 3:5.) I am sure he did not expect what he got. God is able to give us exceeding abundantly above all we can ask or expect and He loves to do it. Our part is to look away from everything else to Jesus; and if we do that, we cannot expect too much.

Peter said, "Silver and gold have I none; but such as I have give I thee." (v. 6.) He had no money; he said so. But he still had something to give. What was that something? Had he some magic power perhaps granted him because he had left all to follow Christ? In verse 12 he says he had no power of his own to cure the man. Yet he gave him something that made that cripple leap up, stand, and walk into the temple leaping and praising God. (v. 8.)

What was that something? Three times over he tells us that it was the power of the name of Jesus Christ of Nazareth. He explains exactly how it was done, "through *faith in His name*." (Acts 3:6,16; 4:10.)

Once for some time I held a government position where I had the right to sign the name of a high officer, which carried with it the power to enforce obedience. Because of this, the orders I sent out had to be obeyed. I had no power of my own; and if I had used my own name, no one would have moved an inch.

I did many things of great value to many people. But it was all through the power of the name I was told to use. If I had not had faith in that name, I would not have been able to do these things, because I would not have used it. If I had not used it, I would have disobeyed.

What Peter had was power to use the name that is above every name. The name that has to be obeyed. He was not only allowed to use it, but it was his duty to do so. The Lord Jesus had said to Peter and the others, "In my name, shall they lay hands on the sick and they shall recover." (Mark 16:17,18.)

He was telling them and us to preach the Gospel to every creature, so this Word is to us today. To whom? "Them that believe." If we do not use this name, it is because we are not believing what Jesus said.

This wonderful healing of the lame man led to many, many healings and signs and wonders. They even brought the sick ones out into the streets and laid them on beds and couches so that Peter's shadow might fall on them. A great many people believed and were added to the church. Also, awful persecution arose. Satan did not like these healings because he hates to see the glorious name of the Lord Jesus Christ praised and worshipped. He does not like divine healing any better today. But the apostles and early Christians went right along doing what the Lord had told them to do, and the Lord went with them doing miracles. Shall we follow our Lord and Master as closely as they did? If we do, we may count on His power.

Not long after this miracle of the lame man at the temple gate, Peter went down to a place called Lydia. There he found a man called Aeneas, who was paralyzed and had been bedfast for eight long years. How he must have suffered! I have seen so many sad cases like his, and my heart went out to them; but there was nothing I could do for them though I was a doctor. Peter was no doctor; but as we saw in the story of the lame man, he had something to give—if they would take it—that made sick people perfectly sound.

Knowing that the medicine never failed, he said "Aeneas, Jesus Christ maketh thee whole! Arise! And make thy bed." (Acts 9:34.) And he arose immediately. What was the use of lying around another moment? He had had enough of that to last him a lifetime.

Has that medicine lost its power? No; and it will never fail, for it is the power of the name of the Lord Jesus Christ. And we read in Psalm 72:17: His name shall endure for ever...and men shall be blessed in him; all nations shall call him blessed.

Let us use that name in faith.

Chapter 8

THE JOY OF THE LORD

When you have a sure cure for all disease, you only need one remedy. Who forgiveth all thine iniquities; who healeth all thy diseases (Ps. 103:3). It is because doctors have no medicine that will cure every disease that they are always working so hard trying to find new remedies. Then the medicines they have are more or less uncertain in their action. They do not always do what the doctors expect.

But when the medicine is God's Word, it cannot fail. He says about it: So shall my word be that goeth forth out of my mouth: it shall not return unto me void, but it shall accomplish that which I please, and it shall prosper in the thing whereto I sent it (Isa. 55:11). So when God sends His Word to heal you, it always does its work if you will let it.

"Can I prevent it from healing me?" Certainly you can. God does not force salvation for soul or body upon us. It is written, ...whosoever will, let him take of the water of life freely (Rev. 22:17). To get the action of any remedy you have to take that remedy according to directions. Sometimes when I was practicing medicine, I would go to see a sick person and leave them a prescription to be taken according to instructions. When I returned, I would see at a glance—for I knew what the medicine would do if they took it—that they had not taken it according to directions. When they saw that I was angry with them, they would sometimes say they had taken it. Then I was angry for sure!

God says that He sends His Word and heals. His Word cannot fail; so if we are not healed, we must look for the cause of it in ourselves. It must be that we have not taken it according to instructions. What is lacking? Turn to the Bible and you will find out. In Hebrews 4:2 it says, ...the word preached did not profit them, not being mixed with faith in them that heard it. To take the Word, you must mix it with faith. The Lord Jesus Himself said when healing two blind men, ...According to your faith be it unto you (Matt. 9:29).

One thing the Bible tells us about our wonderful bodies is that to keep them healthy, well oiled, and running smoothly, we have to be happy. It is our duty to be happy. God commands it. You will find this in many places in the Bible, our book of instructions. In the prophecy of Joel 2:21, we read, "Be glad and rejoice." That is a command of God. Then in Nehemiah 8:10, we find it given again in the negative form. Joel tells us what we must do, and Nehemiah tells us what we must not do. ...neither be ye sorry; for the joy of the Lord is your strength.

Oh, what a difference it would make if all God's people would obey these commands!

There is a great power in happiness. When I practiced medicine, I had a great many baby cases. That means I was often with mothers to welcome the precious little ones God gave them. I always wanted my mothers and babies to be well and strong, and I found that the best tonic I could give the mothers was their babies. Some doctors had them taken away to a nursery in the hospital to be cared for by nurses, but I was not so fond of that. Looking at their babies and listening to their voices made my little mothers very happy, and happiness is the best tonic I know. If human happiness makes us strong, what will the joy the Bible speaks of do? This joy is as far above earthly joys and pleasures as the heavens are high above the earth. God wants us to have it constantly. He even tells us that we shall be punished if we are not happy. And one of the punishments He speaks of is sickness.

Because thou servedst not the Lord thy God with joyfulness, and with gladness of heart, for the abundance of all things; therefore shalt thou serve thine enemies which the Lord shall send against thee…Moreover He will bring upon thee all the diseases of Egypt, which thou wast afraid of; and they shall cleave unto thee. Also every sickness, and every plague, which is not written in…this law, them will the Lord bring upon thee… (Deut. 28:47,48,60,61).

How are we to get this joy that makes our hearts rejoice and our bodies strong? God has provided it for us and tells us how to get it in the book of instructions—the Bible.

David says, "I will go unto the altar of God, unto God my exceeding joy." (Ps. 43:4.)

Peter tells us about it: Whom having not seen, ye love; in whom, though now ye see him not, yet believing, ye rejoice with joy unspeakable and full of glory (1 Peter 1:8).

Believing what the Bible says about the Lord Jesus and what He has done for you and yours, you *rejoice, you just can't help it.* And you are strong, for the "joy of the Lord is your strength." (Neh. 8:10.) Believing you rejoice, but doubting you despair and become weak and ready to fall a victim to sickness.

There is only one thing that will give you this wonderful joy that fills your soul and spirit with glory and makes your very "bones rejoice," and that is faith in the Lord Jesus Christ and what He did for you when He died on the cross *for you,* and rose again, showing that your "old account" was settled.

Money cannot give you this joy. It is not to be bought for gold. You may have kind friends who would be glad to help you in every way possible, but they cannot bestow this gladness upon you. It has to come down from heaven, for "Every perfect gift is from above, and cometh down from the Father of lights." (James 1:17.) On the other hand, nothing can take this joy from you, for He says of the joy He gives us, "Your joy no man taketh from you." (John 16:22.)

We are living in awful days, and we need the joy of the Lord as much, or more, than any of His children ever needed it. For a great many years I have received letters from people asking for prayer and counsel. But the letters that have come to me of late have been the saddest I have ever received. Some of them are so sad that I hasten to destroy them when I have prayed over them for fear anyone might happen to see them and be saddened by them. When I get these letters, I am so glad that I have the "gladdest letter" that ever was written. It is in my Bible. I hasten to drink of its sweetness and to pass the sparkling cup to the poor sufferers to whom I am writing. I know you are asking, "Where is that gladdest of all letters?" Was it written by someone who had everything heart could wish and was surrounded by loved ones and shielded from every danger?"

It was written by a man nearing seventy, in a dark, damp, slimy cellar under the city of Rome, Italy. A man who had "suffered the loss of all things." He was the prisoner of the Emperor Nero, the most awful monster that ever lived, and was chained to a Roman soldier. He was so filled with joy that his praises have rung down all the years and changed wails of woe to songs of victory in countless hearts, since he went home to glory. That man is the apostle Paul, and the "gladdest letter" ever written, all "joy unspeakable and full of glory," is his Epistle to the "saints in Christ Jesus...at Philippi." Thank God, it is ours as well as theirs!

I do not believe we begin to know what a mighty thing the joy of the Lord is, to keep us well and heal us, if we are sick. I am going to relate *a joy* healing that comes to me at this time. It happened at least six years ago in Chicago, where I was holding a campaign for

Brother S. A. Jamieson. As though to freshen my mind as to all the details, the minister who with me visited the sick man happened to call upon me not long ago. I had not seen him for a long time until then. Of course, we talked over this case. He was acting as pastor of a congregation in Chicago, and the sick man attended his church. When we reached the home, which was in a humble little flat, we saw one of the saddest scenes we had ever seen. The young couple was only recently married. They were sweet Christian people. Though the furniture was not fine, everything was just as neat as it could be. But the faces of those dear young people, I shall never forget. He was very, very sick, with that pale, drawn, anxious look that comes with awful suffering. His case was a stone in the kidney, and he had the usual anguish, bleeding, etc., that goes with it. He was booked for an operation in a day or so. The little wife knelt at the foot of the bed. She had her face buried in the coverlet, to hide her tears from her husband I suppose. And I noticed that her hands clasped his feet as though to prevent anyone from taking him away. I knew what that meant: the ambulance. She was thinking of the moment it would stop at their door.

Nothing could be sadder than this case, yet the Lord Jesus was so manifestly present that it seemed the man's healing was inevitable. We read about the Lord in the Word, and He seemed to step out of it and stand in our midst. Never shall I forget the joy of that hour! We were in the heavenlies; anxiety was impossible in that atmosphere. We just adored Him to our heart's content. All the pale, drawn look of anguish vanished from the young husband's face, and he laughed and laughed and laughed and *laughed!* The little wife joined in silvery notes, and it was a laughing duet. We lost our sense of time and place. Like Peter on the Mount of Transfiguration we were only conscious that it was good for us to be there.

I know that the song in our hearts was...

Oh, it is Jesus, Oh, it is Jesus, Oh, it is Jesus in my soul,
For I have touched the hem of His garment,
And His power has made me whole.

The young husband was healed and went to church and gave God the glory.

Chapter 9
THE LORD'S PRAYER

While writing these little chapters I have thought so much of you, my readers, that you have become very dear to me. I see mothers who feel too weak to bear the heavy burdens that life brings, seeking strength in these pages.

Tiny children, with eyes too large for their pale, wasted little faces, seem to be looking to me for aid. Fathers of families, too crushed under sickness, which makes it impossible for them to earn for their loved ones what they need, are asking, "Is there healing and health for me?" Yes. God, who changeth not, has promised to heal all who call upon Him in the *name of the Lord Jesus Christ.*

In closing I desire to point out to you that in the Lord's Prayer which our Lord Jesus Himself taught us to pray, there is a plea for healing and health in every clause. Let us read it from Matthew 6:9-13.

Our Father which art in heaven. Who is our Father? If we have been born again, "the Lord that healeth thee." (Ex. 15:26.)

Hallowed be Thy name. For what does His name stand? His name through faith in his name hath made this man strong, whom ye see and know: yea, the faith which is by him hath given him...perfect soundness... (Acts 3:16).

Thy kingdom come. This is a prayer for health of body, as well as spirit. We are told that, Of the increase of his government and peace there shall be no end... (Isa. 9:7). God has promised to keep us in perfect peace if we trust in Him. (Isa. 26:3.) Perfect peace means perfect health of body as well as mind. The Lord Jesus is the Prince of Peace. (Isa. 9:6.)

Thy will be done in earth, as it is in heaven. There is no sickness in heaven. In Revelation 21:4 we read, And God shall wipe away all tears from their eyes; and there shall be no more death, neither sorrow, nor crying, neither shall there be any more pain....

Give us this day our daily bread. Here we are praying for physical as well as spiritual blessing. The Lord Jesus Christ Himself speaks of healing as the "children's bread." (Matt. 15:26.) In praying for our daily bread we are asking for perfect health. It is only if we have this that we can be properly nourished by our food.

And forgive us our debts (or sins). In the 5th chapter of Luke's Gospel, the Lord Jesus Christ said that He healed the paralytic, who was borne of four men, "that ye may know that the Son of man hath power upon earth to forgive sins." (v. 24.) Forgiveness and healing go together. When the sin is pardoned and put away, the mortgage on the house—our bodies—is lifted.

Lead us not into temptation. I do not know any temptations that are harder to fight than those of doubt, fear, unbelief, discouragement, and despair, that come with Satan's attacks on our bodies.

Deliver us from evil. This covers all diseases, for they are mentioned as part of the curse of the broken Law.

We are sure of the answer to this prayer: ...for thine is the kingdom, and the power, and the glory, for ever, Amen (Matt. 6:13).

PRAYER OF SALVATION

God loves you—no matter who you are, no matter what your past. God loves you so much that He gave His one and only begotten Son for you. The Bible tells us that ...whoever believes in him shall not perish but have eternal life (John 3:16 NIV). Jesus laid down His life and rose again so that we could spend eternity with Him in heaven and experience His absolute best on earth. If you would like to receive Jesus into your life, say the following prayer out loud and mean it from your heart.

Heavenly Father, I come to You admitting that I am a sinner. Right now, I choose to turn away from sin, and I ask You to cleanse me of all unrighteousness. I believe that Your Son, Jesus, died on the cross to take away my sins. I also believe that He rose again from the dead so that I might be forgiven of my sins and made righteous through faith in Him. I call upon the name of Jesus Christ to be the Savior and Lord of my life. Jesus, I choose to follow You and ask that You fill me with the power of the Holy Spirit. I declare that right now I am a child of God. I am free from sin and full of the righteousness of God. I am saved in Jesus' name. Amen.

If you prayed this prayer to receive Jesus Christ as your Savior for the first time, please contact us on the Web at **www.harrisonhouse.com** to receive a free book.

Or you may write to us at

Harrison House

P.O. Box 35035

Tulsa, Oklahoma 74153

ABOUT THE AUTHOR

Dr. Lilian B. Yeomans, M.D., was a popular Bible teacher and writer, inspiring thousands to believe God for healing. She is known as one of God's Generals of the Healing Revival in the early 1900s because of the numerous miracle healings that took place in her ministry.

Dr. Yeoman's was a graduate of the University of Michigan Department of Medicine in Ann Arbor, Michigan. As a young woman practicing medicine, she became hopelessly addicted to drugs. Freedom from bondage came miraculously when a minister pointed to the Word of God and fervently prayed for her. Dr. Yeomans gave up her medical career and spent the next 40 years teaching the Word of God and ministering salvation, healing, and restoration.

Yeomans' books were first published in the 1930s but her remarkable insight into the Word of God makes these classic messages relevant to our life today.